TEMPLAR, ARIZONA.
4 – Trouble Every Day.

By Spike.

www.TemplarAZ.com

IRON CIRCUS COMICS

TM

WWW.IRONCIRCUS.COM

This volume collects the fourth chapter of Templar, Arizona.
More of the story is available at http://www.templaraz.com.

Write Spike: ironcircus@gmail.com

First Edition: March 2010

ISBN: 978-0-9794080-3-8

Printed in Canada

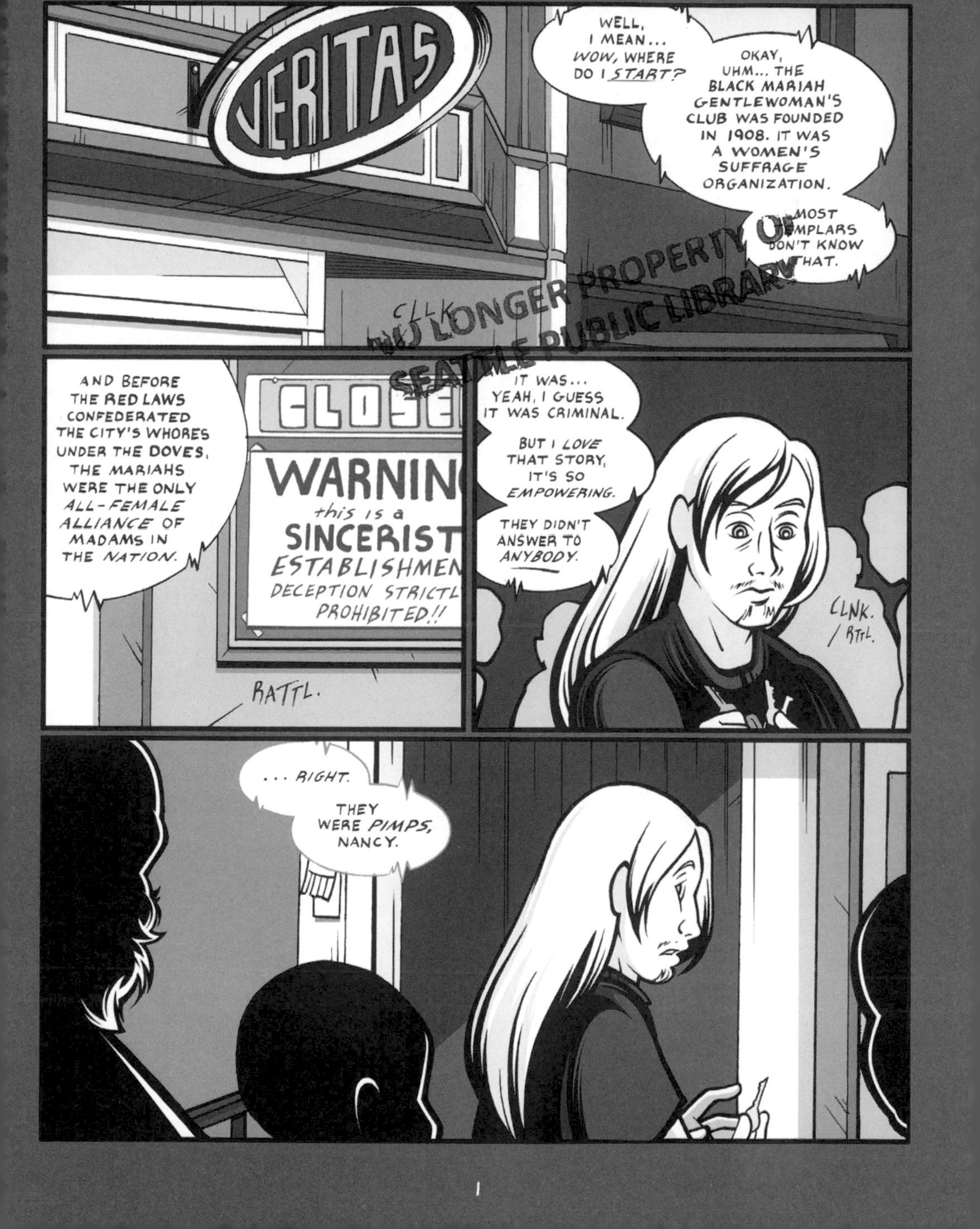
VERITAS
WELL, I MEAN... WOW, WHERE DO I START?
OKAY, UHM... THE BLACK MARIAH GENTLEWOMAN'S CLUB WAS FOUNDED IN 1908. IT WAS A WOMEN'S SUFFRAGE ORGANIZATION.
MOST TEMPLARS DON'T KNOW THAT.
CLLK.
AND BEFORE THE RED LAWS CONFEDERATED THE CITY'S WHORES UNDER THE DOVES, THE MARIAHS WERE THE ONLY ALL-FEMALE ALLIANCE OF MADAMS IN THE NATION.
WARNIN
this is a
SINCERIST
ESTABLISHMEN
DECEPTION STRICTL
PROHIBITED!!
RATTL.
IT WAS... YEAH, I GUESS IT WAS CRIMINAL.
BUT I LOVE THAT STORY, IT'S SO EMPOWERING.
THEY DIDN'T ANSWER TO ANYBODY.
CLNK.
RTTL.
... RIGHT.
THEY WERE PIMPS, NANCY.

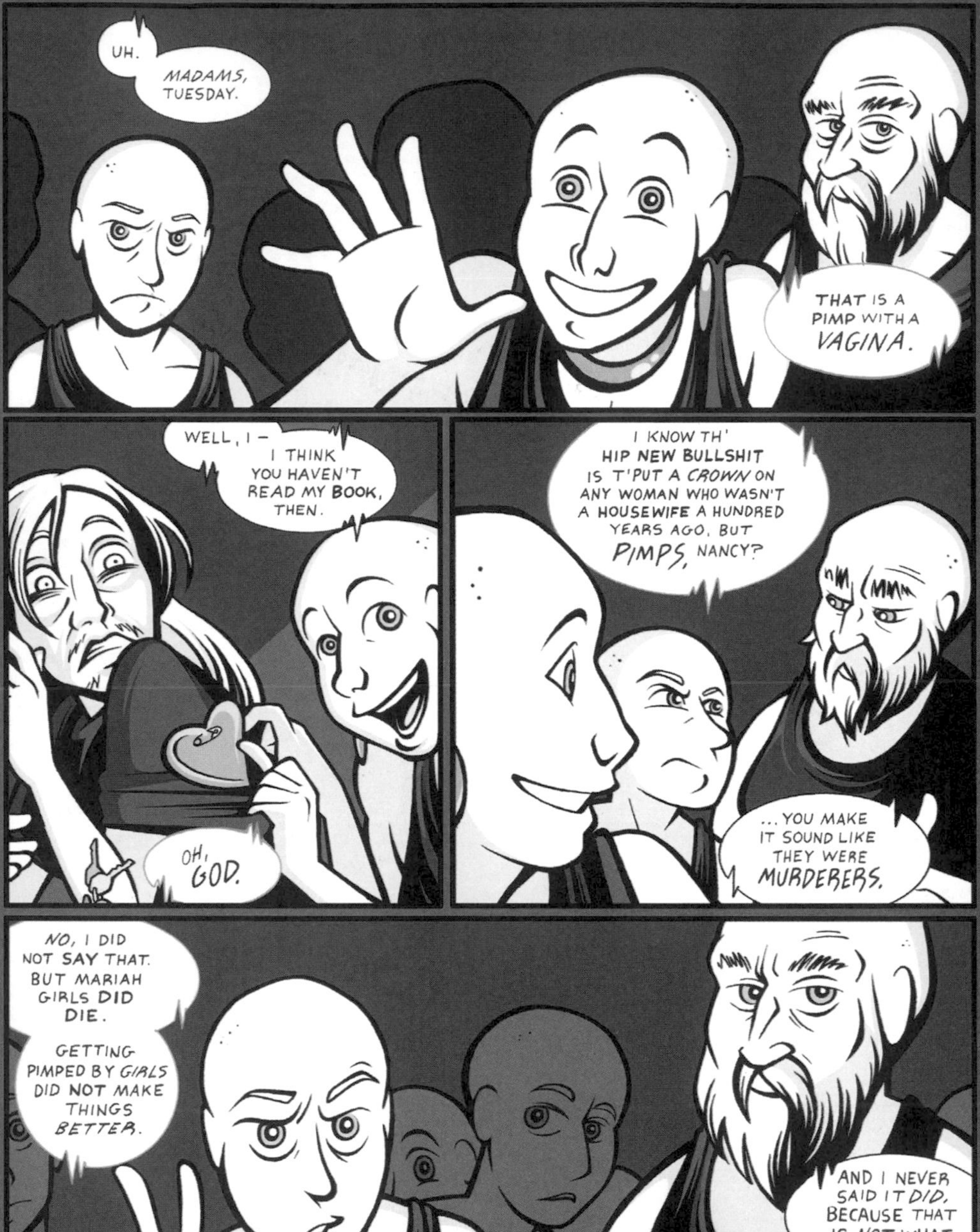
UH.
MADAMS, TUESDAY.
THAT IS A PIMP WITH A VAGINA.
WELL, I -
I THINK YOU HAVEN'T READ MY BOOK, THEN.
OH, GOD.
I KNOW TH' HIP NEW BULLSHIT IS T'PUT A CROWN ON ANY WOMAN WHO WASN'T A HOUSEWIFE A HUNDRED YEARS AGO, BUT PIMPS, NANCY?
... YOU MAKE IT SOUND LIKE THEY WERE MURDERERS.
NO, I DID NOT SAY THAT. BUT MARIAH GIRLS DID DIE.
GETTING PIMPED BY GIRLS DID NOT MAKE THINGS BETTER.
AND I NEVER SAID IT DID, BECAUSE THAT IS NOT WHAT I LIKE.

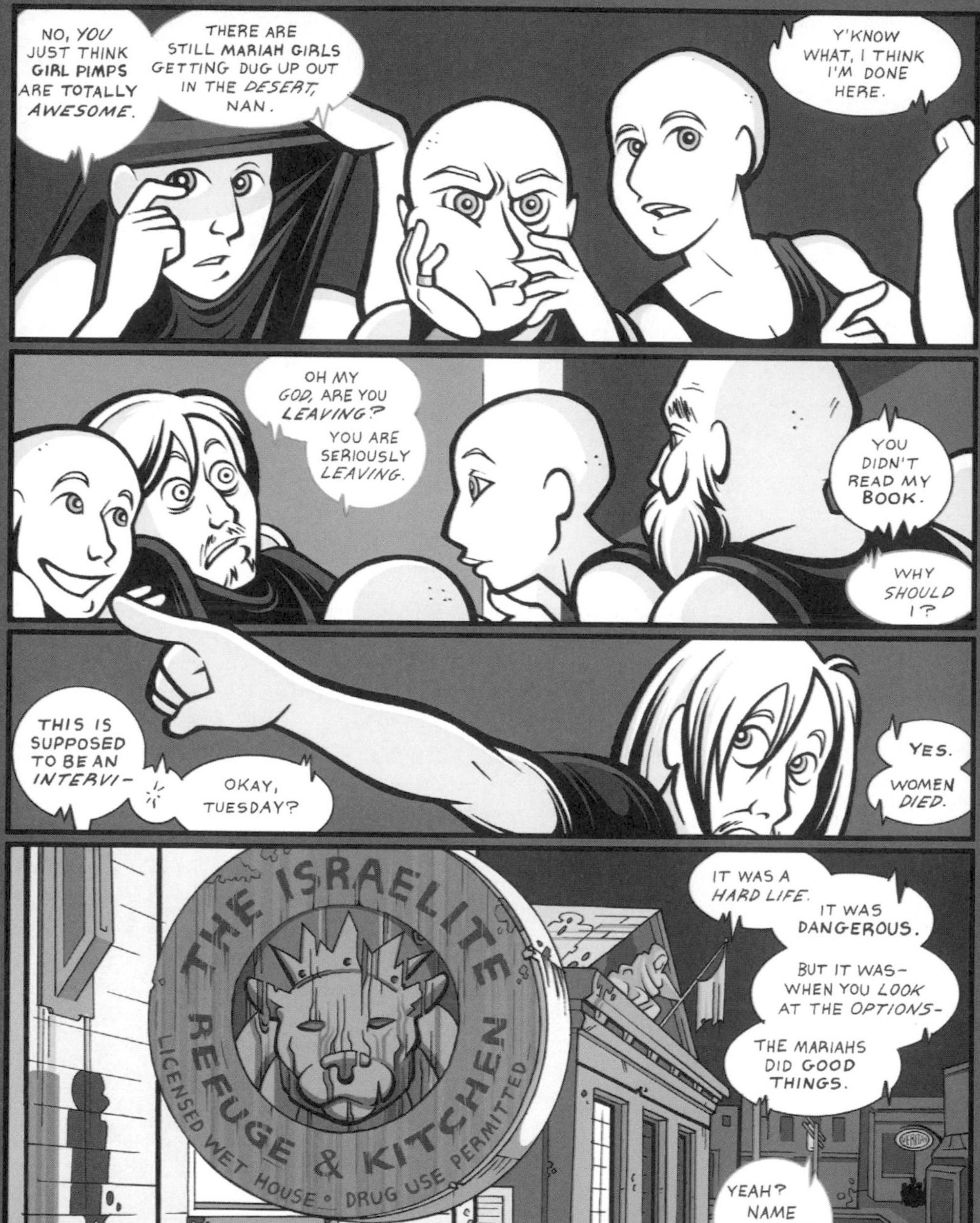
NO, YOU JUST THINK GIRL PIMPS ARE TOTALLY AWESOME.
THERE ARE STILL MARIAH GIRLS GETTING DUG UP OUT IN THE DESERT, NAN.
Y'KNOW WHAT, I THINK I'M DONE HERE.
OH MY GOD, ARE YOU LEAVING?
YOU ARE SERIOUSLY LEAVING.
YOU DIDN'T READ MY BOOK.
WHY SHOULD I?
THIS IS SUPPOSED TO BE AN INTERVI-
OKAY, TUESDAY?
YES.
WOMEN DIED.
THE ISRAELITE REFUGE & KITCHEN
LICENSED WET HOUSE • DRUG USE PERMITTED
IT WAS A HARD LIFE.
IT WAS DANGEROUS.
BUT IT WAS- WHEN YOU LOOK AT THE OPTIONS-
THE MARIAHS DID GOOD THINGS.
YEAH? NAME ONE.

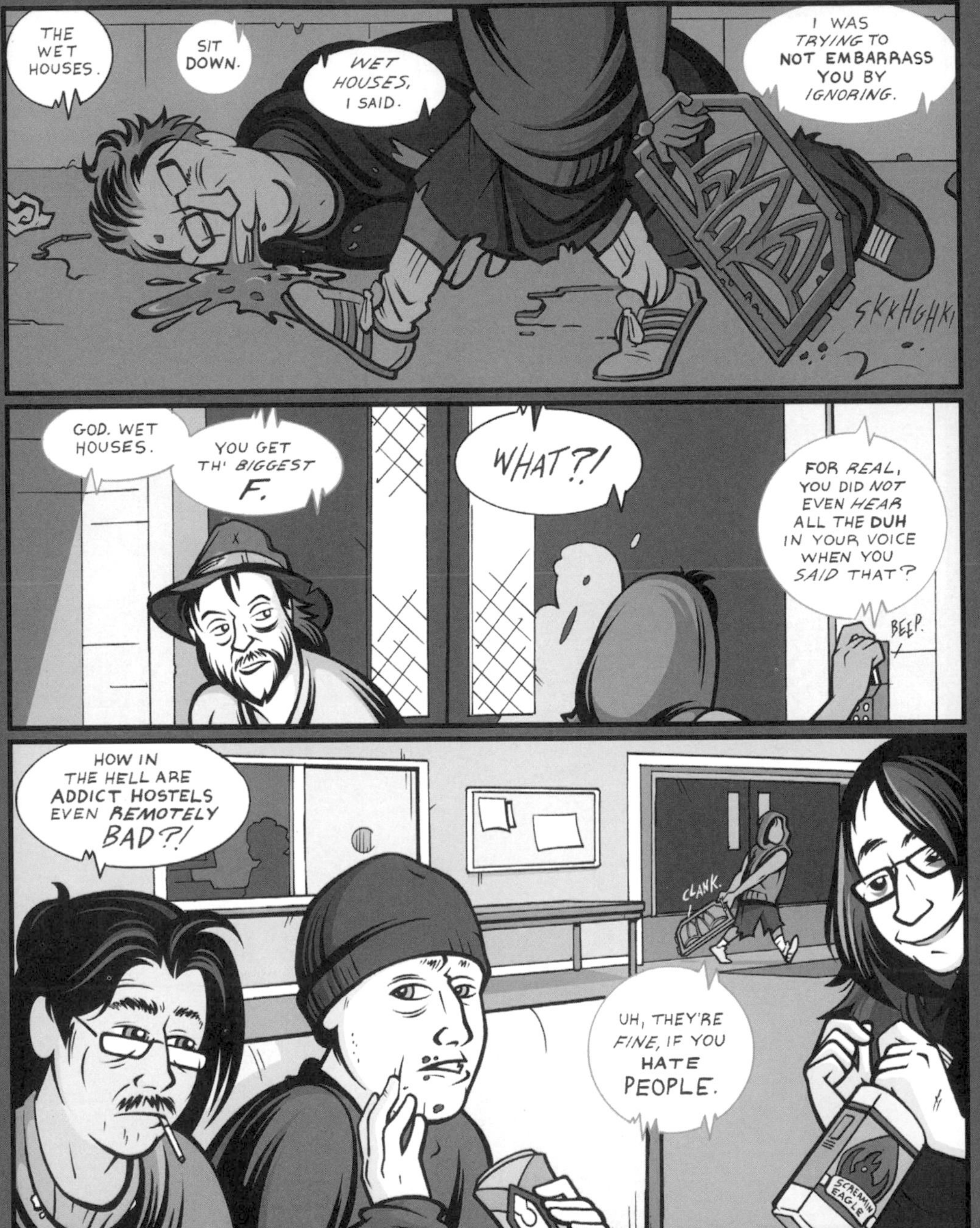

THE WET HOUSES.
SIT DOWN.
WET HOUSES, I SAID.
I WAS TRYING TO NOT EMBARRASS YOU BY IGNORING.
SKKHGHK!
GOD. WET HOUSES.
YOU GET TH' BIGGEST F.
WHAT?!
FOR REAL, YOU DID NOT EVEN HEAR ALL THE DUH IN YOUR VOICE WHEN YOU SAID THAT?
BEEP.
HOW IN THE HELL ARE ADDICT HOSTELS EVEN REMOTELY BAD?!
CLANK.
UH, THEY'RE FINE, IF YOU HATE PEOPLE.
SCREAMIN EAGLE

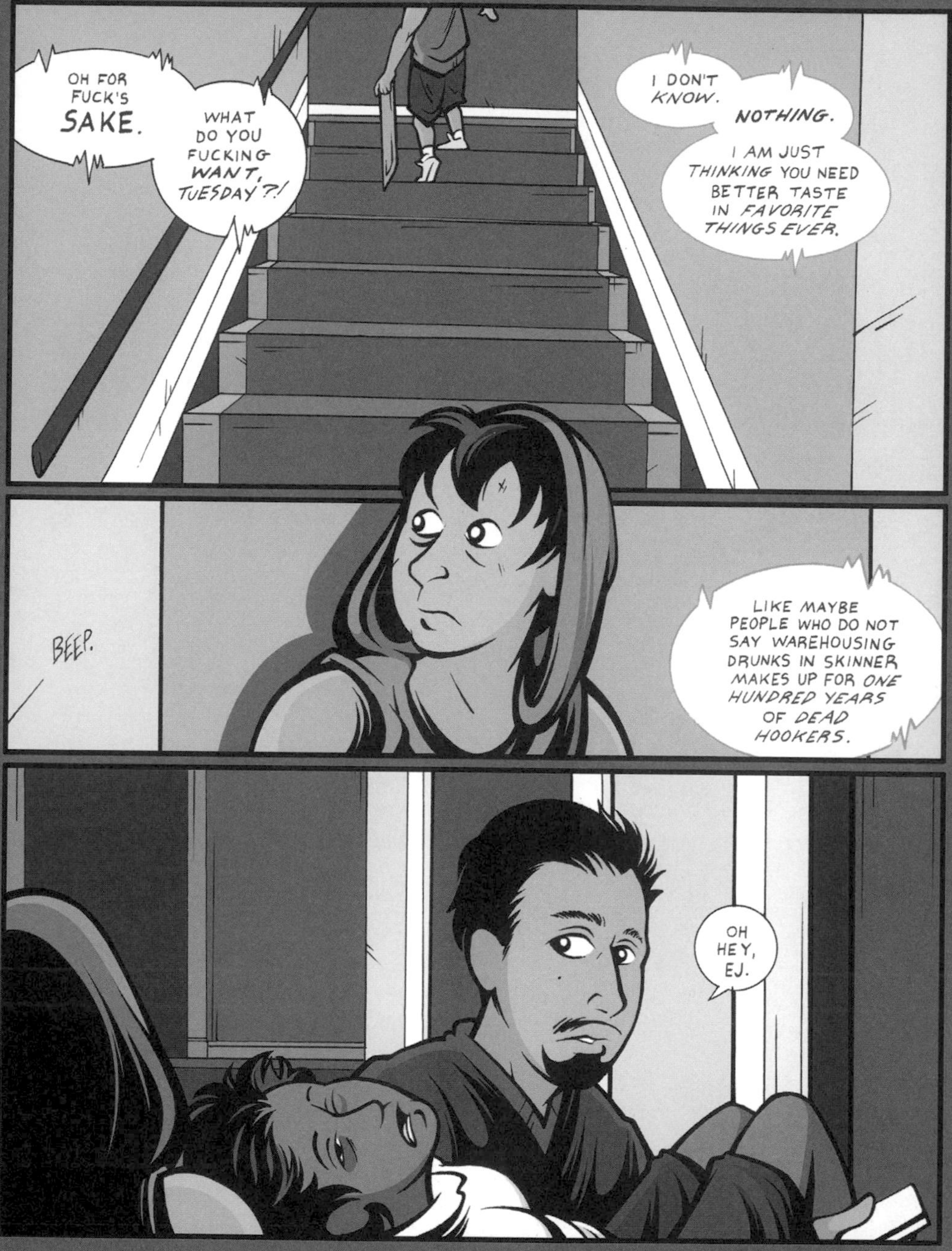
OH FOR FUCK'S SAKE.
WHAT DO YOU FUCKING WANT, TUESDAY?!
I DON'T KNOW.
NOTHING.
I AM JUST THINKING YOU NEED BETTER TASTE IN FAVORITE THINGS EVER.
BEEP.
LIKE MAYBE PEOPLE WHO DO NOT SAY WAREHOUSING DRUNKS IN SKINNER MAKES UP FOR ONE HUNDRED YEARS OF DEAD HOOKERS.
OH HEY, EJ.

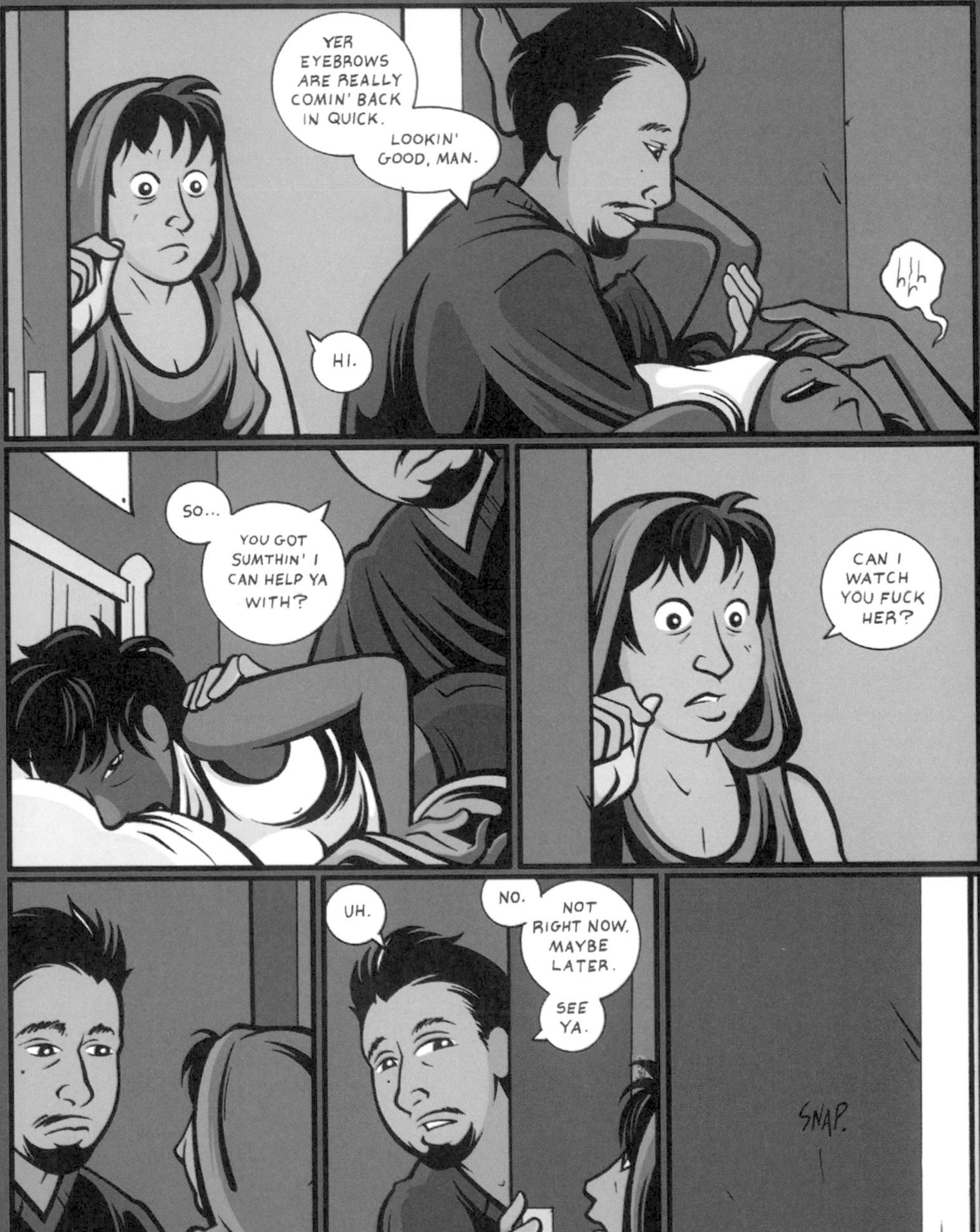
YER EYEBROWS ARE REALLY COMIN' BACK IN QUICK.
LOOKIN' GOOD, MAN.
HI.
SO...
YOU GOT SUMTHIN' I CAN HELP YA WITH?
CAN I WATCH YOU FUCK HER?
UH.
NO.
NOT RIGHT NOW. MAYBE LATER.
SEE YA.
SNAP.

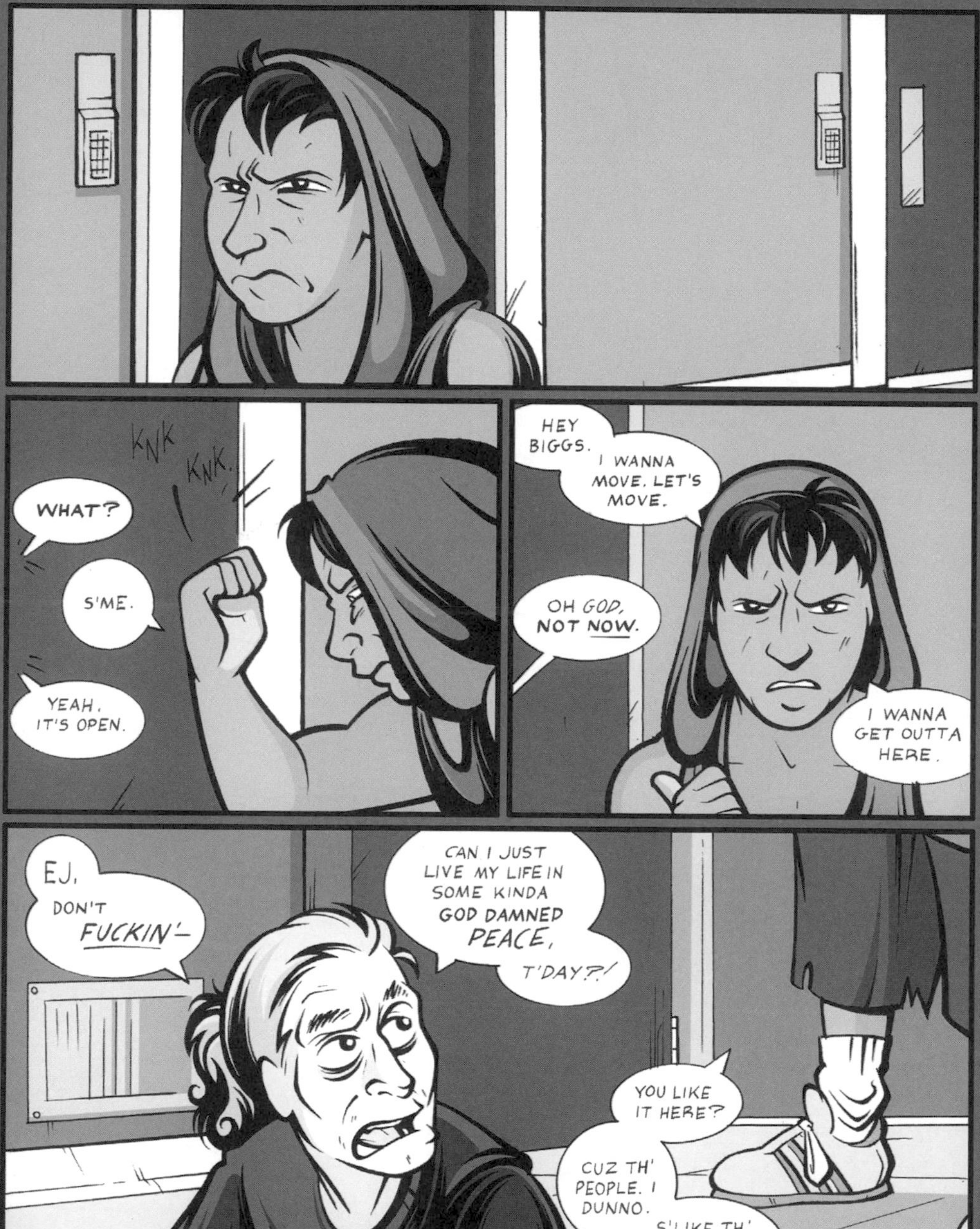
KNK
KNK.
WHAT?
S'ME.
YEAH. IT'S OPEN.
HEY BIGGS.
I WANNA MOVE. LET'S MOVE.
OH GOD, NOT NOW.
I WANNA GET OUTTA HERE.
EJ, DON'T FUCKIN'-
CAN I JUST LIVE MY LIFE IN SOME KINDA GOD DAMNED PEACE,
T'DAY?!
YOU LIKE IT HERE?
CUZ TH' PEOPLE. I DUNNO.
S'LIKE TH' CIRCASSIAN.

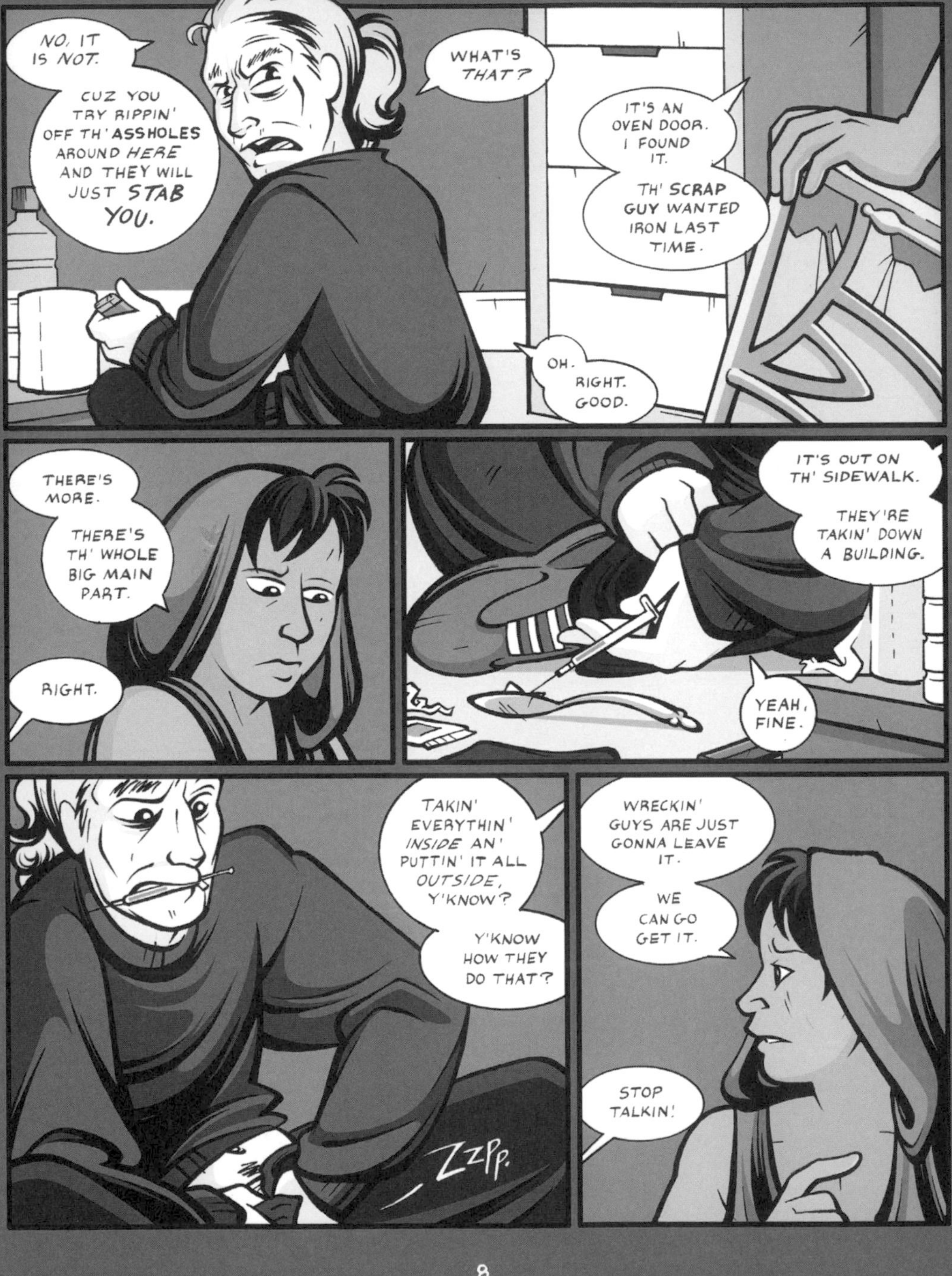
NO, IT IS *NOT*.
CUZ YOU TRY RIPPIN' OFF TH' **ASSHOLES** AROUND *HERE* AND THEY WILL JUST **STAB YOU.**
WHAT'S *THAT?*
IT'S AN OVEN DOOR. I FOUND IT.
TH' **SCRAP** GUY WANTED IRON LAST TIME.
OH. RIGHT. GOOD.
THERE'S MORE.
THERE'S TH' WHOLE BIG MAIN PART.
RIGHT.
IT'S OUT ON TH' SIDEWALK.
THEY'RE TAKIN' DOWN A BUILDING.
YEAH, FINE.
TAKIN' EVERYTHIN' *INSIDE* AN' PUTTIN' IT ALL *OUTSIDE*, Y'KNOW?
Y'KNOW HOW THEY DO THAT?
ZZPP.
WRECKIN' GUYS ARE JUST GONNA LEAVE IT.
WE CAN GO GET IT.
STOP TALKIN'!

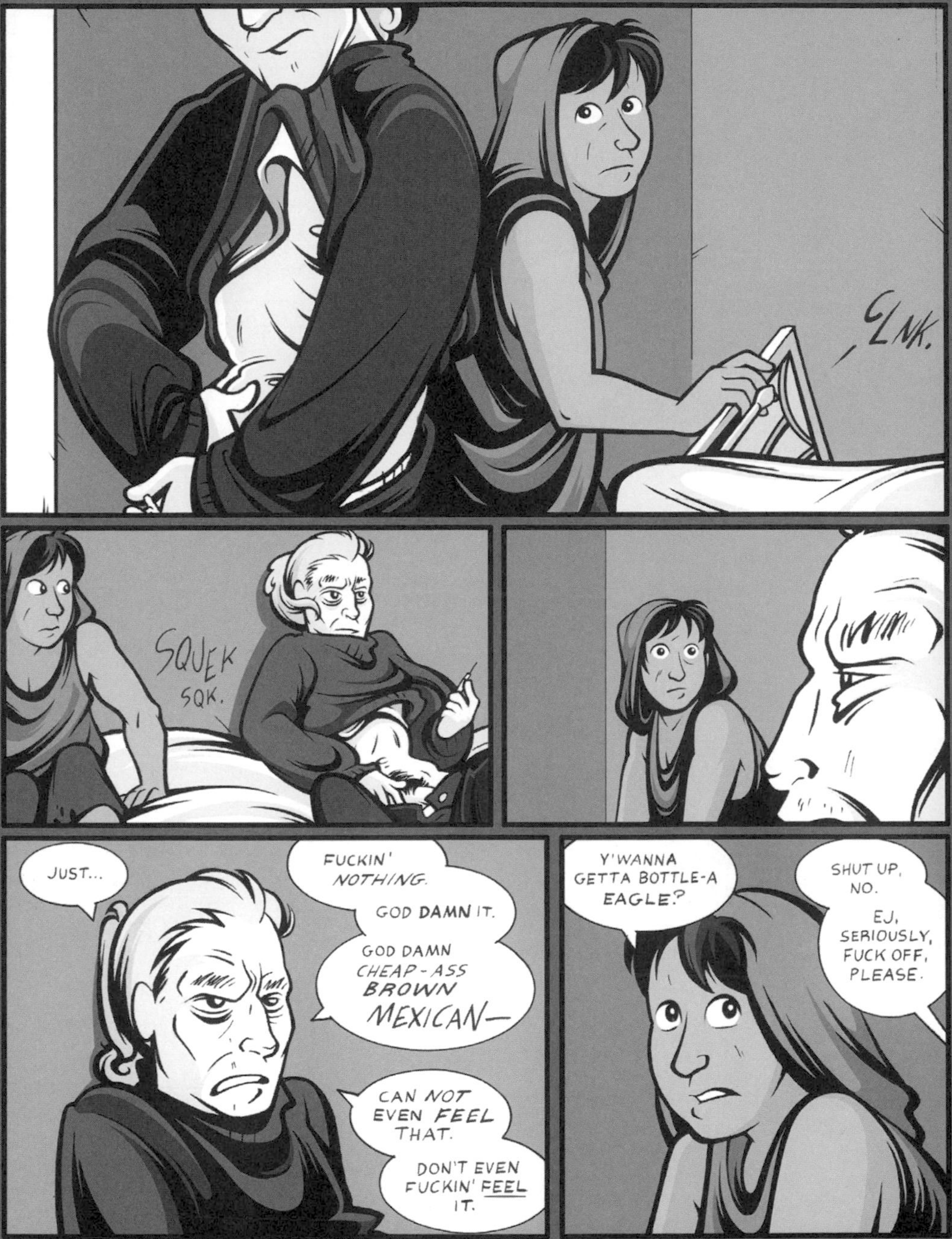
CLNK.
SQUEK
SQK.
JUST...
FUCKIN' NOTHING.
GOD DAMN IT.
GOD DAMN CHEAP-ASS BROWN MEXICAN—
CAN NOT EVEN FEEL THAT.
DON'T EVEN FUCKIN' FEEL IT.
Y'WANNA GETTA BOTTLE-A EAGLE?
SHUT UP, NO.
EJ, SERIOUSLY, FUCK OFF, PLEASE.

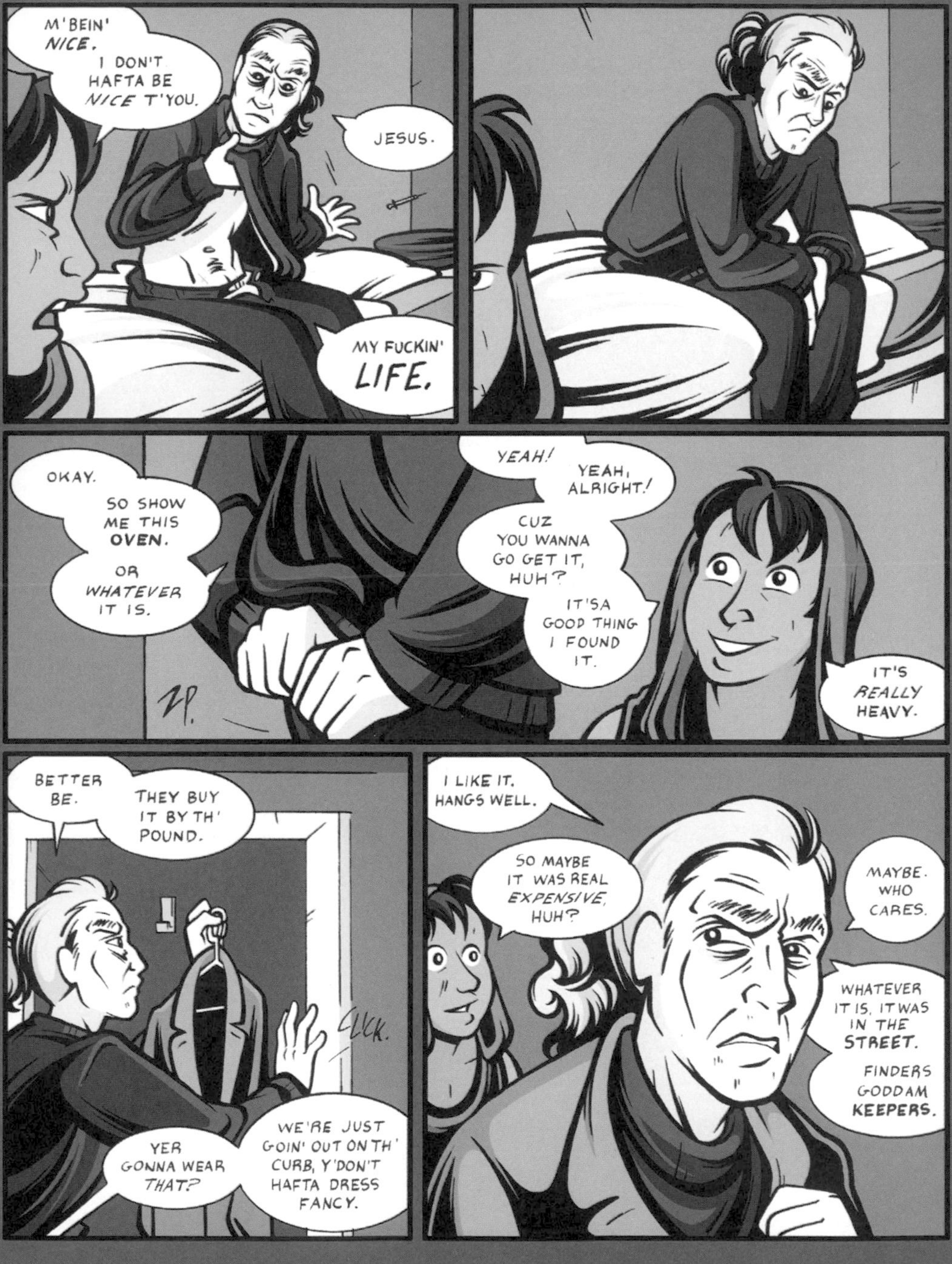

M'BEIN' NICE.
I DON'T HAFTA BE NICE T'YOU.
JESUS.
MY FUCKIN' LIFE.
OKAY.
SO SHOW ME THIS OVEN.
OR WHATEVER IT IS.
ZIP.
YEAH!
YEAH, ALRIGHT!
CUZ YOU WANNA GO GET IT, HUH?
IT'SA GOOD THING I FOUND IT.
IT'S REALLY HEAVY.
BETTER BE.
THEY BUY IT BY TH' POUND.
CLICK.
YER GONNA WEAR THAT?
WE'RE JUST GOIN' OUT ON TH' CURB, Y'DON'T HAFTA DRESS FANCY.
I LIKE IT. HANGS WELL.
SO MAYBE IT WAS REAL EXPENSIVE, HUH?
MAYBE. WHO CARES.
WHATEVER IT IS, IT WAS IN THE STREET.
FINDERS GODDAM KEEPERS.

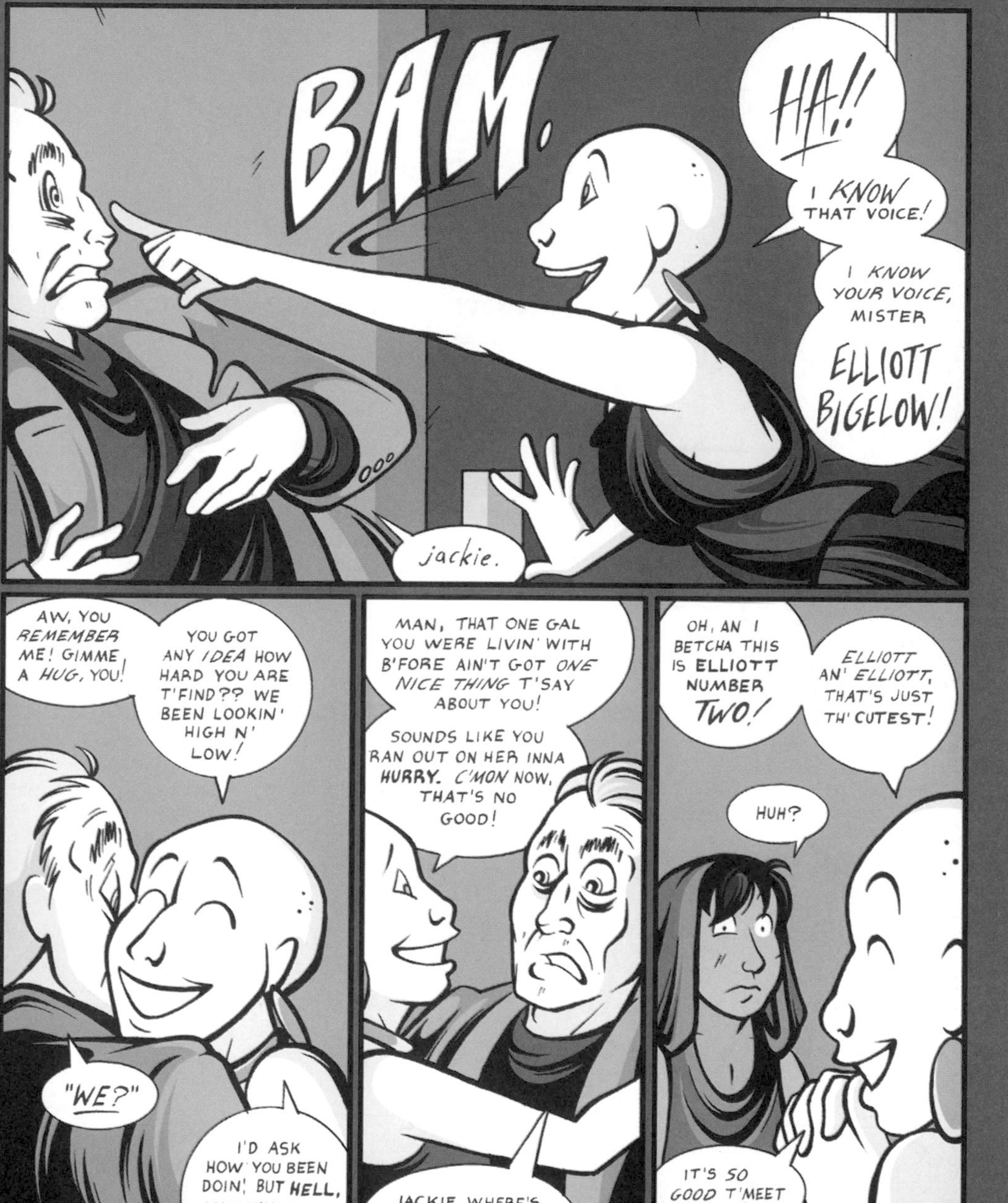
BAM.
HA!!
I KNOW THAT VOICE!
I KNOW YOUR VOICE, MISTER ELLIOTT BIGELOW!
jackie.
AW, YOU REMEMBER ME! GIMME A HUG, YOU!
YOU GOT ANY IDEA HOW HARD YOU ARE T'FIND?? WE BEEN LOOKIN' HIGH N' LOW!
"WE?"
I'D ASK HOW YOU BEEN DOIN', BUT HELL, YOU INNA WET HOUSE, HUH?
MAN, THAT ONE GAL YOU WERE LIVIN' WITH B'FORE AIN'T GOT ONE NICE THING T'SAY ABOUT YOU!
SOUNDS LIKE YOU RAN OUT ON HER INNA HURRY. C'MON NOW, THAT'S NO GOOD!
JACKIE, WHERE'S MARCUS? WHERE'S APOLLO?
OH, AN I BETCHA THIS IS ELLIOTT NUMBER TWO!
ELLIOTT AN' ELLIOTT, THAT'S JUST TH' CUTEST!
HUH?
IT'S SO GOOD T'MEET YOU!

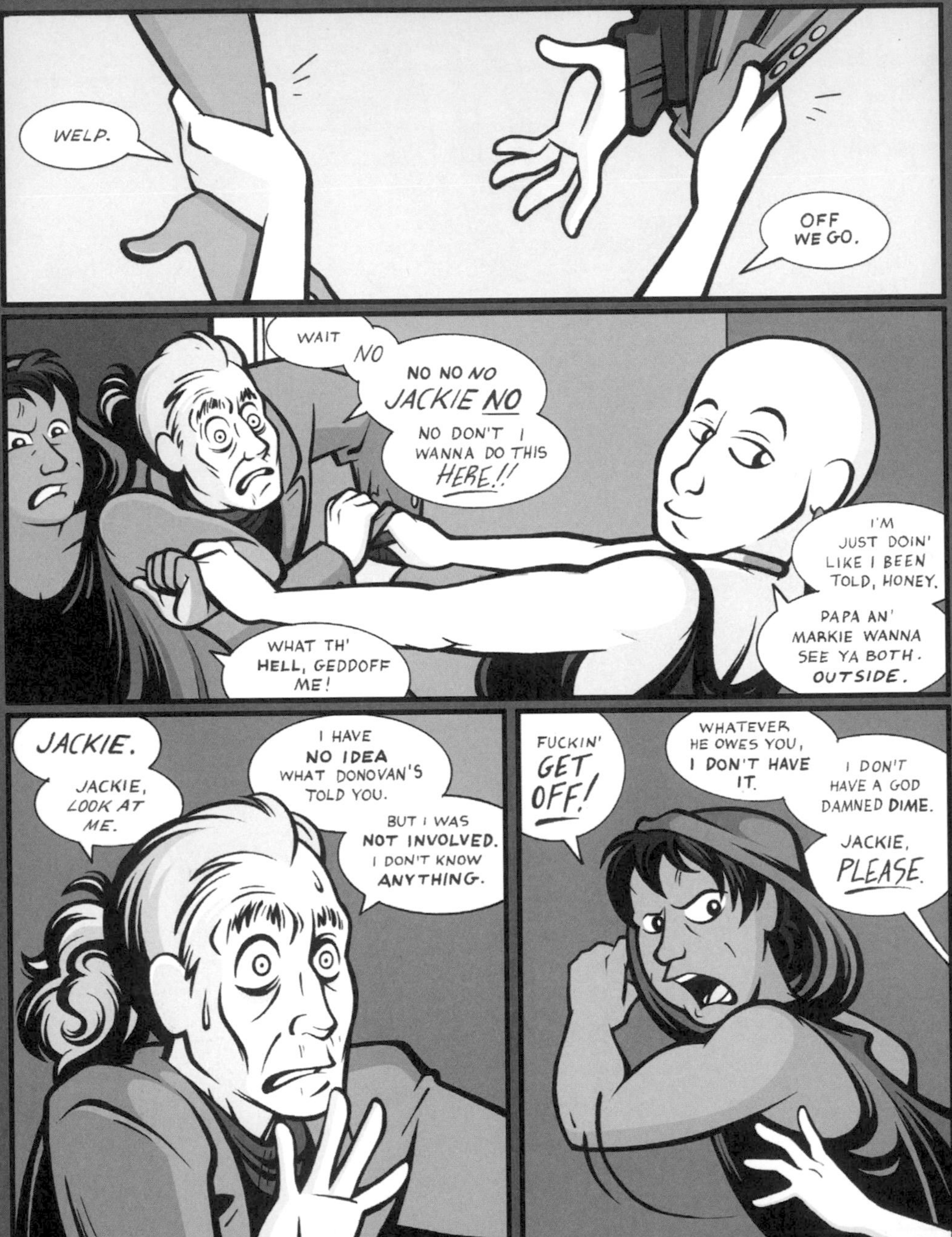

WELP.
OFF WE GO.
WAIT NO
NO NO NO JACKIE NO
NO DON'T I WANNA DO THIS HERE!!
WHAT TH' HELL, GEDDOFF ME!
I'M JUST DOIN' LIKE I BEEN TOLD, HONEY.
PAPA AN' MARKIE WANNA SEE YA BOTH. OUTSIDE.
JACKIE.
JACKIE, LOOK AT ME.
I HAVE NO IDEA WHAT DONOVAN'S TOLD YOU.
BUT I WAS NOT INVOLVED. I DON'T KNOW ANYTHING.
FUCKIN' GET OFF!
WHATEVER HE OWES YOU, I DON'T HAVE IT.
I DON'T HAVE A GOD DAMNED DIME.
JACKIE, PLEASE.

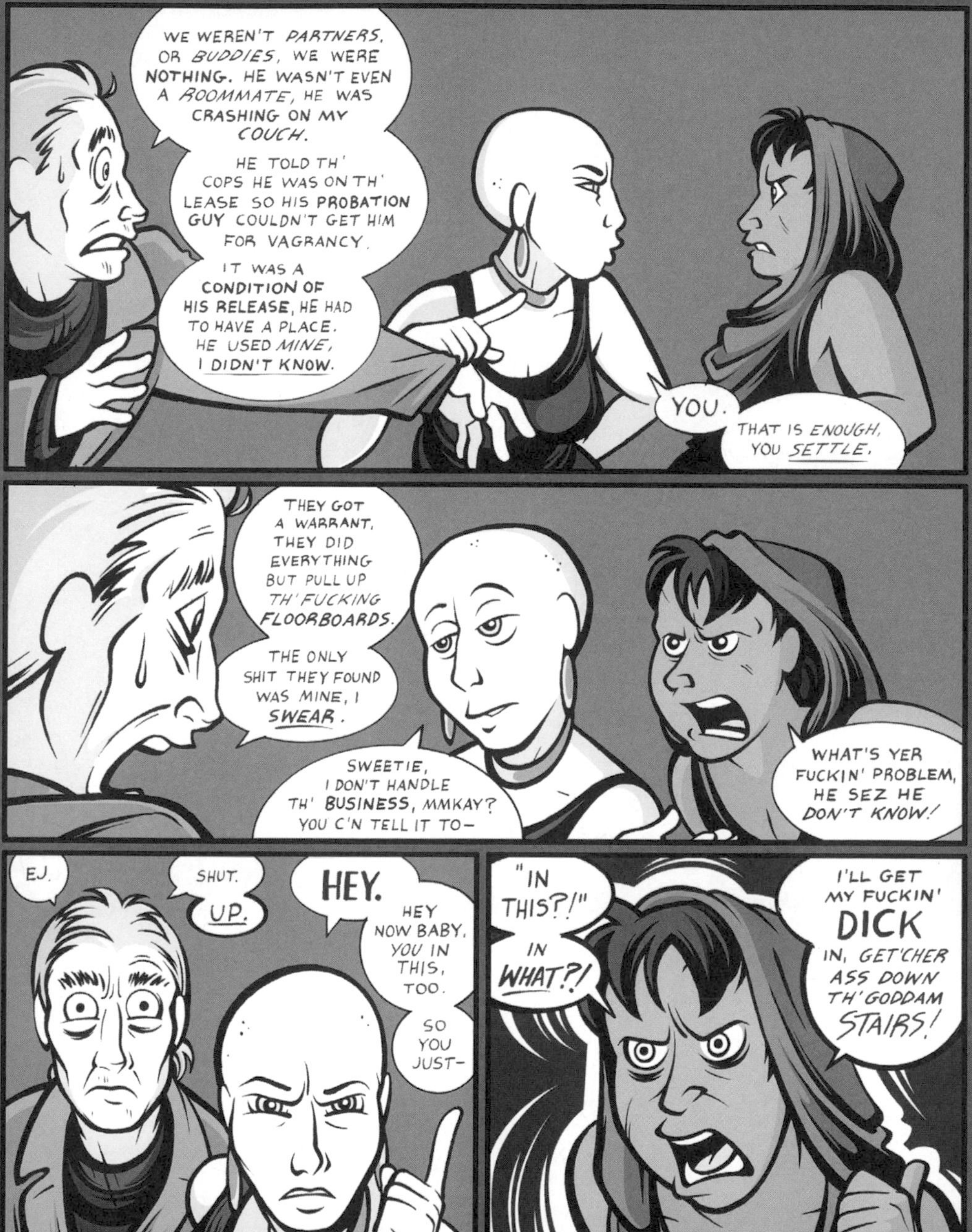
WE WEREN'T PARTNERS, OR BUDDIES, WE WERE NOTHING. HE WASN'T EVEN A ROOMMATE, HE WAS CRASHING ON MY COUCH.
HE TOLD TH' COPS HE WAS ON TH' LEASE SO HIS PROBATION GUY COULDN'T GET HIM FOR VAGRANCY.
IT WAS A CONDITION OF HIS RELEASE, HE HAD TO HAVE A PLACE. HE USED MINE, I DIDN'T KNOW.
YOU.
THAT IS ENOUGH, YOU SETTLE.
THEY GOT A WARRANT, THEY DID EVERYTHING BUT PULL UP TH' FUCKING FLOORBOARDS.
THE ONLY SHIT THEY FOUND WAS MINE, I SWEAR.
SWEETIE, I DON'T HANDLE TH' BUSINESS, MMKAY? YOU C'N TELL IT TO—
WHAT'S YER FUCKIN' PROBLEM, HE SEZ HE DON'T KNOW!
EJ.
SHUT.
UP.
HEY.
HEY NOW BABY. YOU IN THIS, TOO.
SO YOU JUST—
"IN THIS?!"
IN WHAT?!
I'LL GET MY FUCKIN' DICK IN, GET'CHER ASS DOWN TH' GODDAM STAIRS!

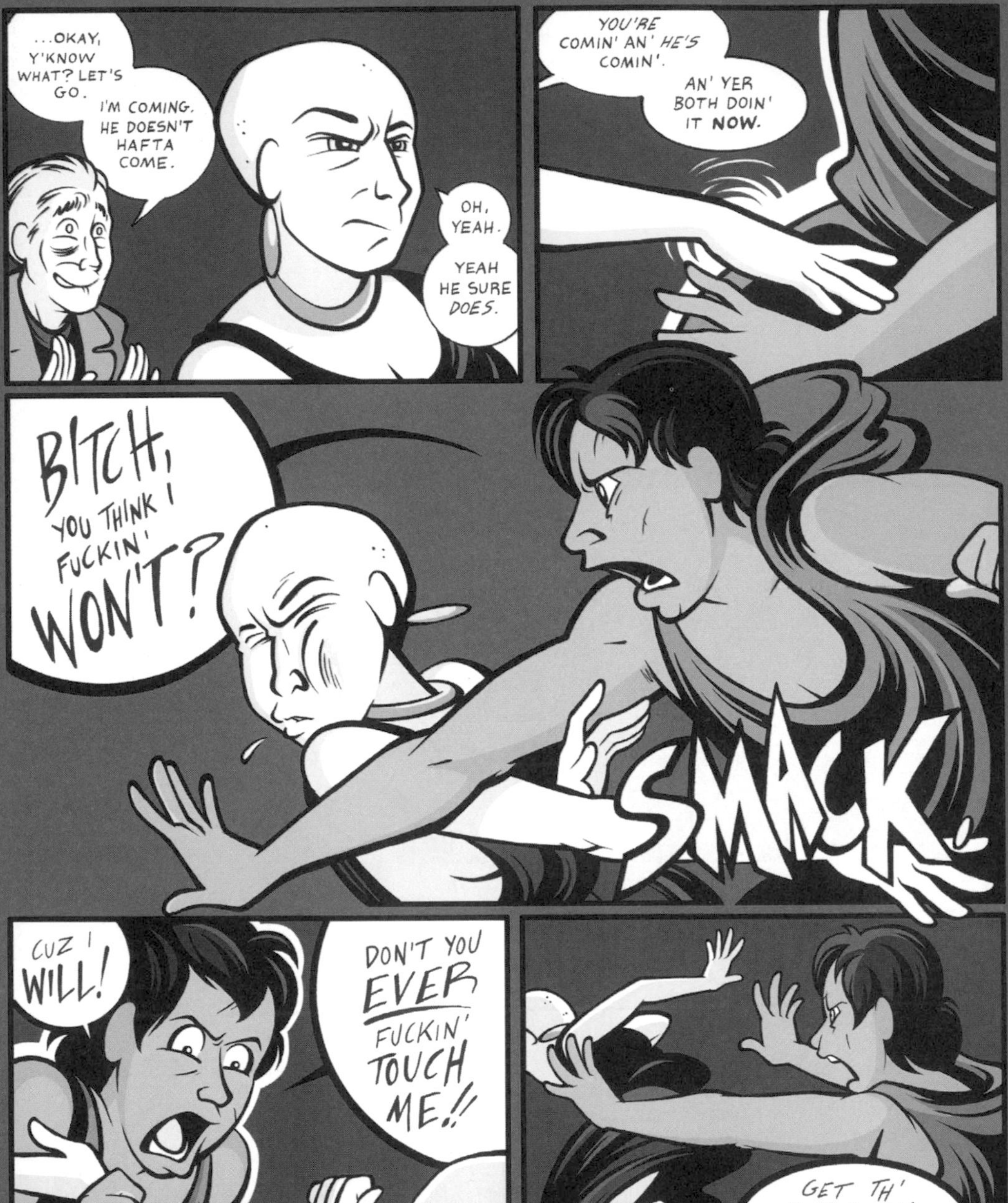
...OKAY, Y'KNOW WHAT? LET'S GO.
I'M COMING. HE DOESN'T HAFTA COME.
OH, YEAH.
YEAH HE SURE *DOES*.
YOU'RE COMIN' AN' *HE'S* COMIN'.
AN' YER BOTH DOIN' IT **NOW**.
BITCH, YOU THINK I FUCKIN' WON'T?
SMACK!
CUZ I WILL!
DON'T YOU EVER FUCKIN' TOUCH ME!!
GET TH' FUCK OUTTA HERE B'FORE I **DO IT TO YA!**

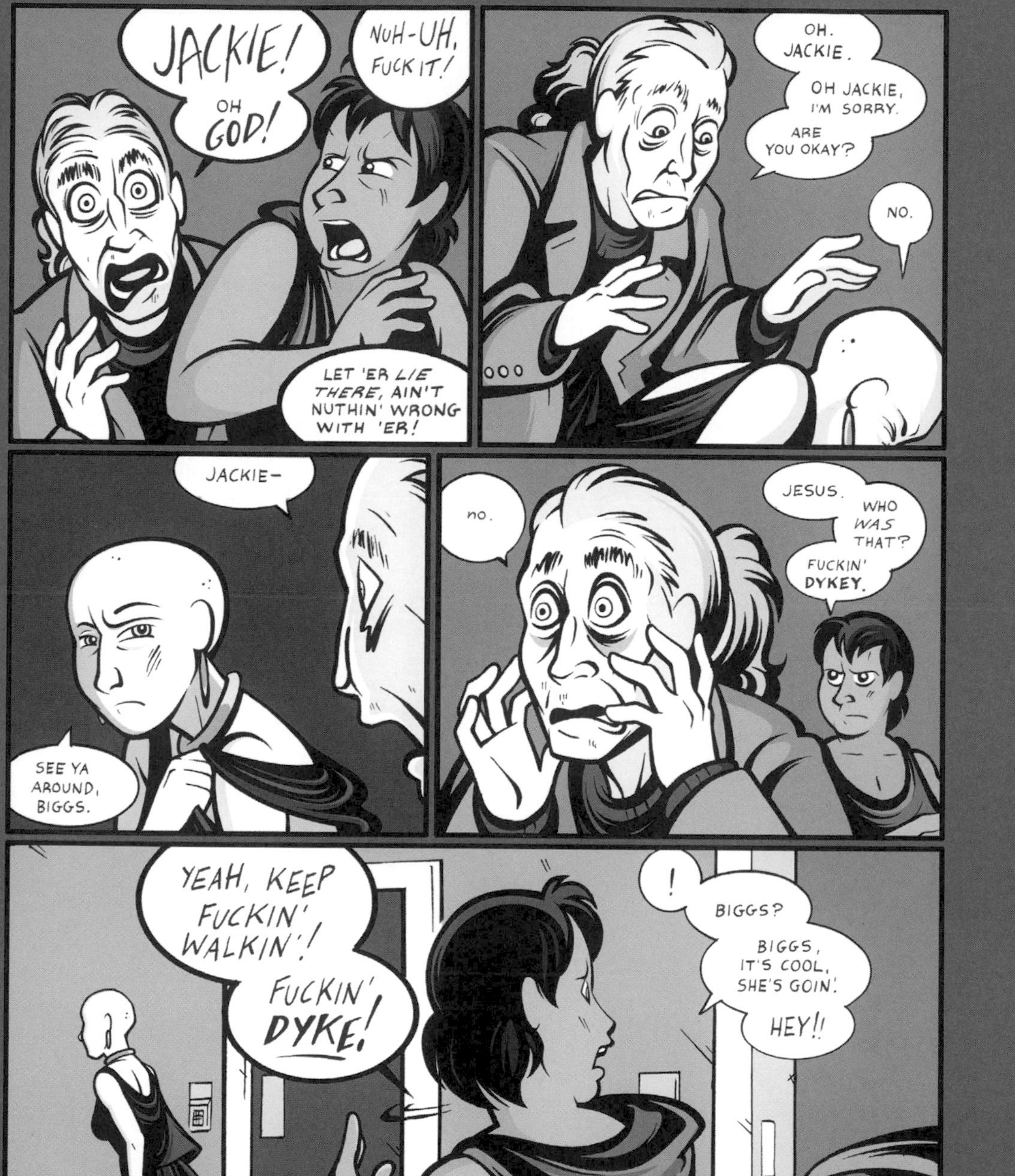
JACKIE! OH GOD!
NUH-UH, FUCK IT!
LET 'ER LIE THERE, AIN'T NUTHIN' WRONG WITH 'ER!
OH. JACKIE.
OH JACKIE, I'M SORRY.
ARE YOU OKAY?
NO.
JACKIE-
SEE YA AROUND, BIGGS.
no.
JESUS.
WHO WAS THAT?
FUCKIN' DYKEY.
YEAH, KEEP FUCKIN' WALKIN'!
FUCKIN' DYKE!
!
BIGGS?
BIGGS, IT'S COOL, SHE'S GOIN'.
HEY!!

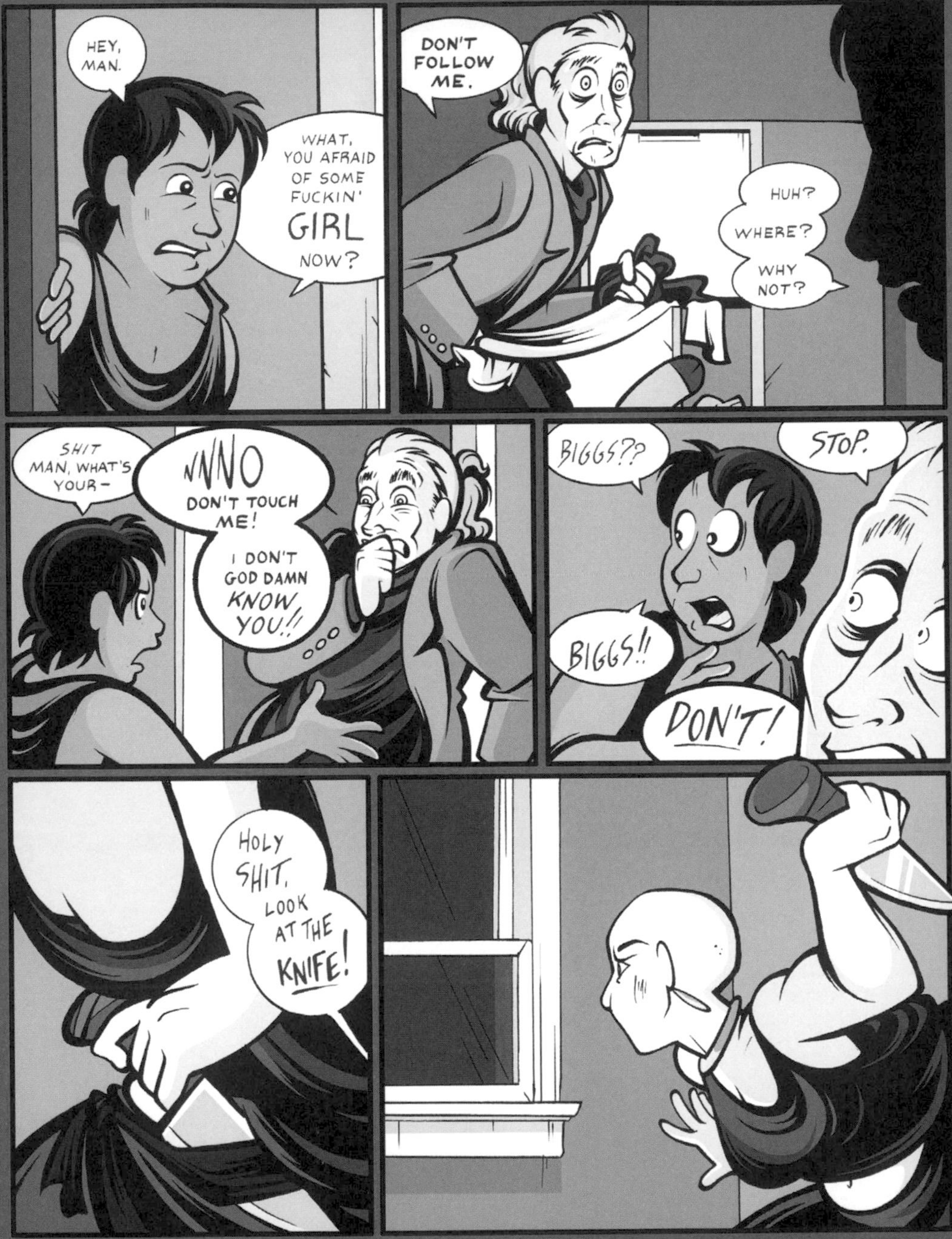
HEY, MAN.
WHAT, YOU AFRAID OF SOME FUCKIN' GIRL NOW?
DON'T FOLLOW ME.
HUH?
WHERE?
WHY NOT?
SHIT MAN, WHAT'S YOUR–
NNNO DON'T TOUCH ME!
I DON'T GOD DAMN KNOW YOU!!
BIGGS??
STOP.
BIGGS!!
DON'T!
HOLY SHIT, LOOK AT THE KNIFE!

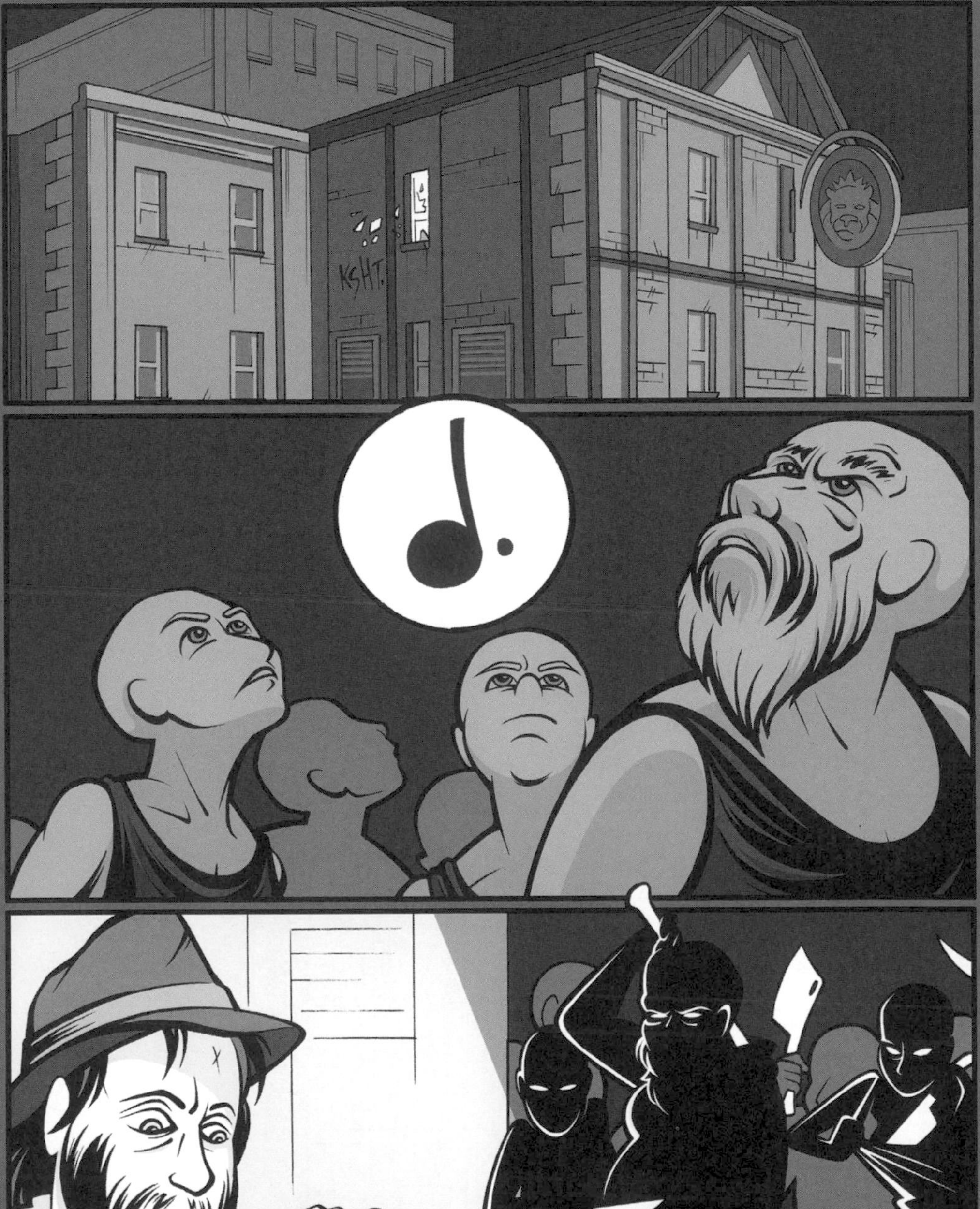
KSHT.

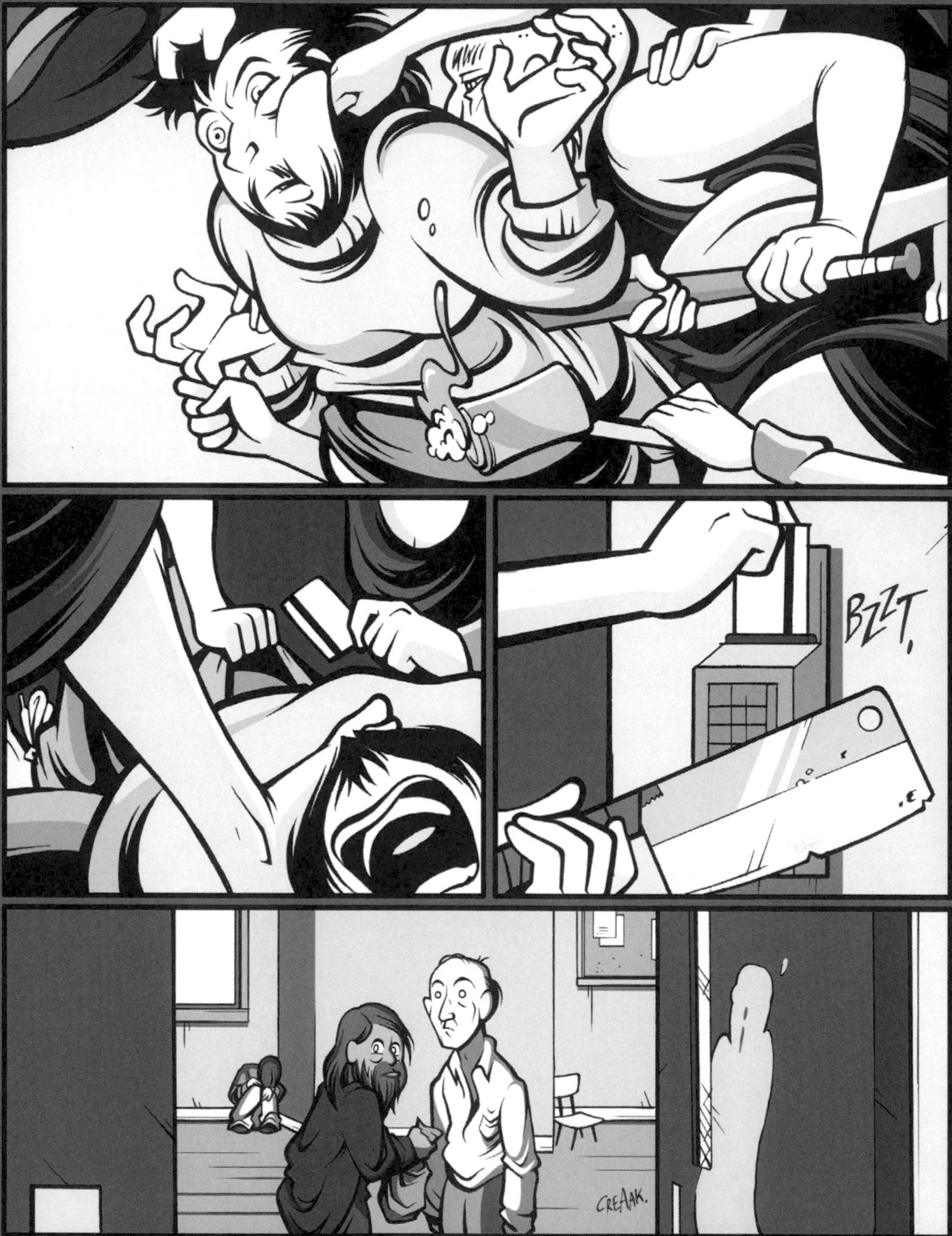
BZZT.
CREAAK.

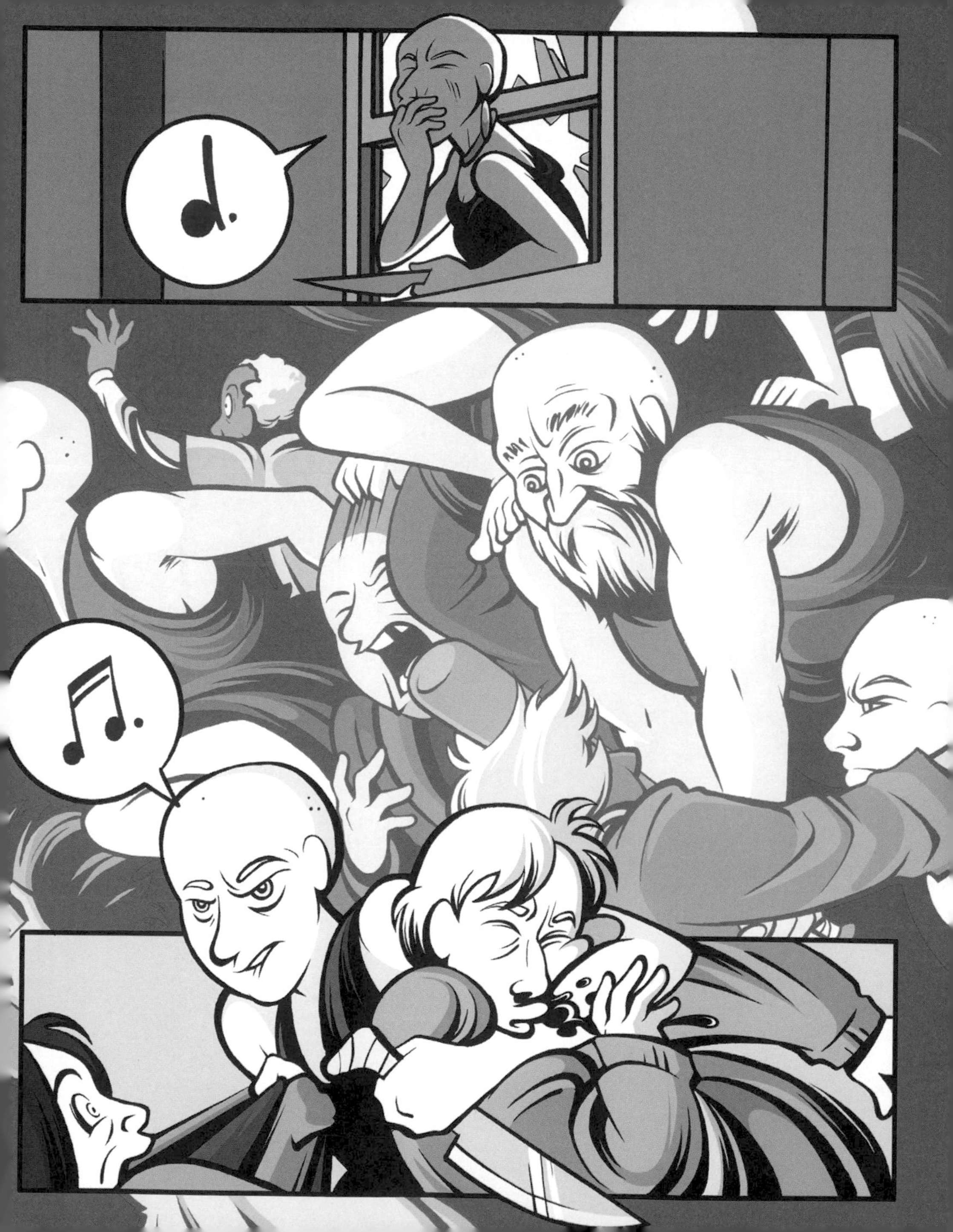

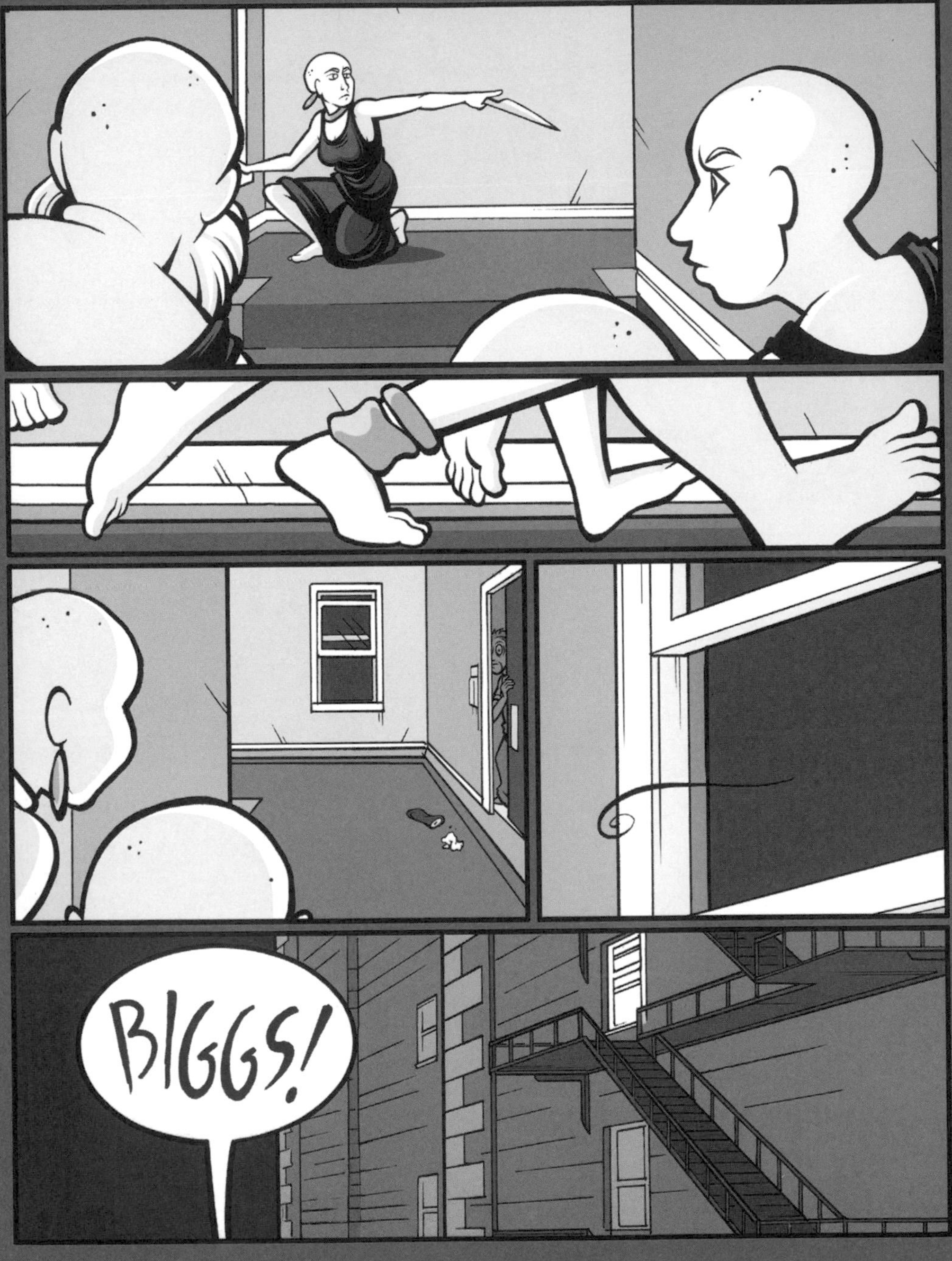
BIGGS!

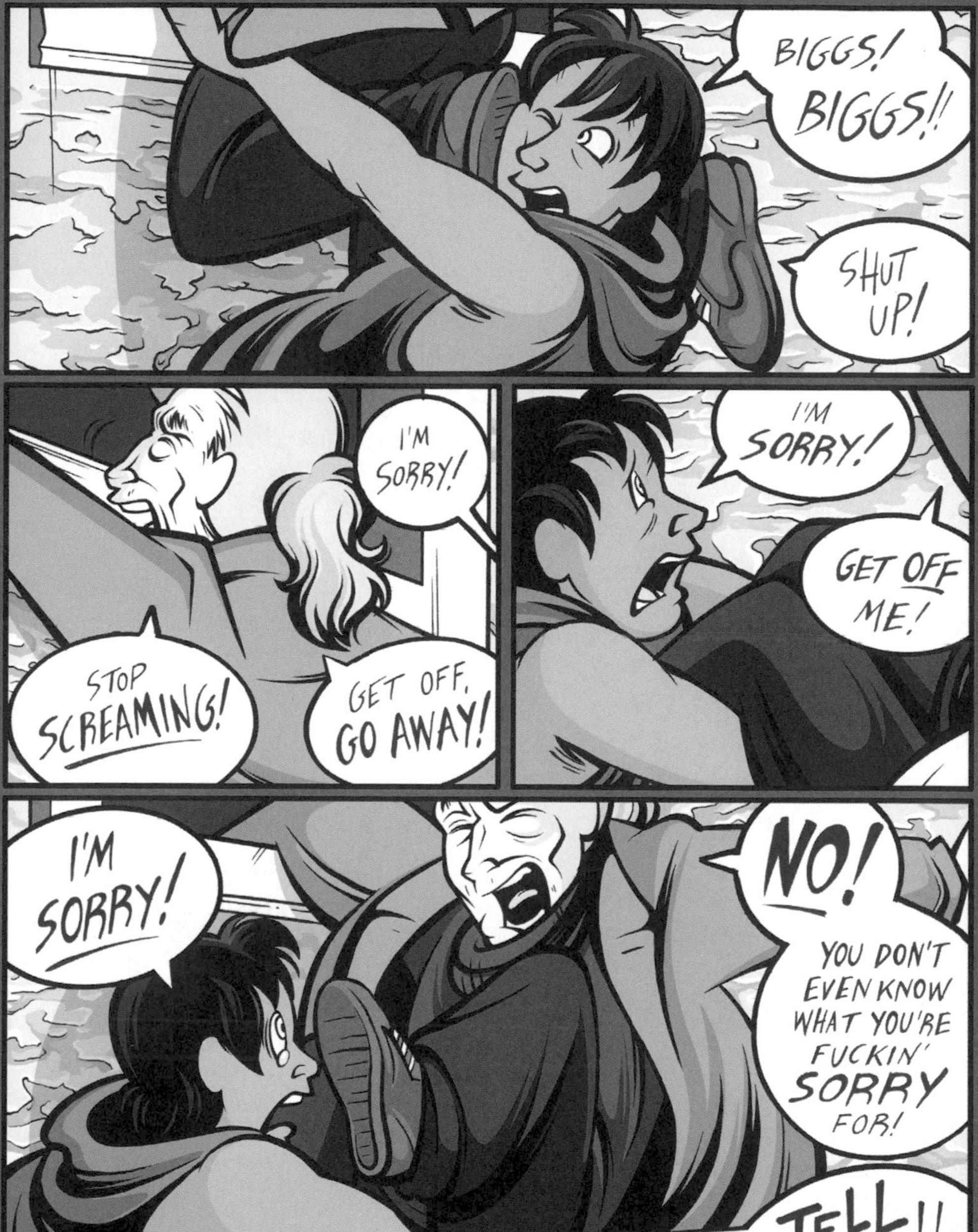
BIGGS! BIGGS!!
SHUT UP!
I'M SORRY!
STOP SCREAMING!
GET OFF, GO AWAY!
I'M SORRY!
GET OFF ME!
I'M SORRY!
NO!
YOU DON'T EVEN KNOW WHAT YOU'RE FUCKIN' SORRY FOR!
TELL ME!!

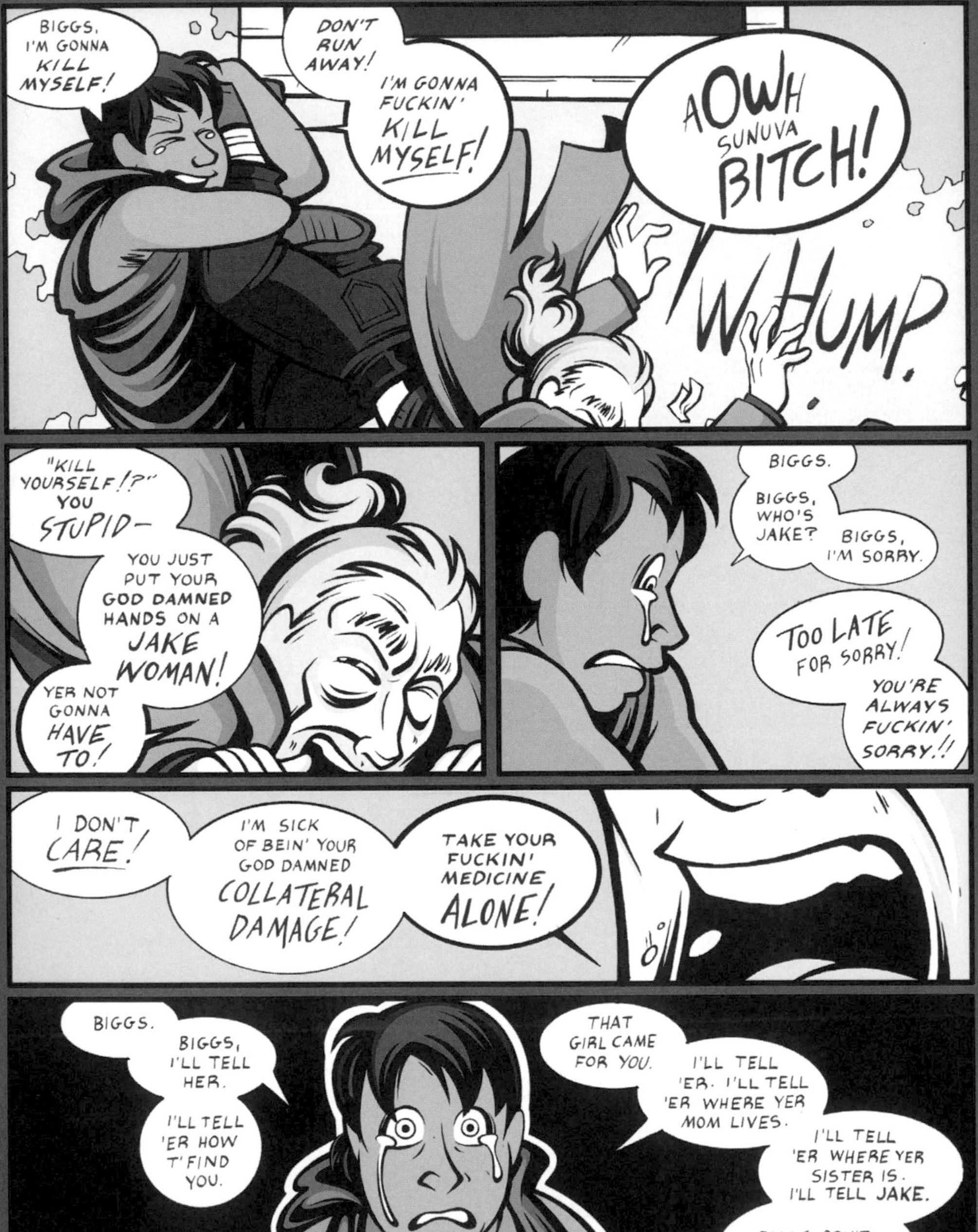
BIGGS, I'M GONNA KILL MYSELF!
DON'T RUN AWAY!
I'M GONNA FUCKIN' KILL MYSELF!
AOWH SUNUVA BITCH!
WHUMP.
"KILL YOURSELF!?" YOU STUPID—
YOU JUST PUT YOUR GOD DAMNED HANDS ON A JAKE WOMAN!
YER NOT GONNA HAVE TO!
BIGGS.
BIGGS, WHO'S JAKE?
BIGGS, I'M SORRY.
TOO LATE FOR SORRY!
YOU'RE ALWAYS FUCKIN' SORRY!!
I DON'T CARE!
I'M SICK OF BEIN' YOUR GOD DAMNED COLLATERAL DAMAGE!
TAKE YOUR FUCKIN' MEDICINE ALONE!
BIGGS.
BIGGS, I'LL TELL HER.
I'LL TELL 'ER HOW T' FIND YOU.
THAT GIRL CAME FOR YOU.
I'LL TELL 'ER. I'LL TELL 'ER WHERE YER MOM LIVES.
I'LL TELL 'ER WHERE YER SISTER IS. I'LL TELL JAKE.
BIGGS, DON'T LEAVE ME ALONE.

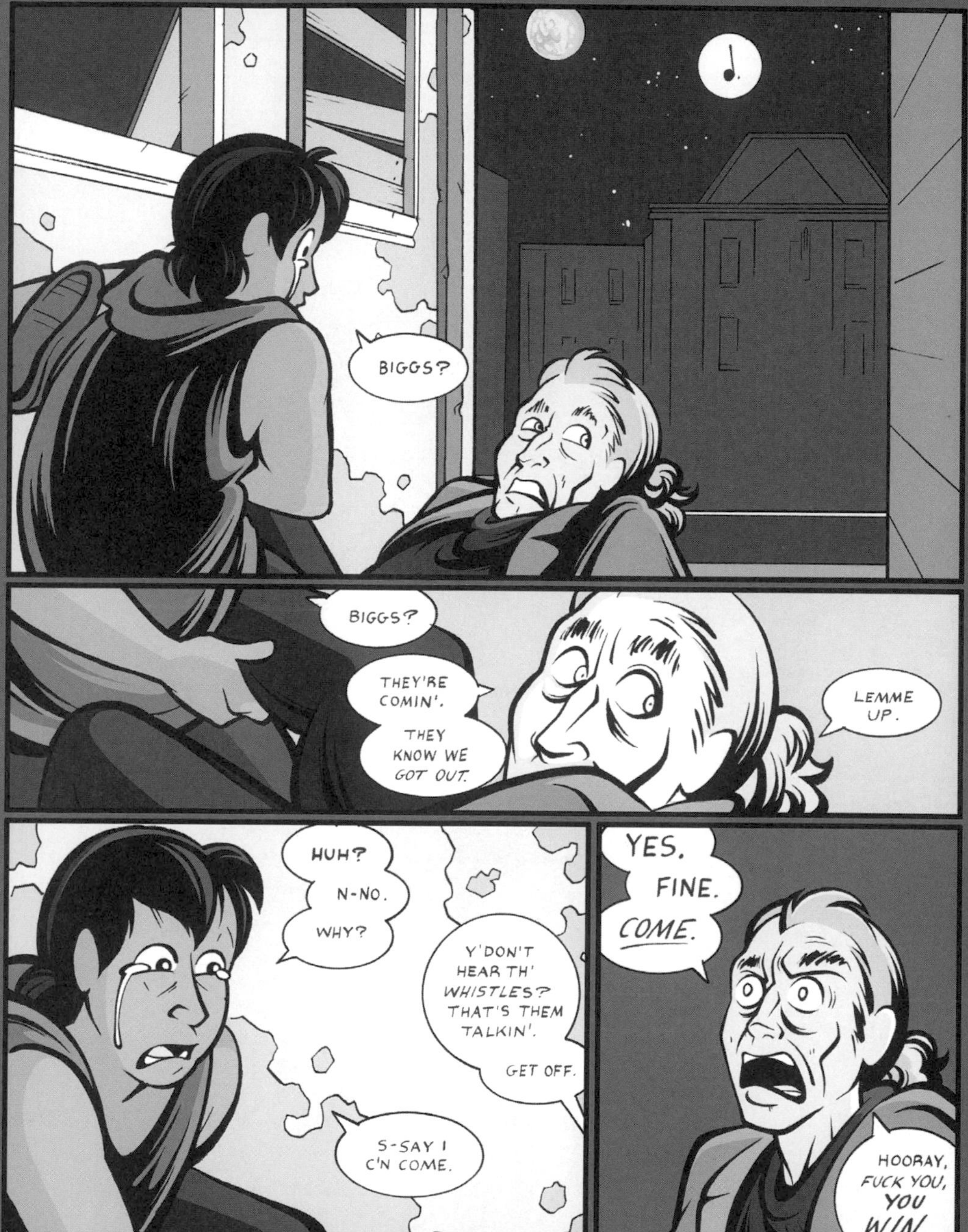
BIGGS?
BIGGS?
THEY'RE COMIN'.
THEY KNOW WE GOT OUT.
LEMME UP.
HUH?
N-NO.
WHY?
Y'DON'T HEAR TH' WHISTLES? THAT'S THEM TALKIN'.
GET OFF.
S-SAY I C'N COME.
YES.
FINE.
COME.
HOORAY, FUCK YOU, YOU WIN.

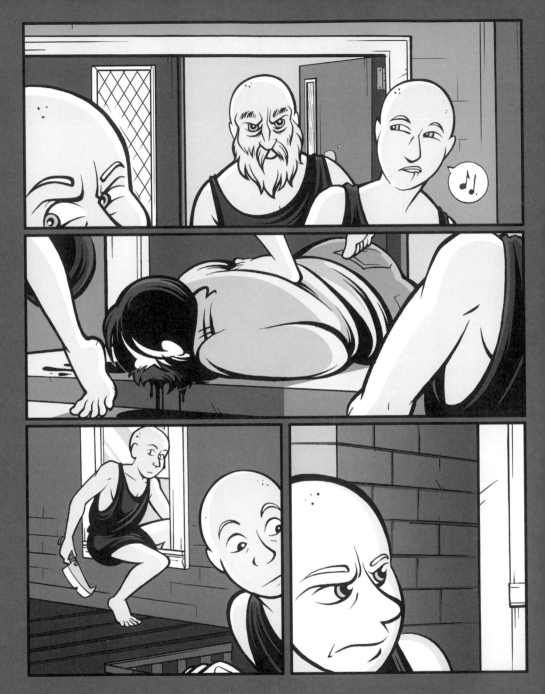

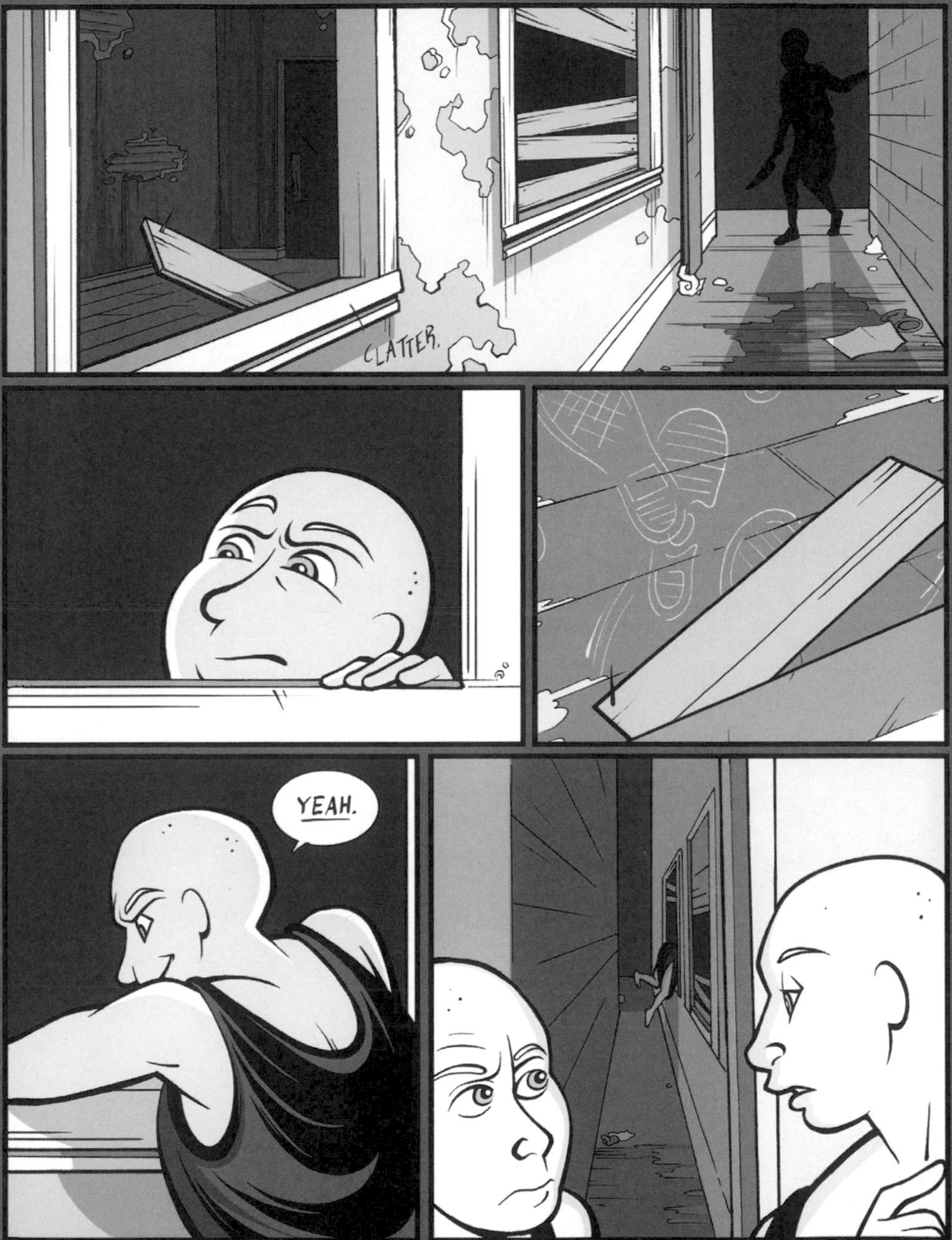
CLATTER.
YEAH.

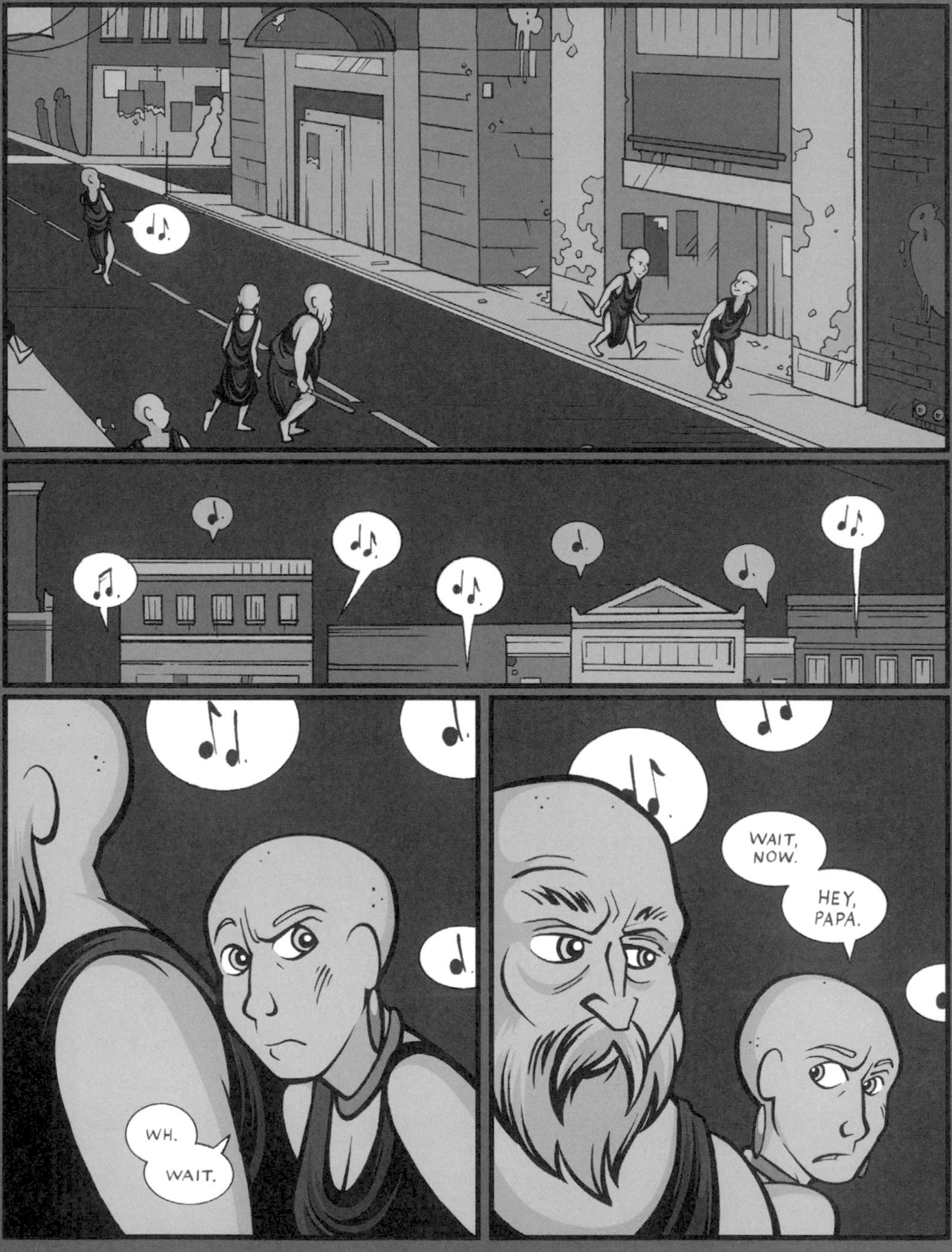
WH.
WAIT.
WAIT, NOW.
HEY, PAPA.

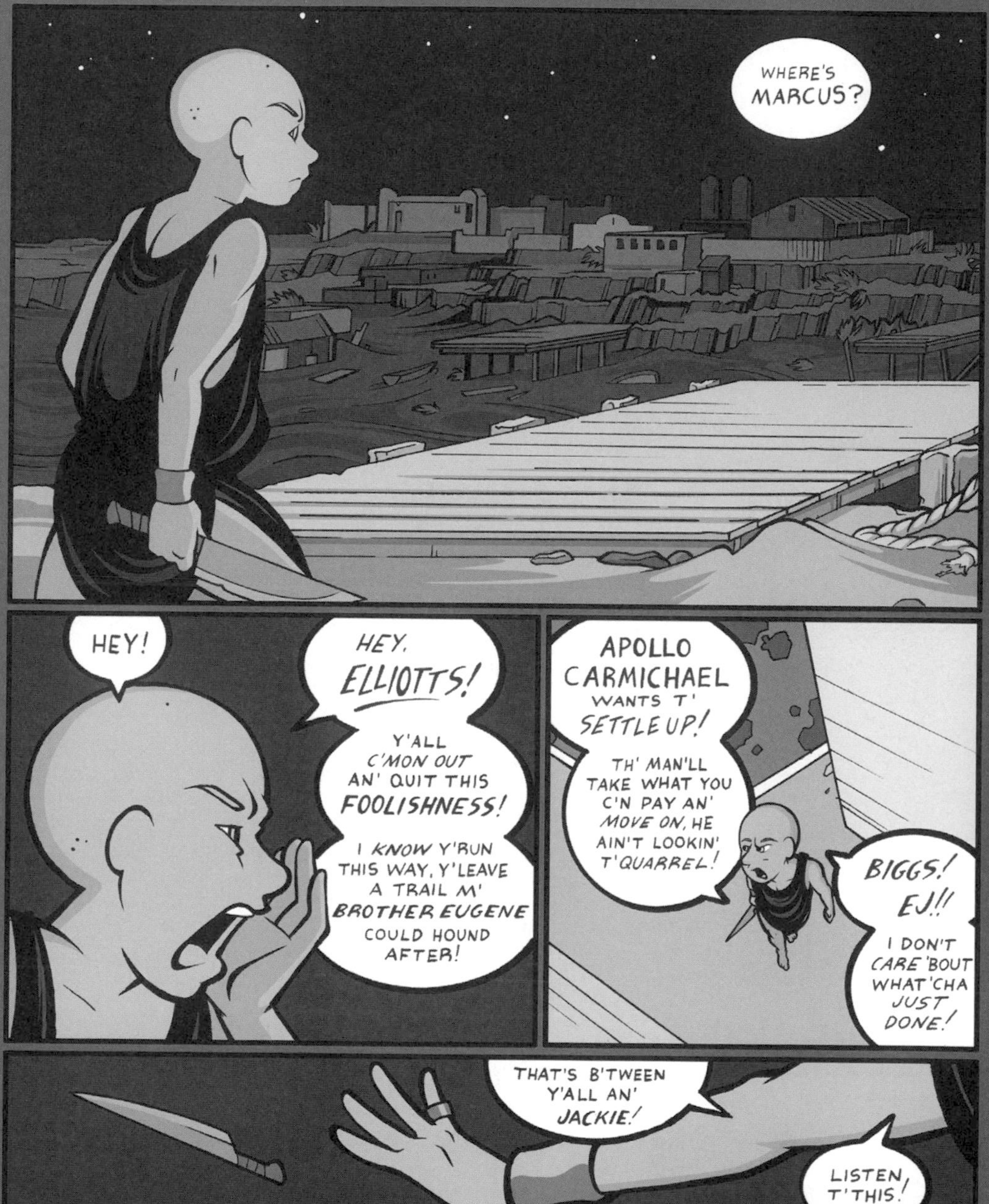
WHERE'S MARCUS?
HEY!
HEY, ELLIOTTS!
Y'ALL C'MON OUT AN' QUIT THIS FOOLISHNESS!
I KNOW Y'RUN THIS WAY, Y'LEAVE A TRAIL M' BROTHER EUGENE COULD HOUND AFTER!
APOLLO CARMICHAEL WANTS T' SETTLE UP!
TH' MAN'LL TAKE WHAT YOU C'N PAY AN' MOVE ON, HE AIN'T LOOKIN' T'QUARREL!
BIGGS! EJ!!
I DON'T CARE 'BOUT WHAT'CHA JUST DONE!
THAT'S B'TWEEN Y'ALL AN' JACKIE!
LISTEN, T'THIS!

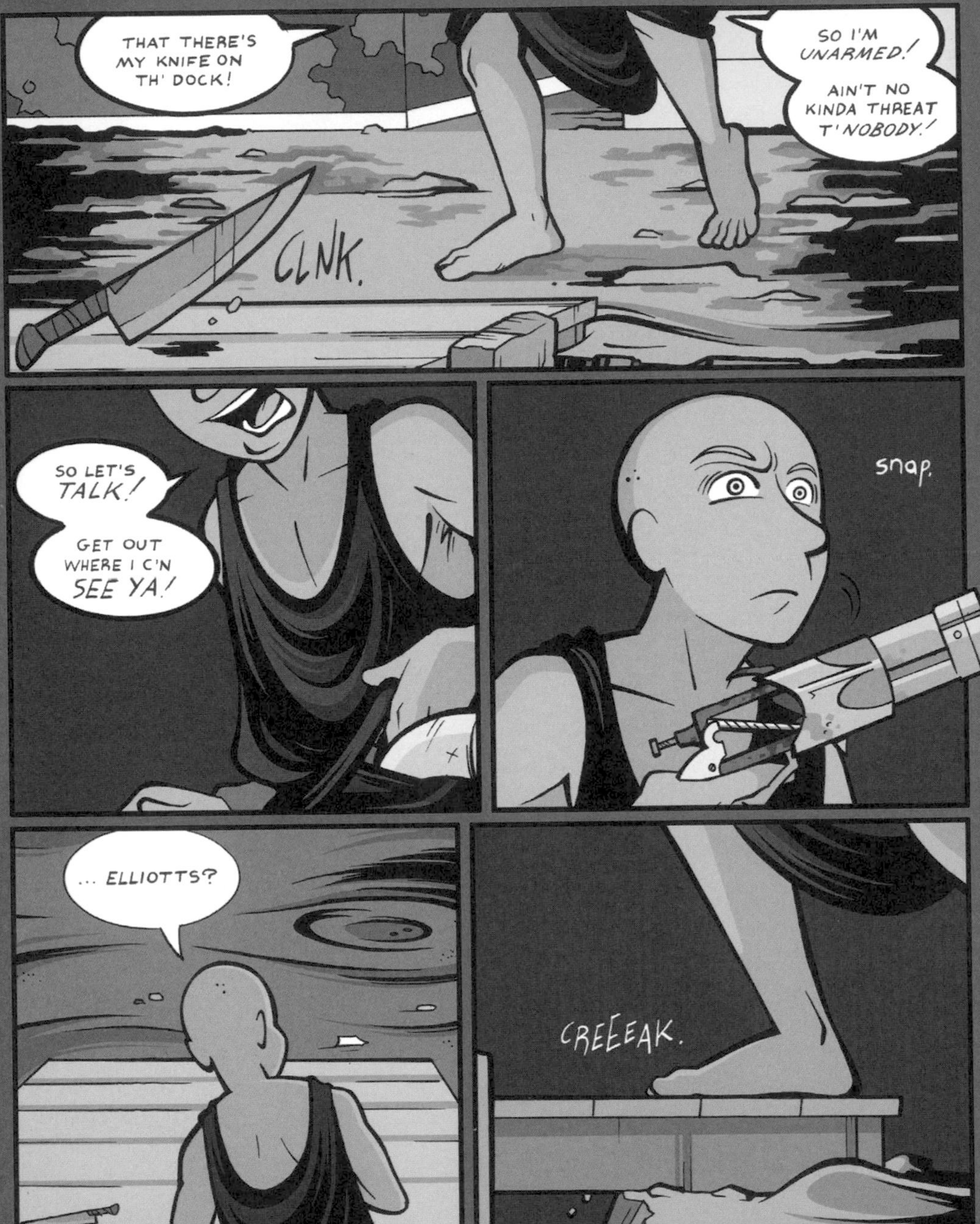
THAT THERE'S MY KNIFE ON TH' DOCK!
SO I'M UNARMED!
AIN'T NO KINDA THREAT T'NOBODY!
CLNK.
SO LET'S TALK!
GET OUT WHERE I C'N SEE YA!
snap.
... ELLIOTTS?
CREEEAK.

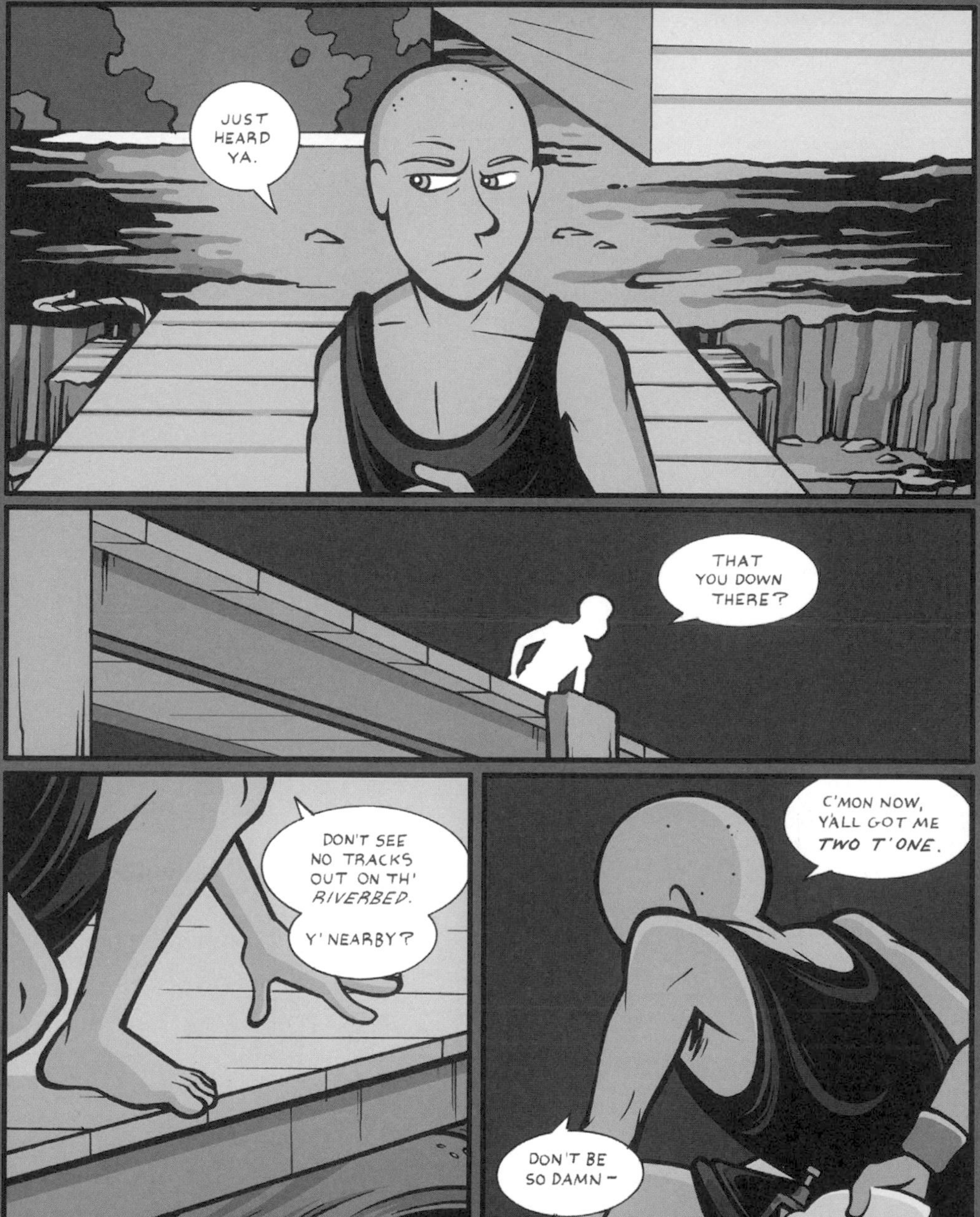
JUST HEARD YA.
THAT YOU DOWN THERE?
DON'T SEE NO TRACKS OUT ON TH' RIVERBED.
Y' NEARBY?
C'MON NOW, Y'ALL GOT ME TWO T' ONE.
DON'T BE SO DAMN -

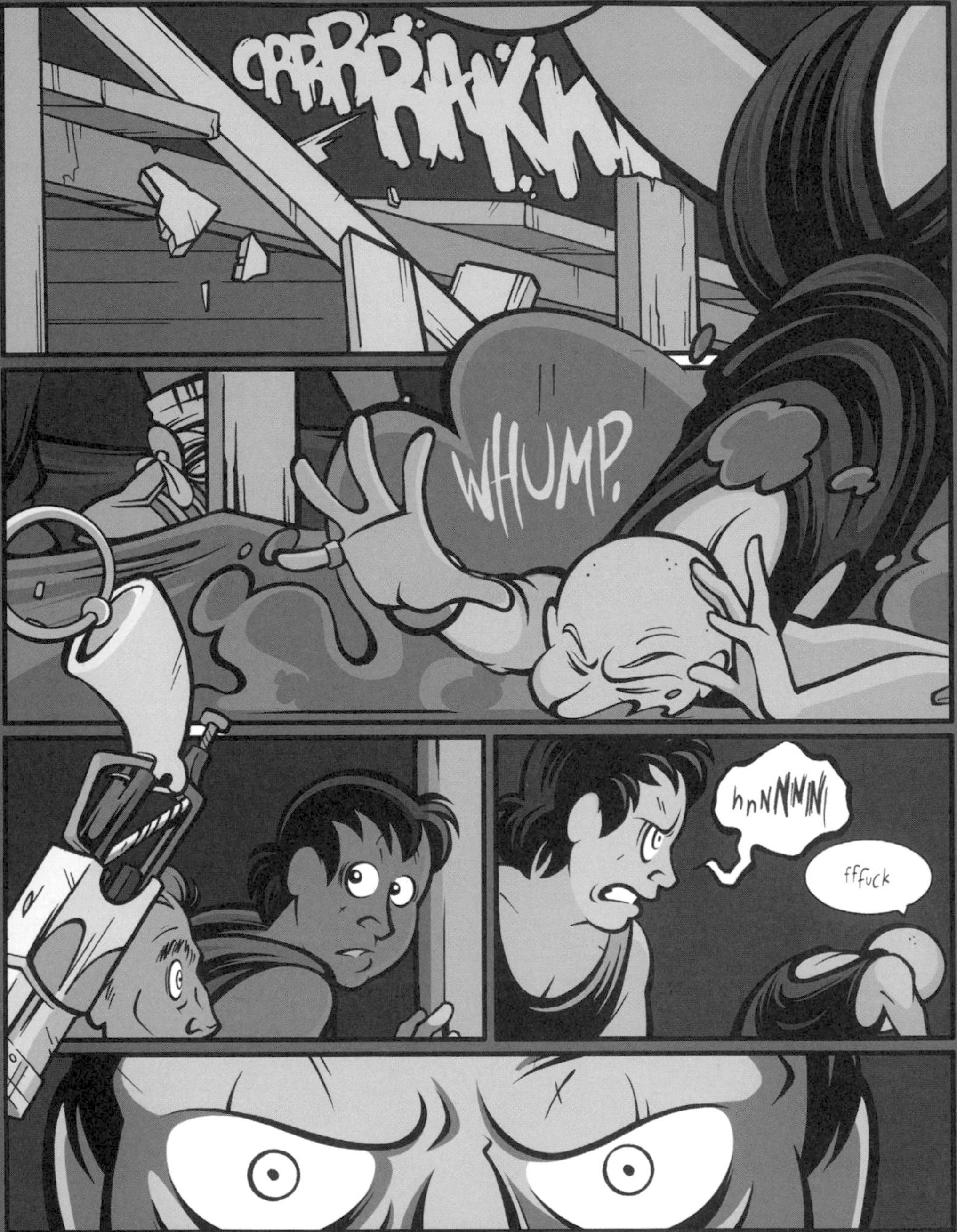
CRRRRAKK
WHUMP.
hnNNNN
fffuck

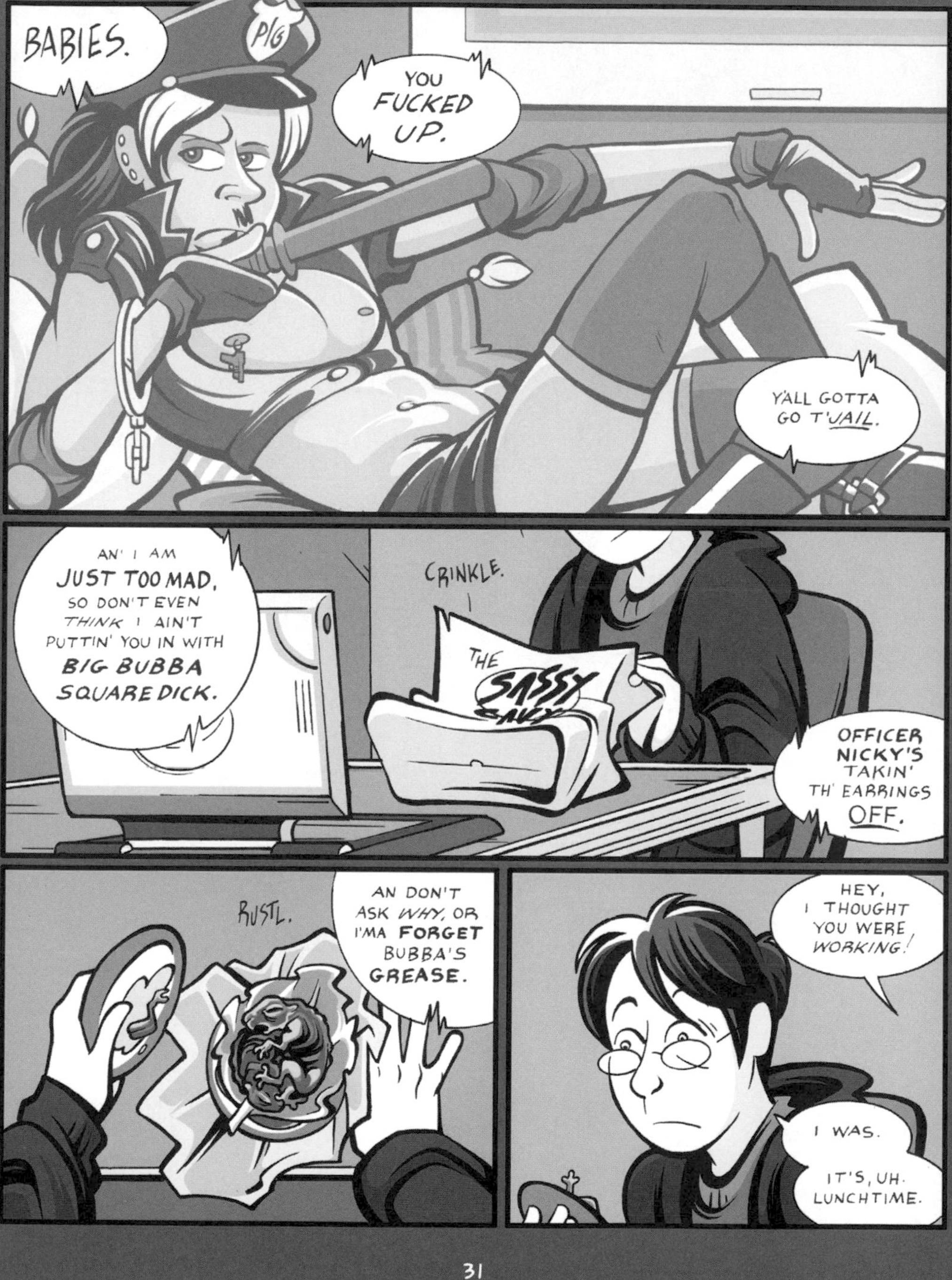
BABIES.
YOU FUCKED UP.
P/G
Y'ALL GOTTA GO T'JAIL.
AN' I AM JUST TOO MAD, SO DON'T EVEN THINK I AIN'T PUTTIN' YOU IN WITH BIG BUBBA SQUARE DICK.
CRINKLE.
THE SASSY
OFFICER NICKY'S TAKIN' TH' EARRINGS OFF.
RUSTL.
AN DON'T ASK WHY, OR I'MA FORGET BUBBA'S GREASE.
HEY, I THOUGHT YOU WERE WORKING!
I WAS.
IT'S, UH. LUNCHTIME.

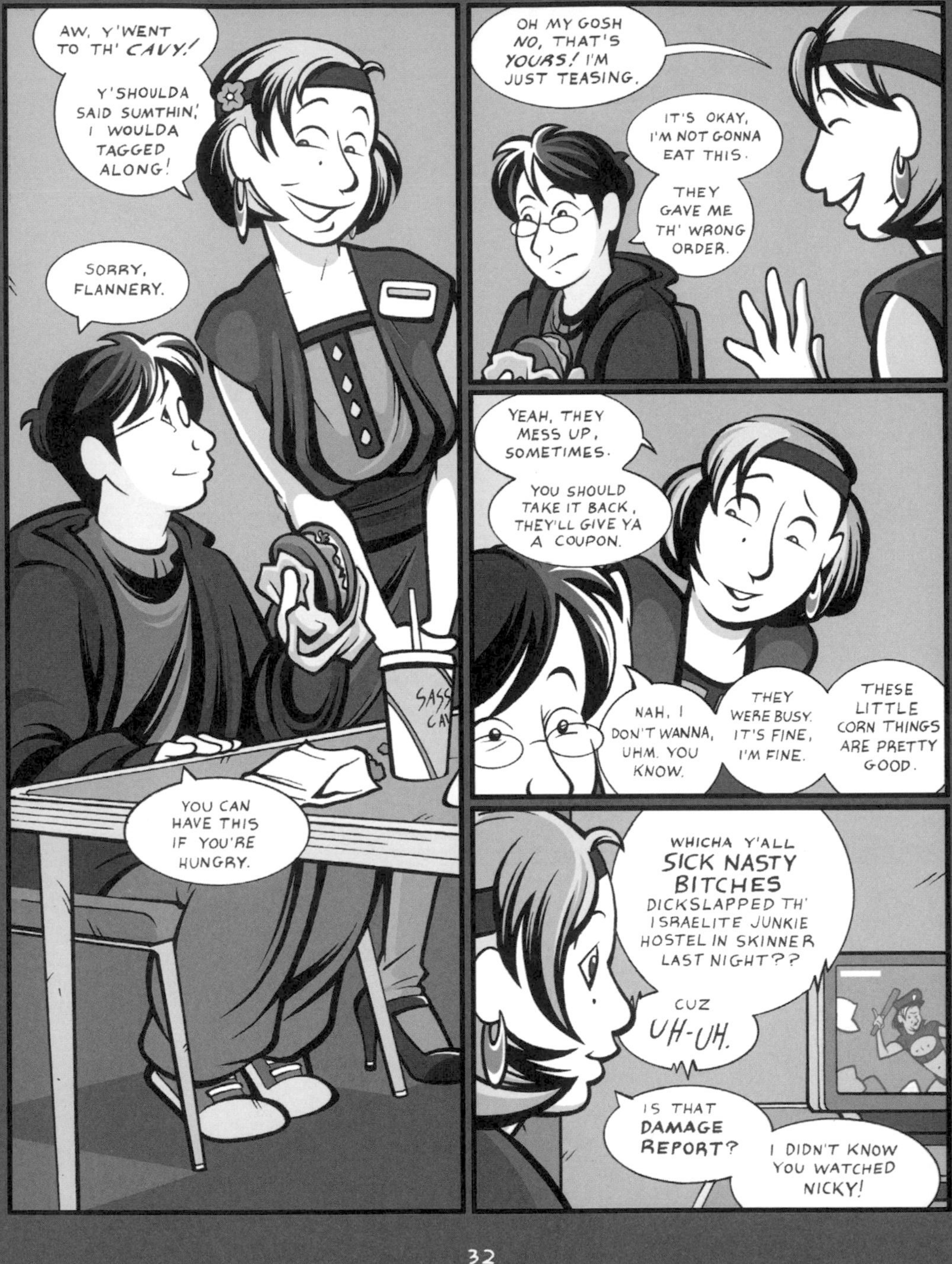
AW, Y'WENT TO TH' CAVY!
Y'SHOULDA SAID SUMTHIN,' I WOULDA TAGGED ALONG!
SORRY, FLANNERY.
YOU CAN HAVE THIS IF YOU'RE HUNGRY.
OH MY GOSH NO, THAT'S YOURS! I'M JUST TEASING.
IT'S OKAY, I'M NOT GONNA EAT THIS.
THEY GAVE ME TH' WRONG ORDER.
YEAH, THEY MESS UP, SOMETIMES.
YOU SHOULD TAKE IT BACK, THEY'LL GIVE YA A COUPON.
NAH, I DON'T WANNA, UHM. YOU KNOW.
THEY WERE BUSY. IT'S FINE, I'M FINE.
THESE LITTLE CORN THINGS ARE PRETTY GOOD.
WHICHA Y'ALL SICK NASTY BITCHES DICKSLAPPED TH' ISRAELITE JUNKIE HOSTEL IN SKINNER LAST NIGHT??
CUZ UH-UH.
IS THAT DAMAGE REPORT?
I DIDN'T KNOW YOU WATCHED NICKY!

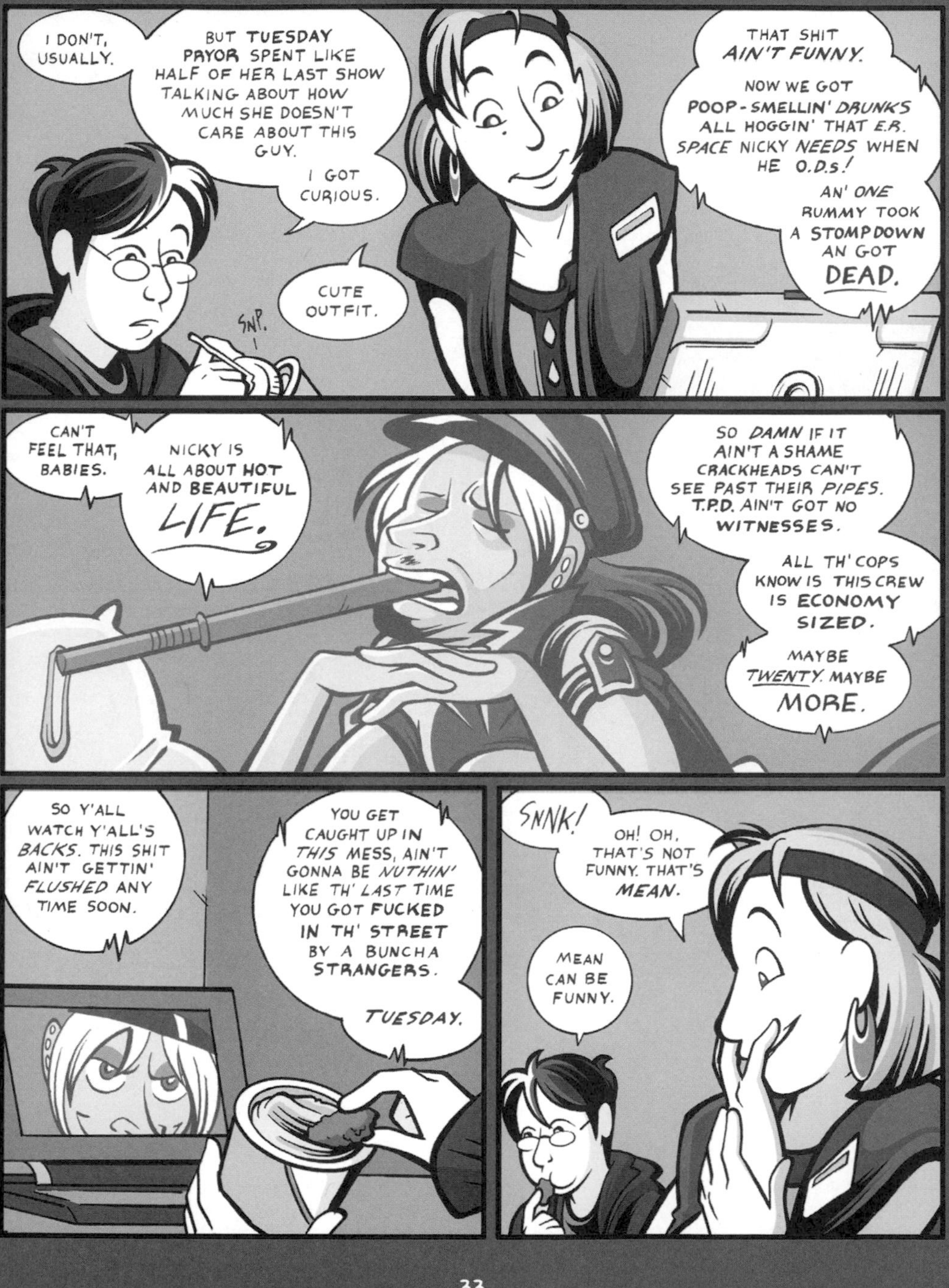
I DON'T, USUALLY.
BUT TUESDAY PRYOR SPENT LIKE HALF OF HER LAST SHOW TALKING ABOUT HOW MUCH SHE DOESN'T CARE ABOUT THIS GUY.
I GOT CURIOUS.
CUTE OUTFIT.
SNP.
THAT SHIT AIN'T FUNNY.
NOW WE GOT POOP-SMELLIN' DRUNKS ALL HOGGIN' THAT E.R. SPACE NICKY NEEDS WHEN HE O.D.s!
AN' ONE RUMMY TOOK A STOMPDOWN AN GOT DEAD.
CAN'T FEEL THAT, BABIES.
NICKY IS ALL ABOUT HOT AND BEAUTIFUL LIFE.
SO DAMN IF IT AIN'T A SHAME CRACKHEADS CAN'T SEE PAST THEIR PIPES. T.P.D. AIN'T GOT NO WITNESSES.
ALL TH' COPS KNOW IS THIS CREW IS ECONOMY SIZED.
MAYBE TWENTY. MAYBE MORE.
SO Y'ALL WATCH Y'ALL'S BACKS. THIS SHIT AIN'T GETTIN' FLUSHED ANY TIME SOON.
YOU GET CAUGHT UP IN THIS MESS, AIN'T GONNA BE NUTHIN' LIKE TH' LAST TIME YOU GOT FUCKED IN TH' STREET BY A BUNCHA STRANGERS.
TUESDAY.
SNNK!
OH! OH, THAT'S NOT FUNNY. THAT'S MEAN.
MEAN CAN BE FUNNY.

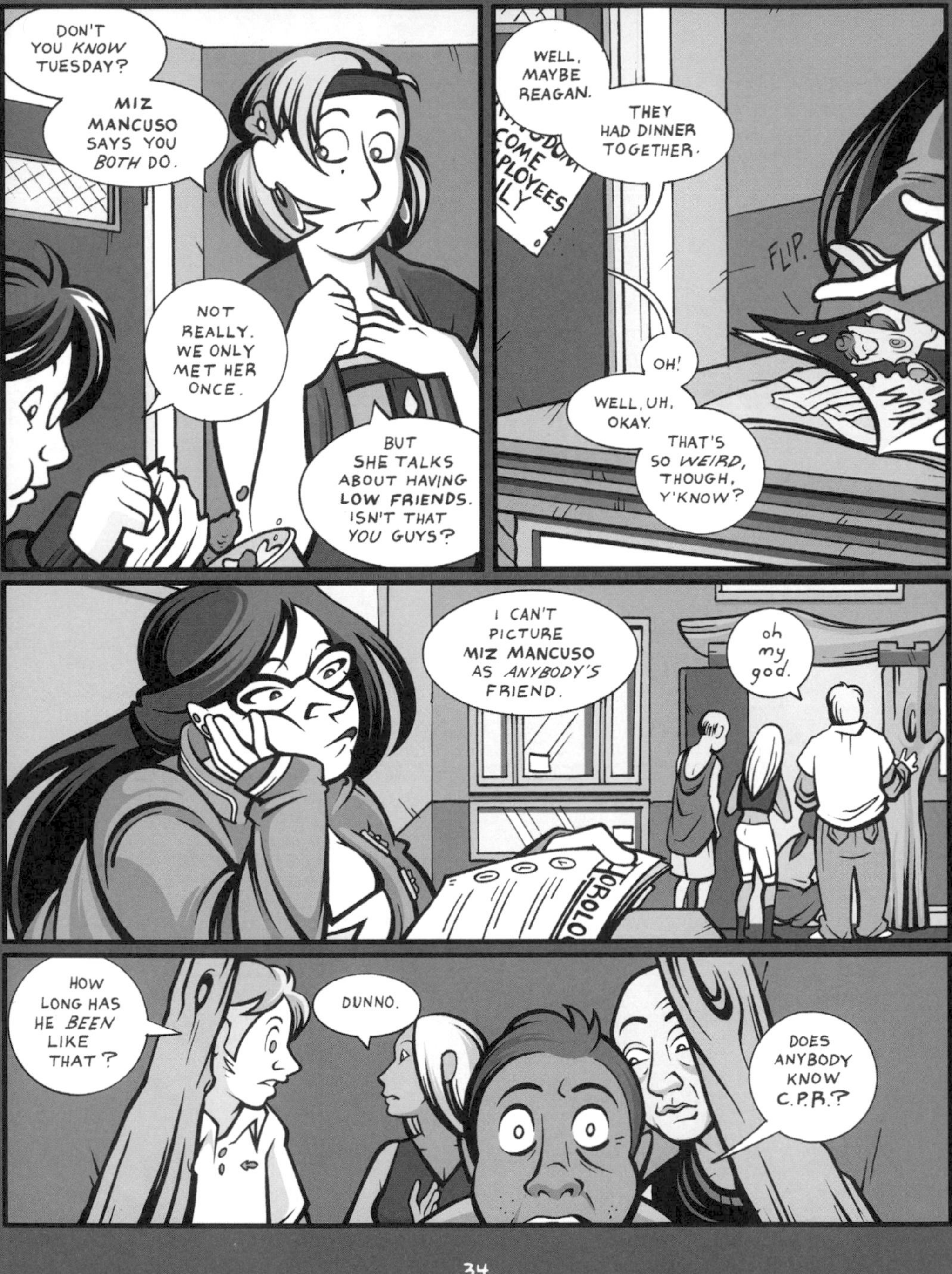
DON'T YOU KNOW TUESDAY?
MIZ MANCUSO SAYS YOU BOTH DO.
NOT REALLY. WE ONLY MET HER ONCE.
BUT SHE TALKS ABOUT HAVING LOW FRIENDS. ISN'T THAT YOU GUYS?
WELL, MAYBE REAGAN.
THEY HAD DINNER TOGETHER.
FLIP.
OH!
WELL, UH, OKAY.
THAT'S SO WEIRD, THOUGH, Y'KNOW?
I CAN'T PICTURE MIZ MANCUSO AS ANYBODY'S FRIEND.
oh my god.
HOW LONG HAS HE BEEN LIKE THAT?
DUNNO.
DOES ANYBODY KNOW C.P.R.?

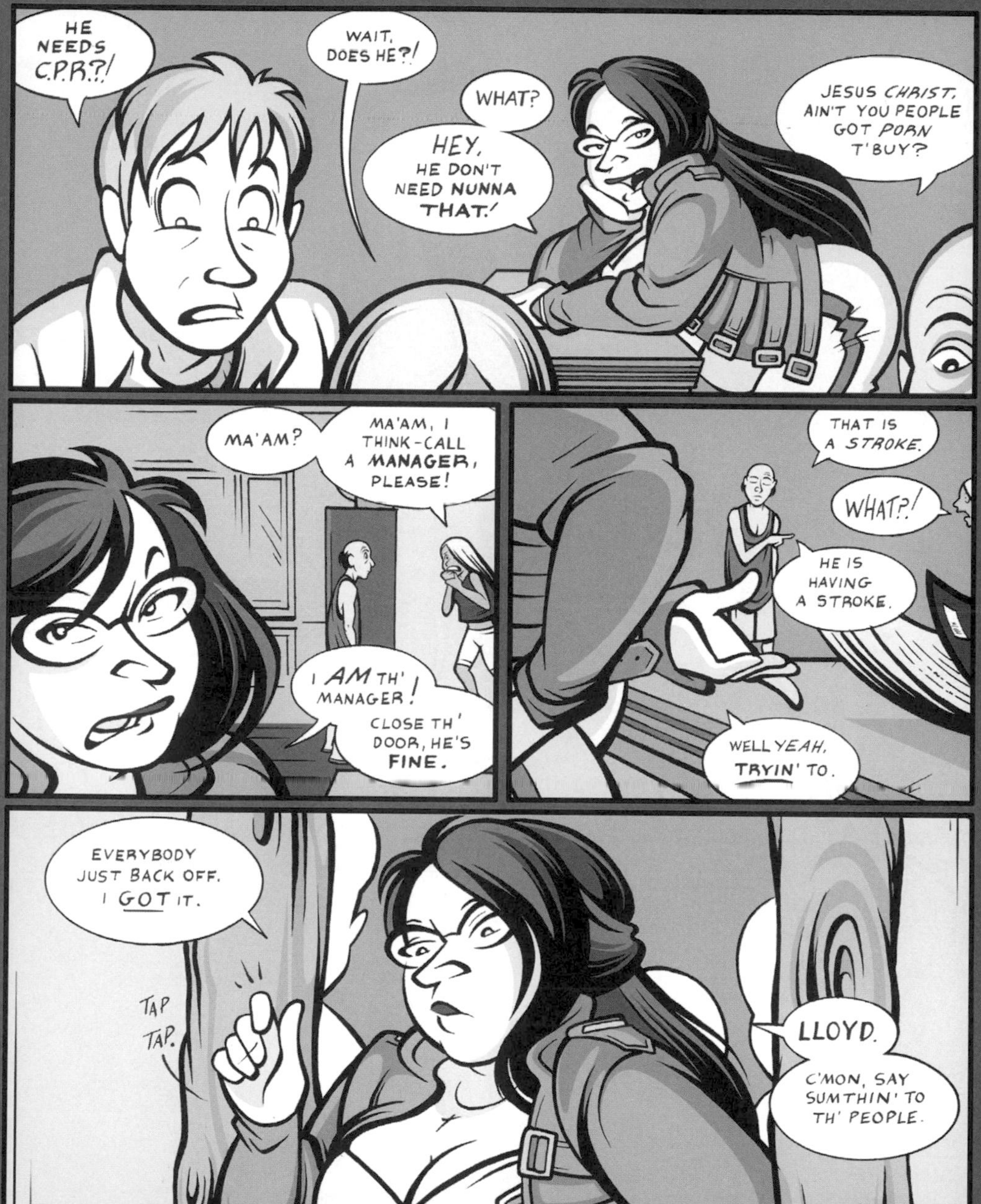
HE NEEDS C.P.R.?!
WAIT, DOES HE?!
WHAT?
HEY, HE DON'T NEED NUNNA THAT!
JESUS CHRIST, AIN'T YOU PEOPLE GOT PORN T'BUY?
MA'AM?
MA'AM, I THINK-CALL A MANAGER, PLEASE!
I AM TH' MANAGER!
CLOSE TH' DOOR, HE'S FINE.
THAT IS A STROKE.
WHAT?!
HE IS HAVING A STROKE.
WELL YEAH, TRYIN' TO.
EVERYBODY JUST BACK OFF. I GOT IT.
TAP TAP.
LLOYD.
C'MON, SAY SUMTHIN' TO TH' PEOPLE.

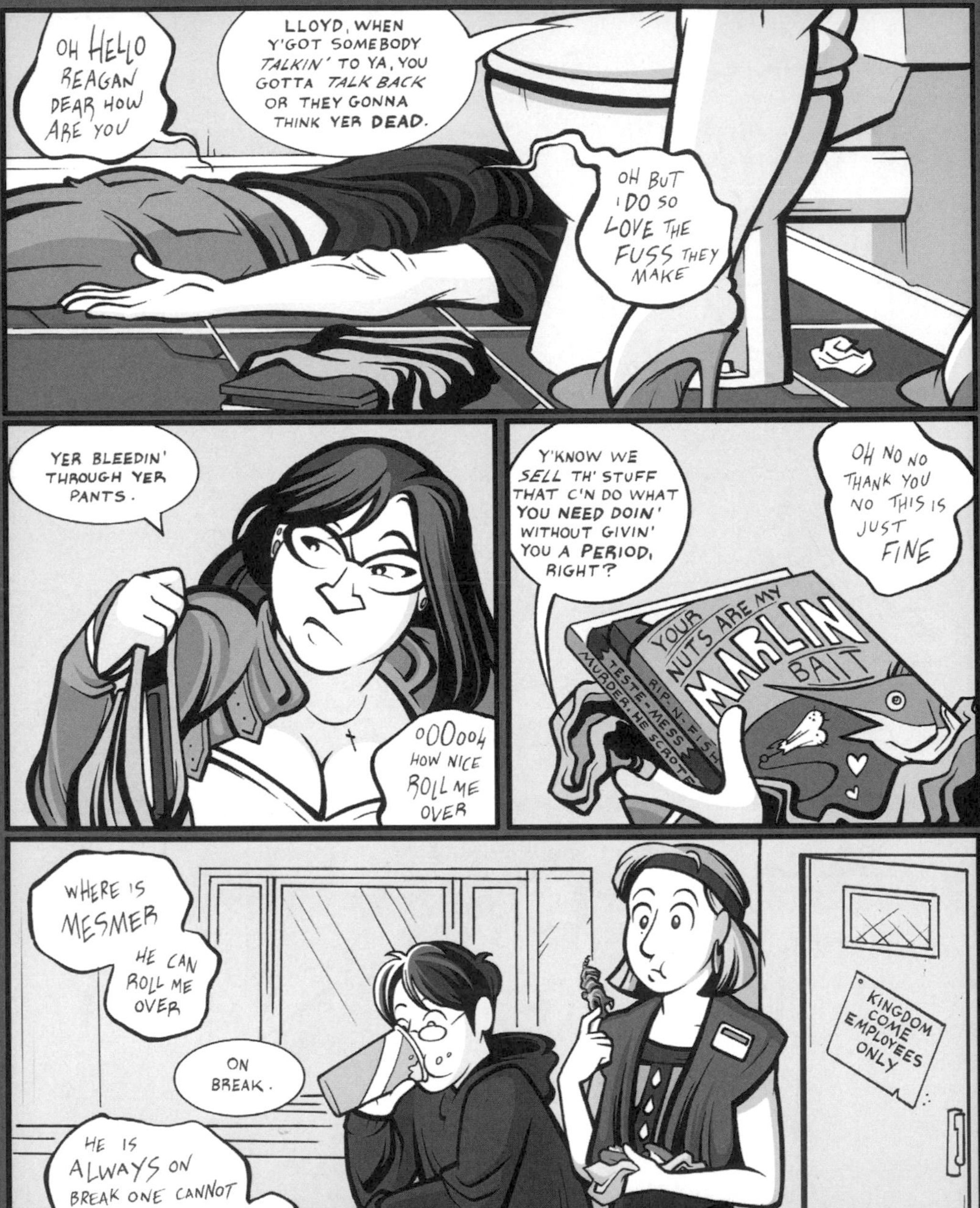
OH HELLO REAGAN DEAR HOW ARE YOU
LLOYD, WHEN Y'GOT SOMEBODY *TALKIN'* TO YA, YOU GOTTA *TALK BACK* OR THEY GONNA THINK YER **DEAD**.
OH BUT I DO SO LOVE THE FUSS THEY MAKE
YER BLEEDIN' THROUGH YER PANTS.
OOOOOH HOW NICE ROLL ME OVER
Y'KNOW WE *SELL* TH' STUFF THAT C'N DO WHAT **YOU NEED DOIN'** WITHOUT GIVIN' YOU A **PERIOD**, RIGHT?
OH NO NO THANK YOU NO THIS IS JUST FINE
YOUR NUTS ARE MY MARLIN BAIT
RIP-N-FISH
TESTE-MESS
MURDER, HE SCROTE
WHERE IS MESMER
HE CAN ROLL ME OVER
ON BREAK.
HE IS ALWAYS ON BREAK ONE CANNOT HELP BUT NOTICE
OOH
KINGDOM COME EMPLOYEES ONLY

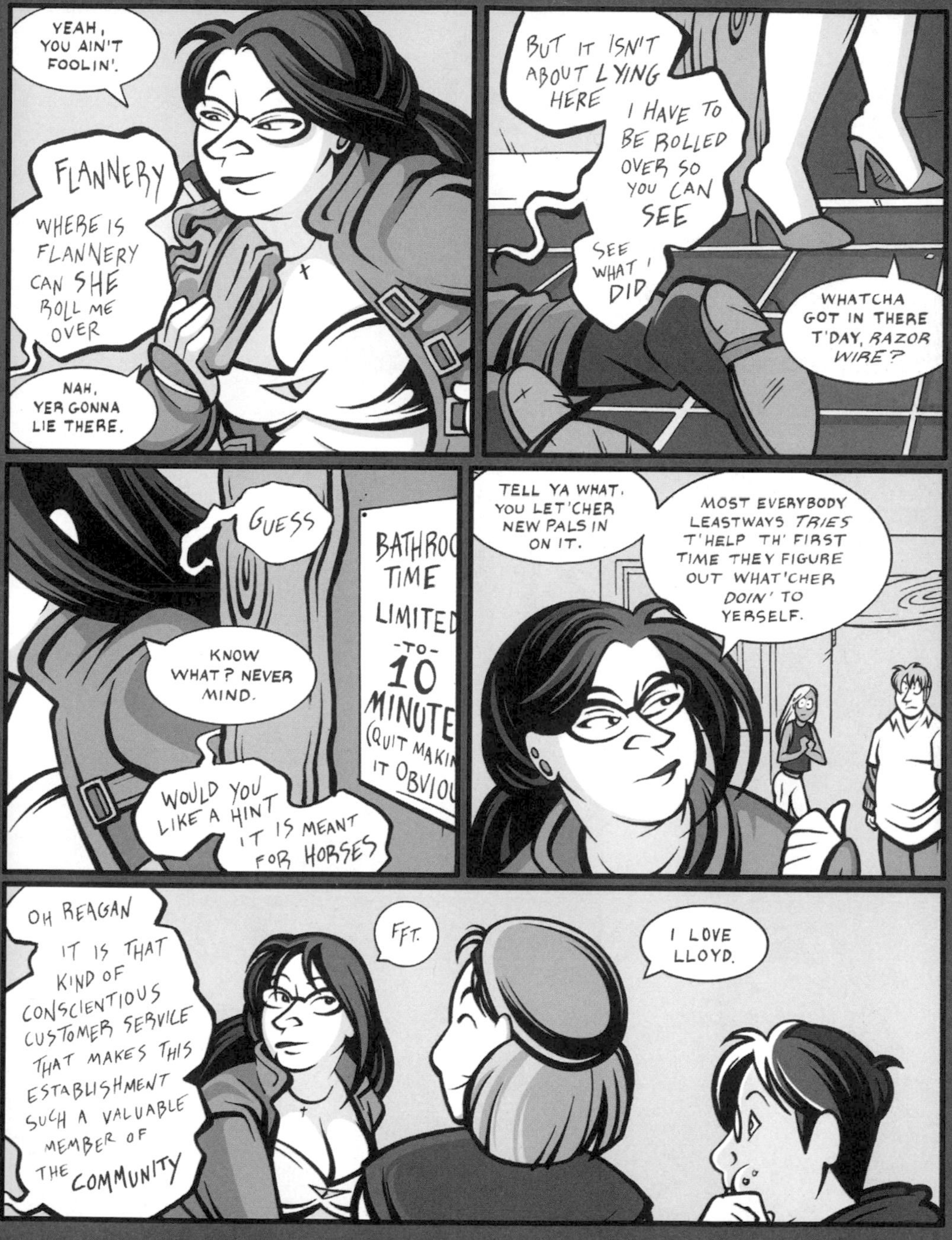

YEAH, YOU AIN'T FOOLIN'.
FLANNERY
WHERE IS FLANNERY CAN SHE ROLL ME OVER
NAH, YER GONNA LIE THERE.
BUT IT ISN'T ABOUT LYING HERE
I HAVE TO BE ROLLED OVER SO YOU CAN SEE
SEE WHAT I DID
WHATCHA GOT IN THERE T'DAY, RAZOR WIRE?
GUESS
BATHROO
TIME
LIMITED
-TO-
10
MINUTE
(QUIT MAKIN
IT OBVIOU
KNOW WHAT? NEVER MIND.
WOULD YOU LIKE A HINT
IT IS MEANT FOR HORSES
TELL YA WHAT. YOU LET'CHER NEW PALS IN ON IT.
MOST EVERYBODY LEASTWAYS TRIES T'HELP TH' FIRST TIME THEY FIGURE OUT WHAT'CHER DOIN' TO YERSELF.
OH REAGAN
IT IS THAT KIND OF CONSCIENTIOUS CUSTOMER SERVICE THAT MAKES THIS ESTABLISHMENT SUCH A VALUABLE MEMBER OF THE COMMUNITY
FFT.
I LOVE LLOYD.

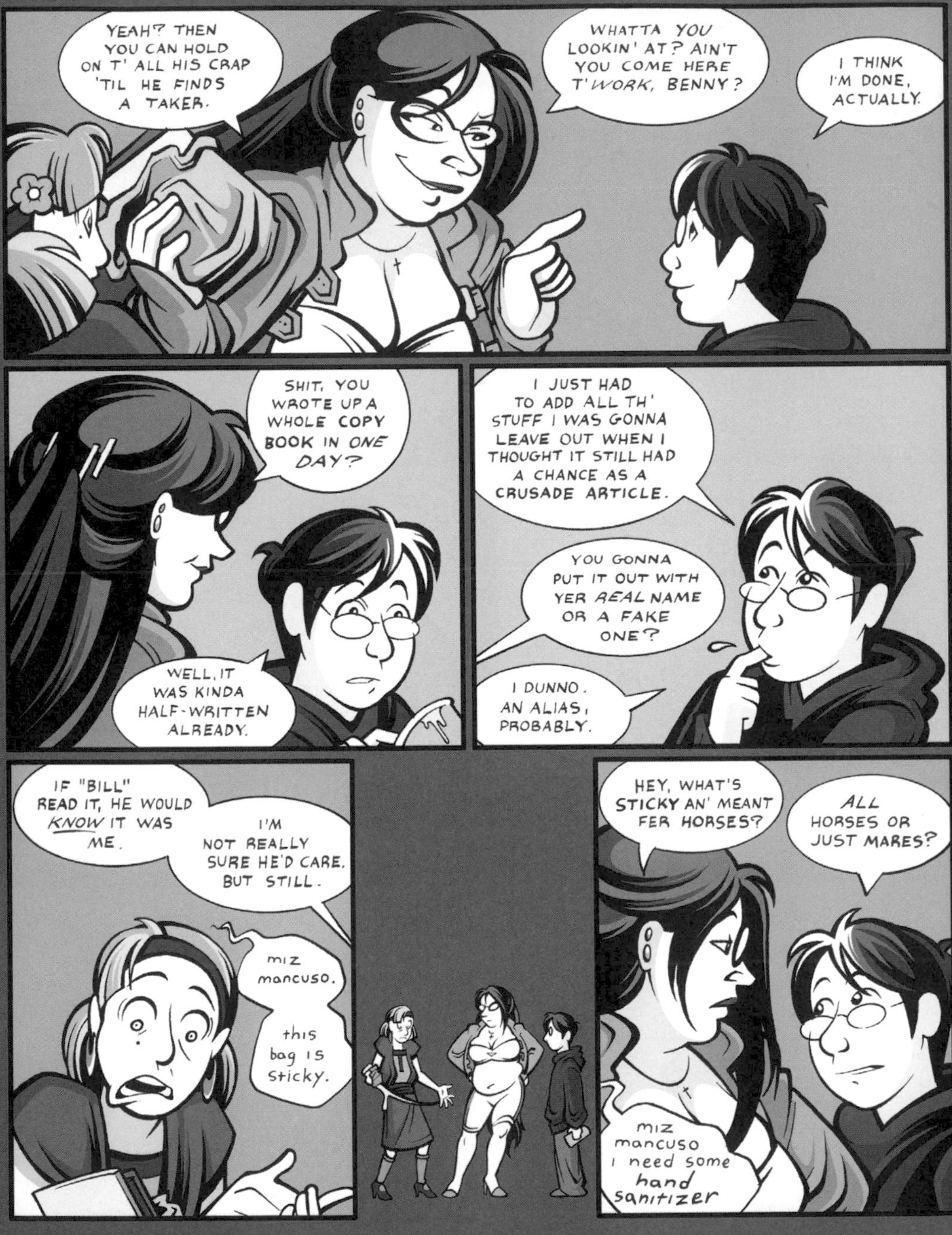
YEAH? THEN YOU CAN HOLD ON T' ALL HIS CRAP 'TIL HE FINDS A TAKER.
WHATTA YOU LOOKIN' AT? AIN'T YOU COME HERE T'WORK, BENNY?
I THINK I'M DONE, ACTUALLY.
SHIT, YOU WROTE UP A WHOLE COPY BOOK IN ONE DAY?
WELL, IT WAS KINDA HALF-WRITTEN ALREADY.
I JUST HAD TO ADD ALL TH' STUFF I WAS GONNA LEAVE OUT WHEN I THOUGHT IT STILL HAD A CHANCE AS A CRUSADE ARTICLE.
YOU GONNA PUT IT OUT WITH YER REAL NAME OR A FAKE ONE?
I DUNNO. AN ALIAS, PROBABLY.
IF "BILL" READ IT, HE WOULD KNOW IT WAS ME.
I'M NOT REALLY SURE HE'D CARE. BUT STILL.
miz mancuso.
this bag is sticky.
HEY, WHAT'S STICKY AN' MEANT FER HORSES?
ALL HORSES OR JUST MARES?
miz mancuso i need some hand sanitizer

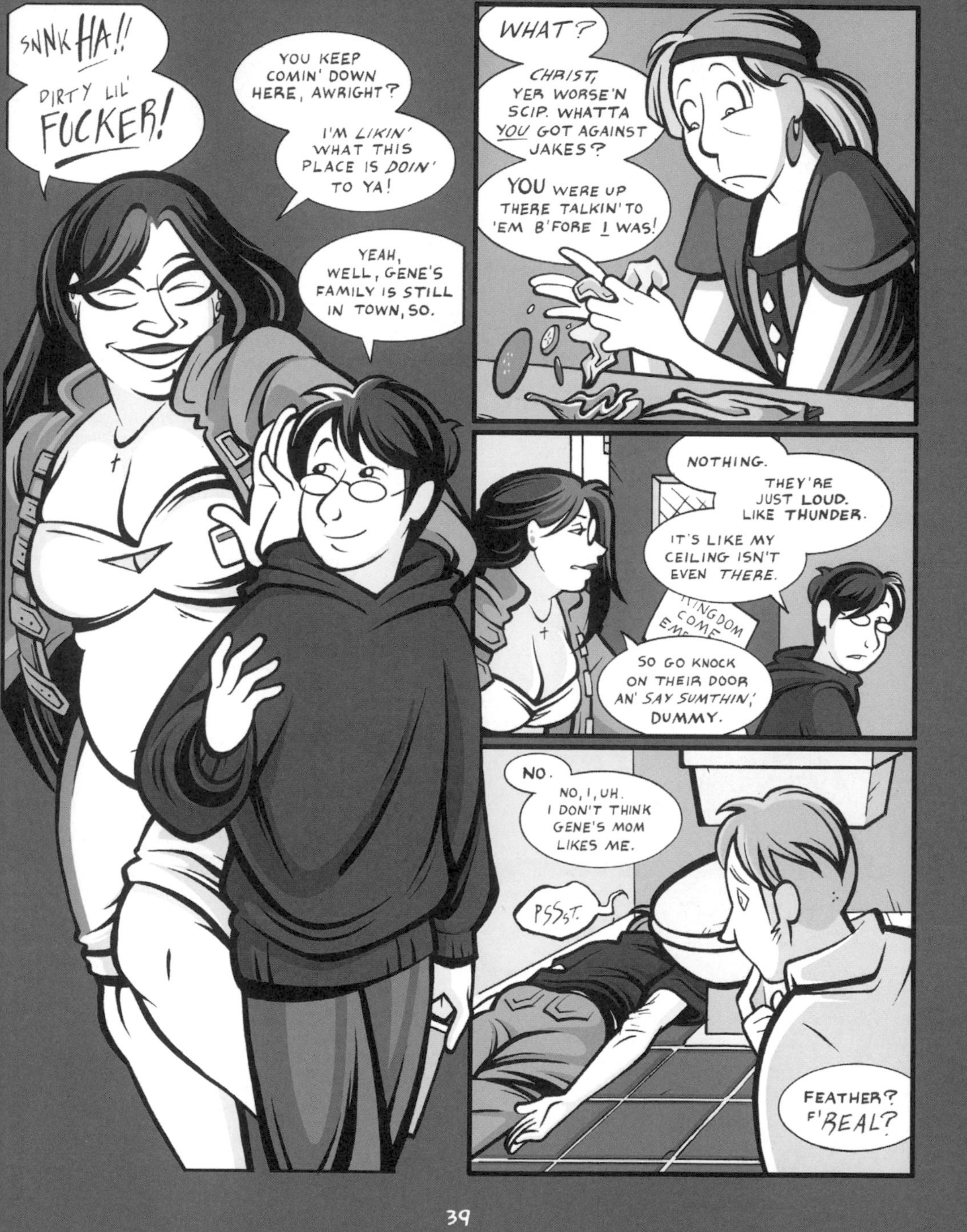
SNNK HA!!
DIRTY LIL' FUCKER!
YOU KEEP COMIN' DOWN HERE, AWRIGHT?
I'M LIKIN' WHAT THIS PLACE IS DOIN' TO YA!
YEAH, WELL, GENE'S FAMILY IS STILL IN TOWN, SO.
WHAT?
CHRIST, YER WORSE'N SCIP. WHATTA YOU GOT AGAINST JAKES?
YOU WERE UP THERE TALKIN' TO 'EM B'FORE I WAS!
NOTHING.
THEY'RE JUST LOUD. LIKE THUNDER.
IT'S LIKE MY CEILING ISN'T EVEN THERE.
KINGDOM COME
SO GO KNOCK ON THEIR DOOR AN' SAY SUMTHIN', DUMMY.
NO.
NO, I, UH. I DON'T THINK GENE'S MOM LIKES ME.
PSSST.
FEATHER? F'REAL?

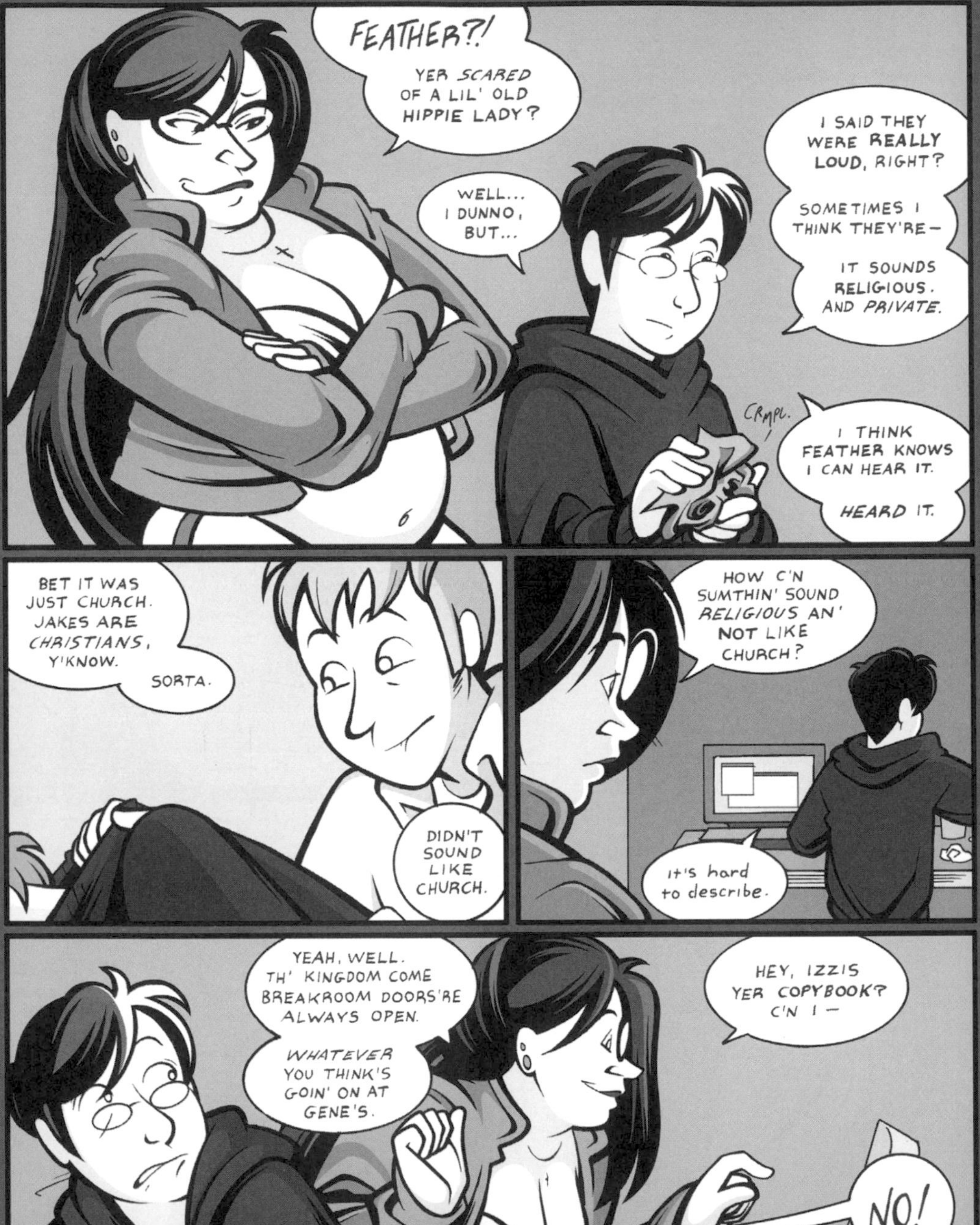
FEATHER?!
YER *SCARED* OF A LIL' OLD HIPPIE LADY?
WELL... I DUNNO, BUT...
I SAID THEY WERE **REALLY** LOUD, RIGHT?
SOMETIMES I THINK THEY'RE—
IT SOUNDS **RELIGIOUS**. AND *PRIVATE*.
CRMPL.
I THINK **FEATHER** KNOWS I CAN HEAR IT.
HEARD IT.
BET IT WAS JUST CHURCH. JAKES ARE *CHRISTIANS*, Y'KNOW.
SORTA.
DIDN'T SOUND LIKE CHURCH.
HOW C'N SUMTHIN' SOUND *RELIGIOUS* AN' **NOT** LIKE CHURCH?
it's hard to describe.
YEAH, WELL. TH' KINGDOM COME BREAKROOM DOORS'RE ALWAYS OPEN.
WHATEVER YOU THINK'S GOIN' ON AT GENE'S.
HEY, IZZIS YER **COPYBOOK**? C'N I—
NO!

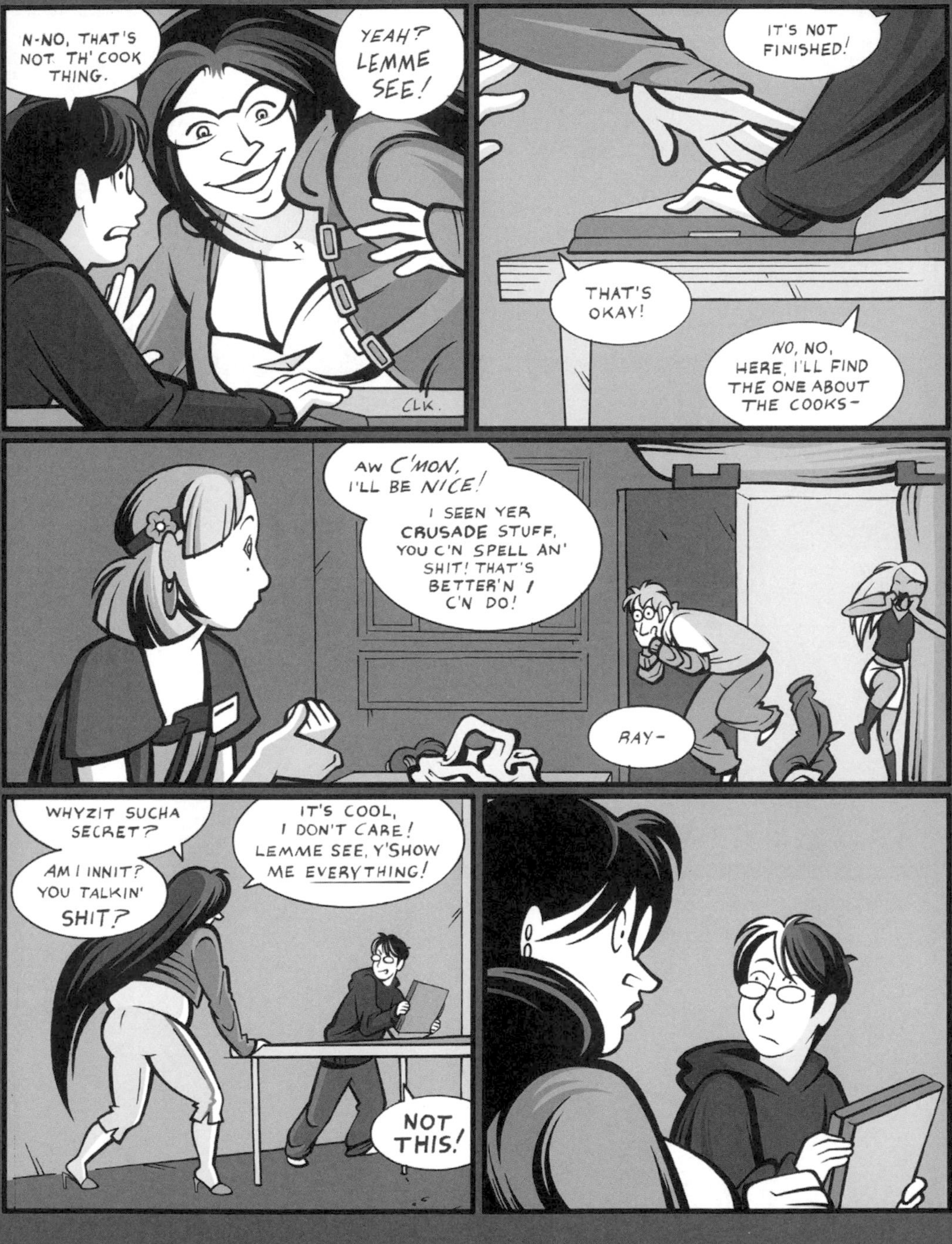
N-NO, THAT'S NOT TH' COOK THING.
YEAH? LEMME SEE!
CLK.
IT'S NOT FINISHED!
THAT'S OKAY!
NO, NO, HERE, I'LL FIND THE ONE ABOUT THE COOKS-
AW C'MON, I'LL BE NICE!
I SEEN YER CRUSADE STUFF, YOU C'N SPELL AN' SHIT! THAT'S BETTER'N I C'N DO!
RAY-
WHYZIT SUCHA SECRET?
AM I INNIT? YOU TALKIN' SHIT?
IT'S COOL, I DON'T CARE! LEMME SEE, Y'SHOW ME EVERYTHING!
NOT THIS!

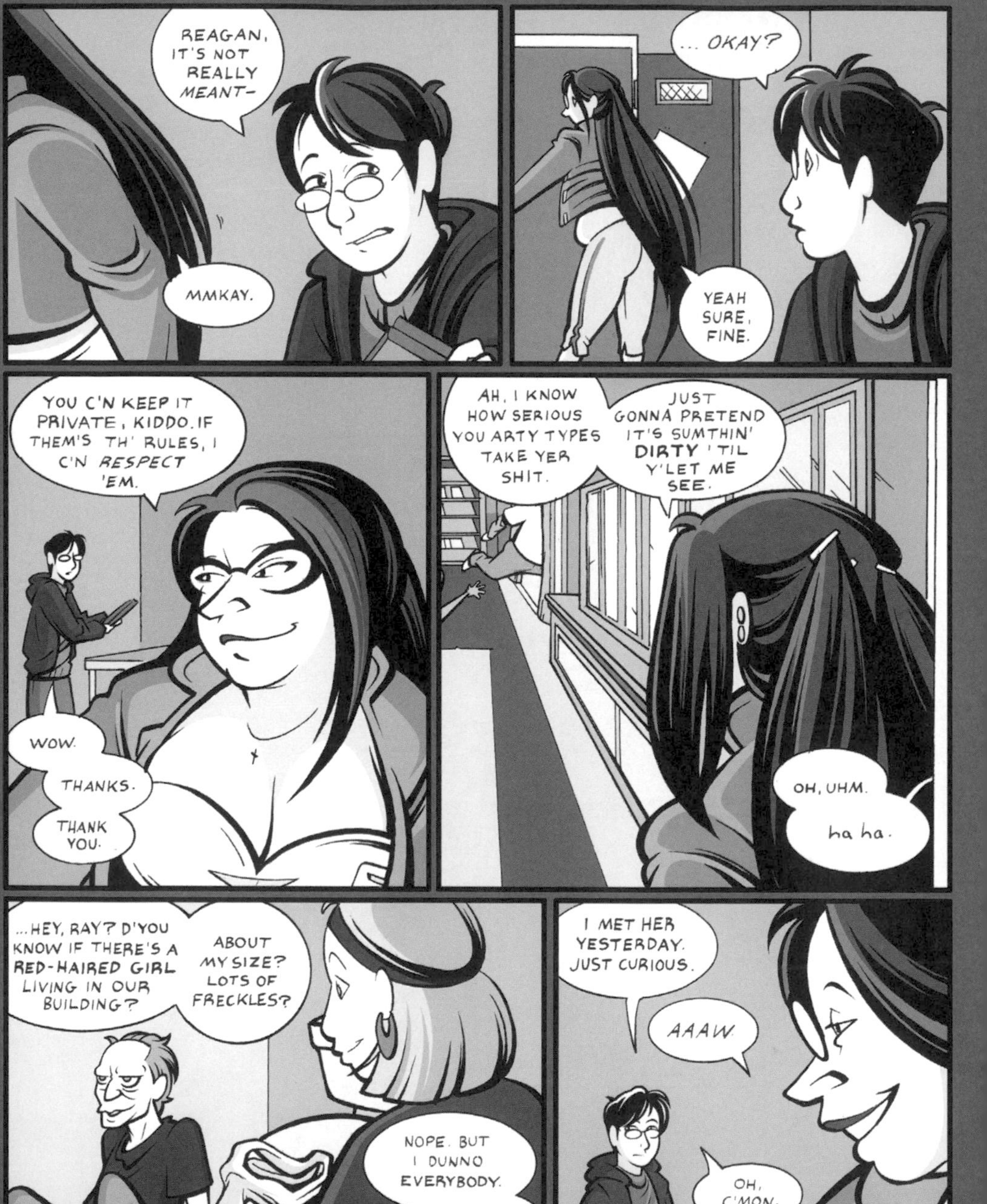
REAGAN, IT'S NOT REALLY *MEANT*-
MMKAY.
... *OKAY?*
YEAH SURE, FINE.
YOU C'N KEEP IT PRIVATE, KIDDO. IF THEM'S TH' RULES, I C'N *RESPECT* 'EM.
WOW.
THANKS.
THANK YOU.
AH, I KNOW HOW SERIOUS YOU ARTY TYPES TAKE YER SHIT.
JUST GONNA PRETEND IT'S SUMTHIN' **DIRTY** 'TIL Y'LET ME SEE.
OH, UHM.
ha ha.
...HEY, RAY? D'YOU KNOW IF THERE'S A **RED-HAIRED GIRL** LIVING IN OUR BUILDING?
ABOUT MY SIZE? LOTS OF FRECKLES?
NOPE. BUT I DUNNO EVERYBODY.
WHY?
I MET HER YESTERDAY. JUST CURIOUS.
AAAW.
OH, C'MON.

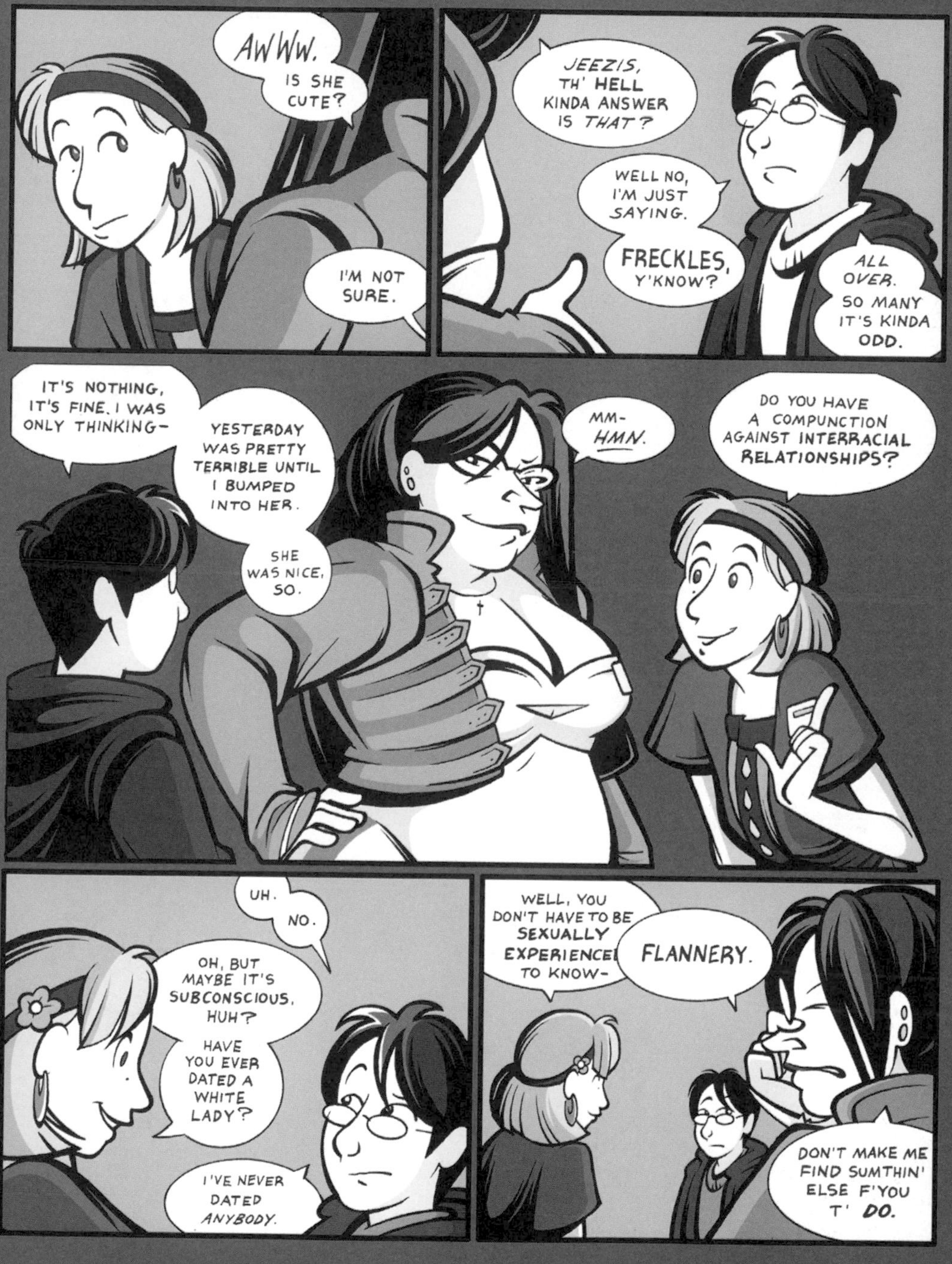

AWWW. IS SHE CUTE?
I'M NOT SURE.
JEEZIS, TH' HELL KINDA ANSWER IS THAT?
WELL NO, I'M JUST SAYING.
FRECKLES, Y'KNOW?
ALL OVER. SO MANY IT'S KINDA ODD.
IT'S NOTHING, IT'S FINE. I WAS ONLY THINKING-
YESTERDAY WAS PRETTY TERRIBLE UNTIL I BUMPED INTO HER.
SHE WAS NICE, SO.
MM-HMN.
DO YOU HAVE A COMPUNCTION AGAINST INTERRACIAL RELATIONSHIPS?
UH.
NO.
OH, BUT MAYBE IT'S SUBCONSCIOUS, HUH?
HAVE YOU EVER DATED A WHITE LADY?
I'VE NEVER DATED ANYBODY.
WELL, YOU DON'T HAVE TO BE SEXUALLY EXPERIENCED TO KNOW-
FLANNERY.
DON'T MAKE ME FIND SUMTHIN' ELSE F'YOU T' DO.

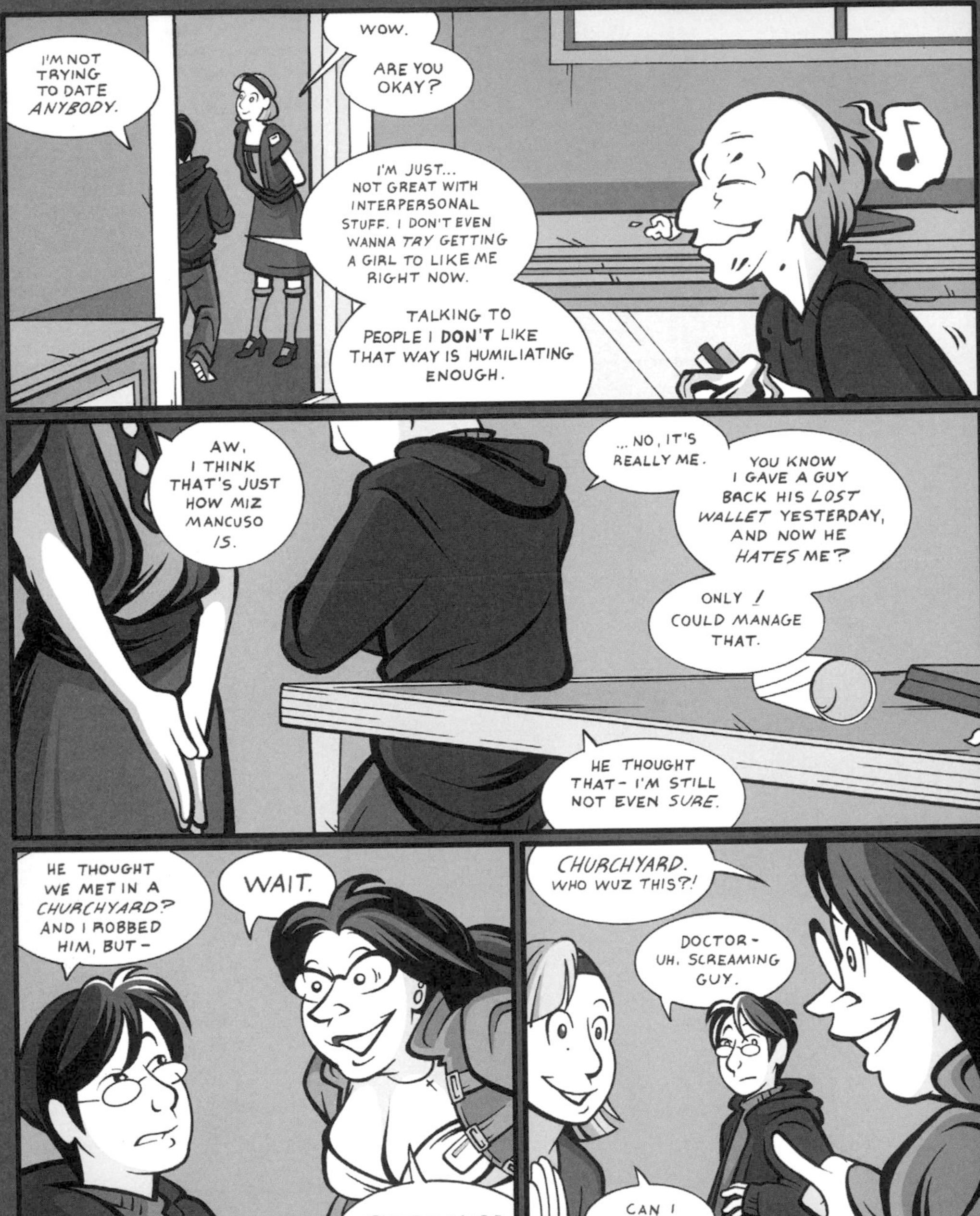
I'M NOT TRYING TO DATE ANYBODY.
WOW.
ARE YOU OKAY?
I'M JUST... NOT GREAT WITH INTERPERSONAL STUFF. I DON'T EVEN WANNA TRY GETTING A GIRL TO LIKE ME RIGHT NOW.
TALKING TO PEOPLE I DON'T LIKE THAT WAY IS HUMILIATING ENOUGH.
AW, I THINK THAT'S JUST HOW MIZ MANCUSO IS.
... NO, IT'S REALLY ME.
YOU KNOW I GAVE A GUY BACK HIS LOST WALLET YESTERDAY, AND NOW HE HATES ME?
ONLY I COULD MANAGE THAT.
HE THOUGHT THAT- I'M STILL NOT EVEN SURE.
HE THOUGHT WE MET IN A CHURCHYARD? AND I ROBBED HIM, BUT-
WAIT.
CHURCHYARD.
CHURCHYARD. WHO WUZ THIS?!
DOCTOR- UH, SCREAMING GUY.
CAN I SAY IT?

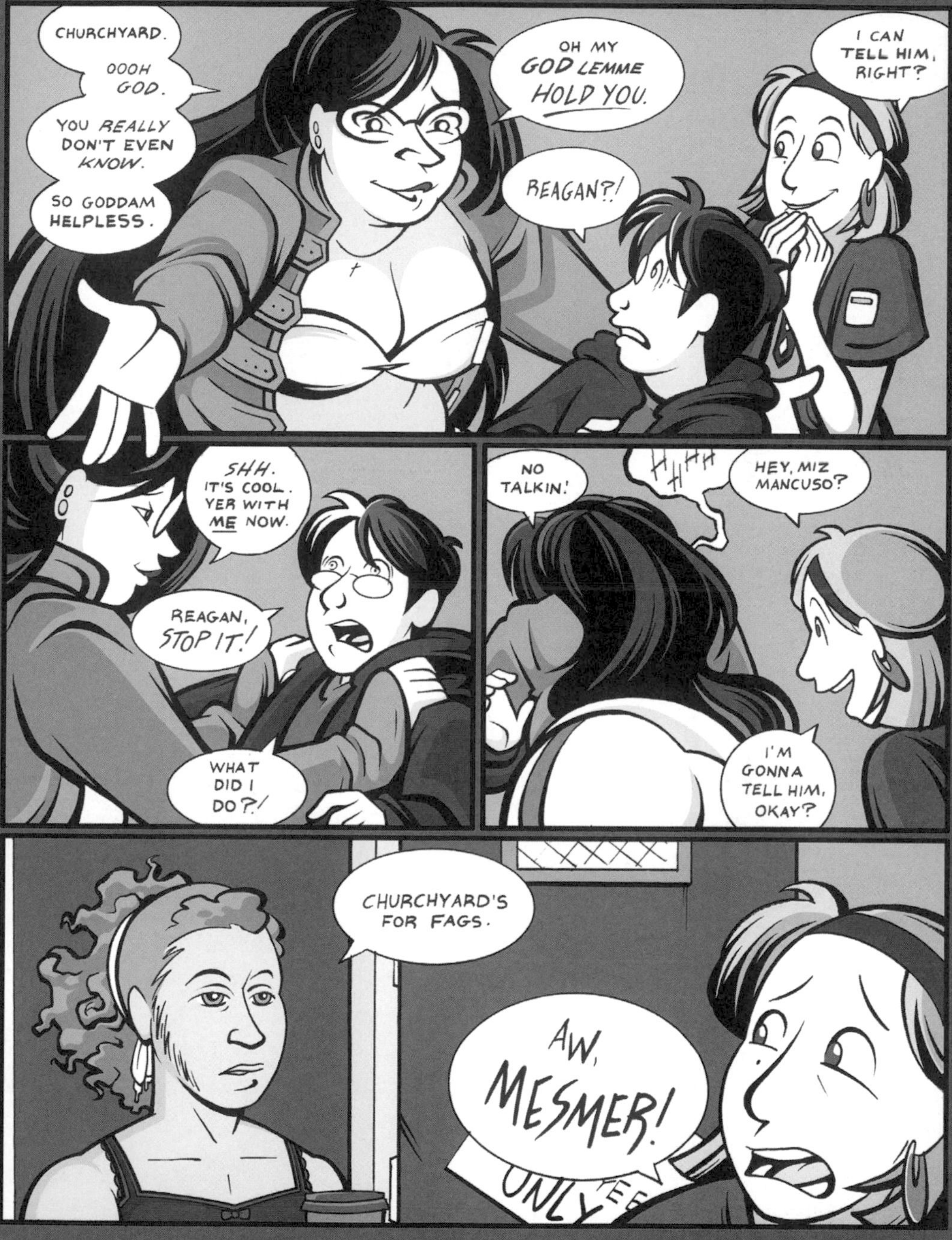
CHURCHYARD.
OOOH GOD.
YOU REALLY DON'T EVEN KNOW.
SO GODDAM HELPLESS.
OH MY GOD LEMME HOLD YOU.
REAGAN?!
I CAN TELL HIM, RIGHT?
SHH. IT'S COOL. YER WITH ME NOW.
REAGAN, STOP IT!
WHAT DID I DO?!
NO TALKIN'!
HEY, MIZ MANCUSO?
I'M GONNA TELL HIM, OKAY?
CHURCHYARD'S FOR FAGS.
AW, MESMER!

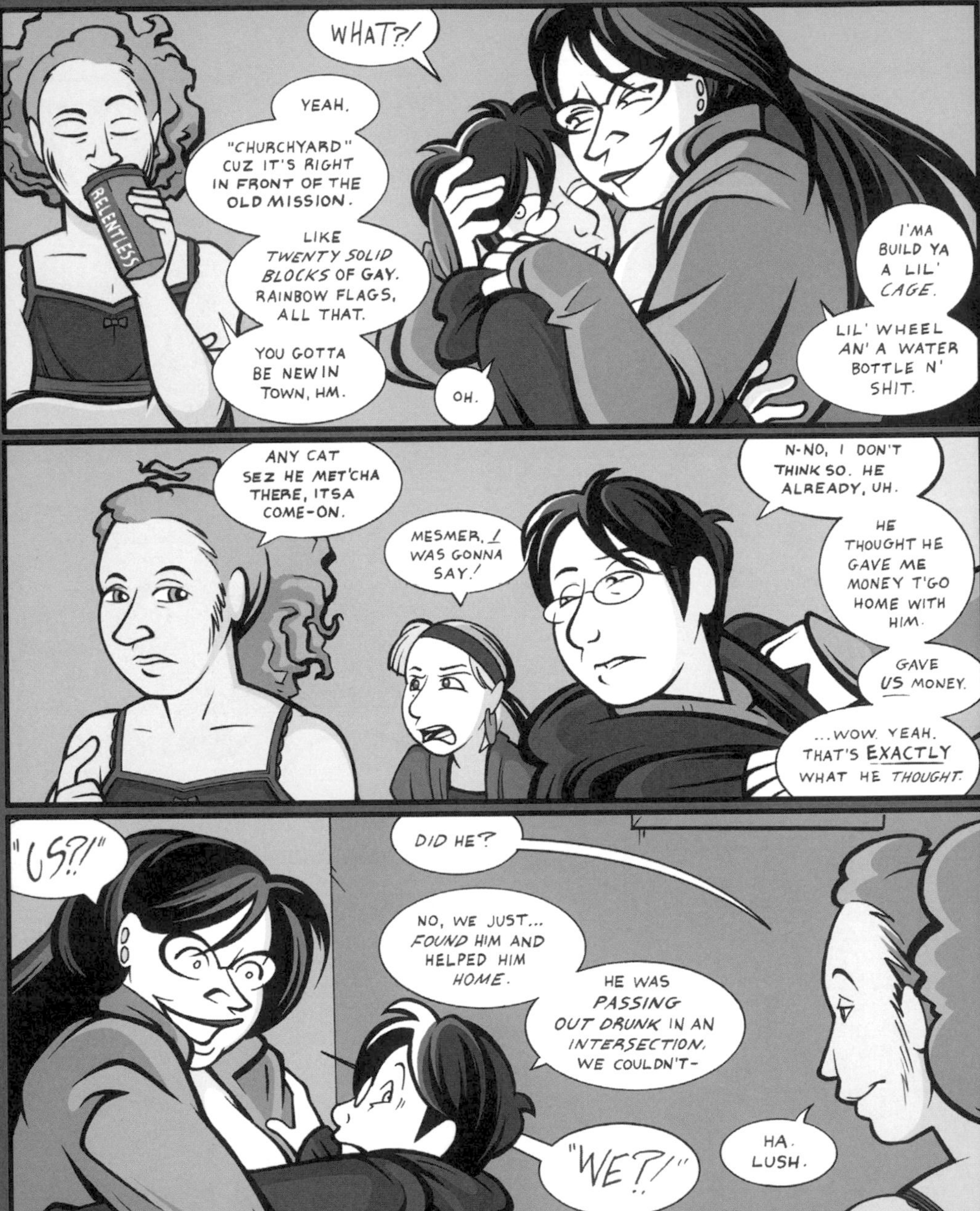
WHAT?!
YEAH.
"CHURCHYARD" CUZ IT'S RIGHT IN FRONT OF THE OLD MISSION.
LIKE TWENTY SOLID BLOCKS OF GAY. RAINBOW FLAGS, ALL THAT.
YOU GOTTA BE NEW IN TOWN, HM.
OH.
I'MA BUILD YA A LIL' CAGE.
LIL' WHEEL AN' A WATER BOTTLE N' SHIT.
ANY CAT SEZ HE MET'CHA THERE, ITSA COME-ON.
MESMER, I WAS GONNA SAY!
N-NO, I DON'T THINK SO. HE ALREADY, UH.
HE THOUGHT HE GAVE ME MONEY T'GO HOME WITH HIM.
GAVE US MONEY.
...WOW. YEAH. THAT'S EXACTLY WHAT HE THOUGHT.
"US?!"
DID HE?
NO, WE JUST... FOUND HIM AND HELPED HIM HOME.
HE WAS PASSING OUT DRUNK IN AN INTERSECTION. WE COULDN'T-
"WE?!"
HA. LUSH.

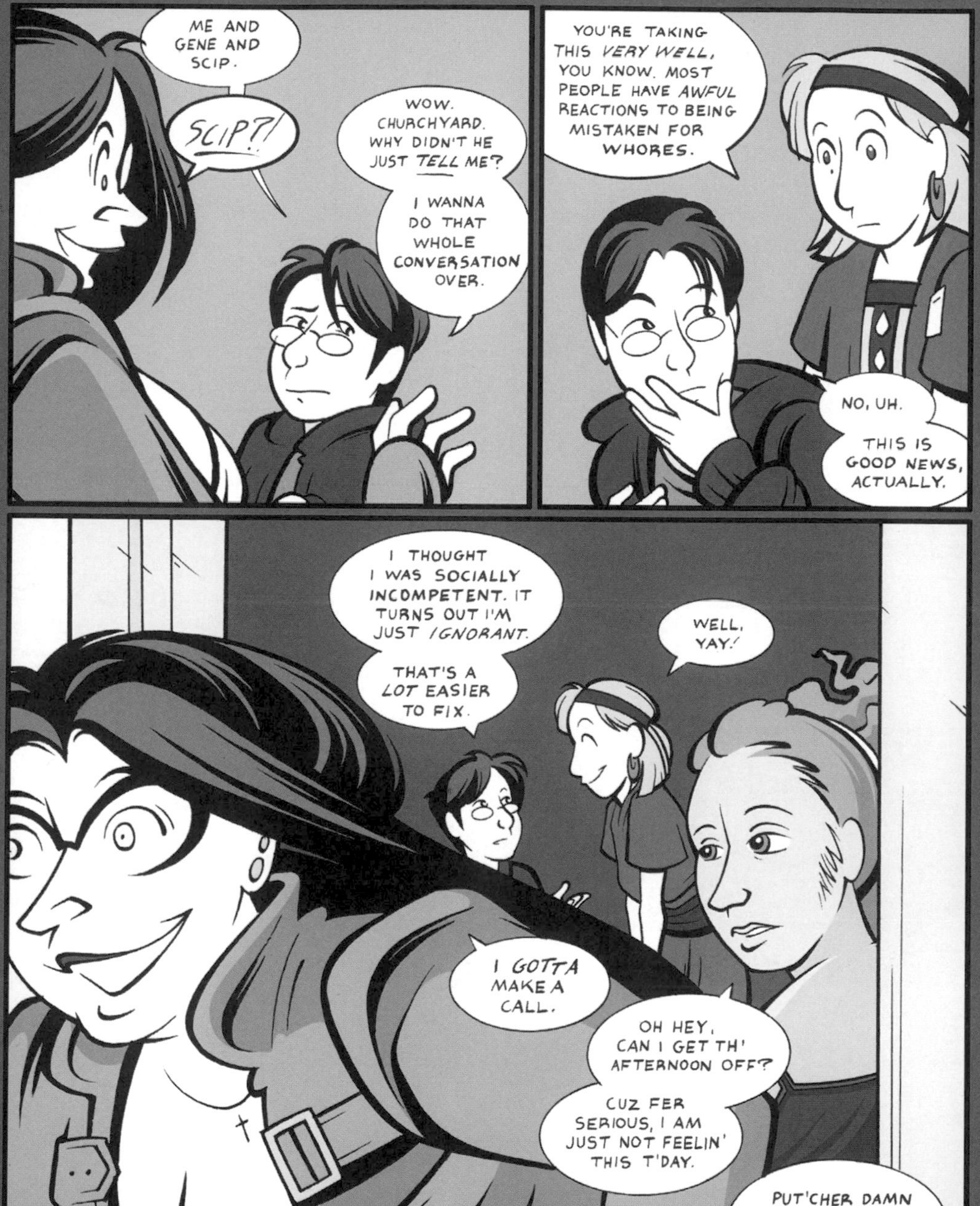
ME AND GENE AND SCIP.
SCIP?!
WOW. CHURCHYARD. WHY DIDN'T HE JUST TELL ME?
I WANNA DO THAT WHOLE CONVERSATION OVER.
YOU'RE TAKING THIS VERY WELL, YOU KNOW. MOST PEOPLE HAVE AWFUL REACTIONS TO BEING MISTAKEN FOR WHORES.
NO, UH.
THIS IS GOOD NEWS, ACTUALLY.
I THOUGHT I WAS SOCIALLY INCOMPETENT. IT TURNS OUT I'M JUST IGNORANT.
THAT'S A LOT EASIER TO FIX.
WELL, YAY!
I GOTTA MAKE A CALL.
OH HEY, CAN I GET TH' AFTERNOON OFF?
CUZ FER SERIOUS, I AM JUST NOT FEELIN' THIS T'DAY.
PUT'CHER DAMN NAMETAG ON, MEZ.

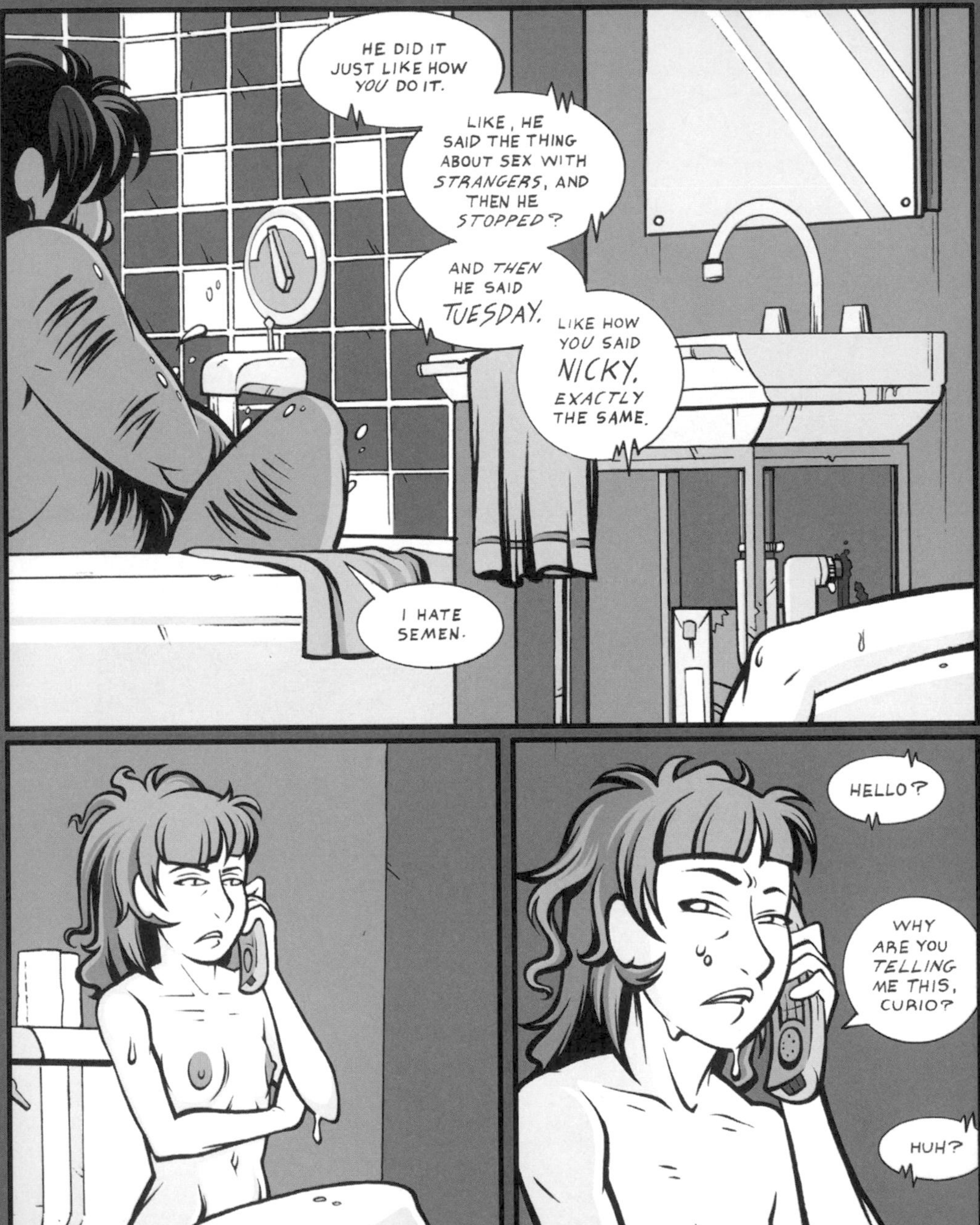
HE DID IT JUST LIKE HOW YOU DO IT.
LIKE, HE SAID THE THING ABOUT SEX WITH STRANGERS, AND THEN HE STOPPED?
AND THEN HE SAID TUESDAY.
LIKE HOW YOU SAID NICKY. EXACTLY THE SAME.
I HATE SEMEN.
HELLO?
WHY ARE YOU TELLING ME THIS, CURIO?
HUH?

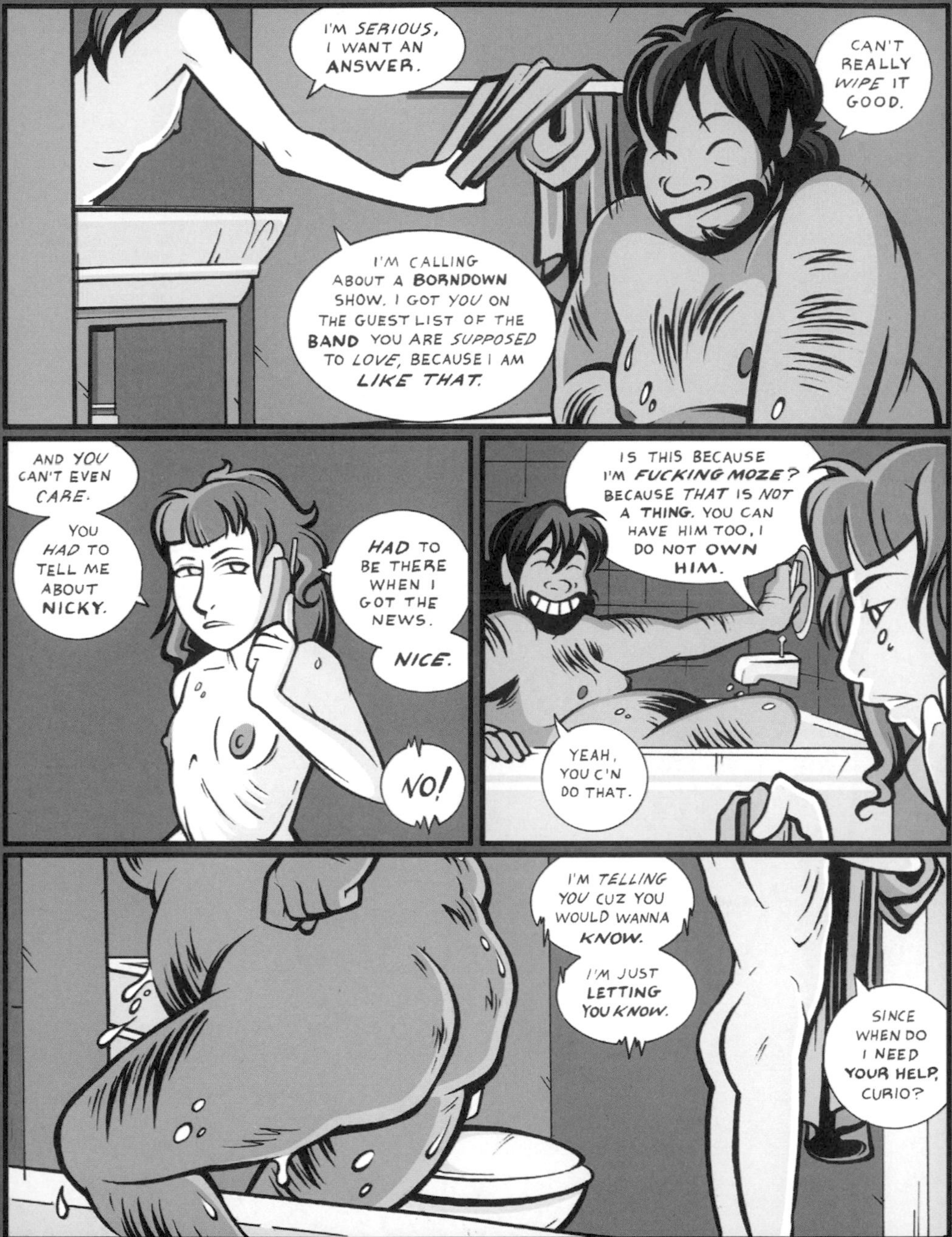
I'M SERIOUS, I WANT AN ANSWER.
CAN'T REALLY WIPE IT GOOD.
I'M CALLING ABOUT A BORNDOWN SHOW. I GOT YOU ON THE GUEST LIST OF THE BAND YOU ARE SUPPOSED TO LOVE, BECAUSE I AM LIKE THAT.
AND YOU CAN'T EVEN CARE.
YOU HAD TO TELL ME ABOUT NICKY.
HAD TO BE THERE WHEN I GOT THE NEWS.
NICE.
NO!
IS THIS BECAUSE I'M FUCKING MOZE? BECAUSE THAT IS NOT A THING. YOU CAN HAVE HIM TOO, I DO NOT OWN HIM.
YEAH, YOU C'N DO THAT.
I'M TELLING YOU CUZ YOU WOULD WANNA KNOW.
I'M JUST LETTING YOU KNOW.
SINCE WHEN DO I NEED YOUR HELP, CURIO?

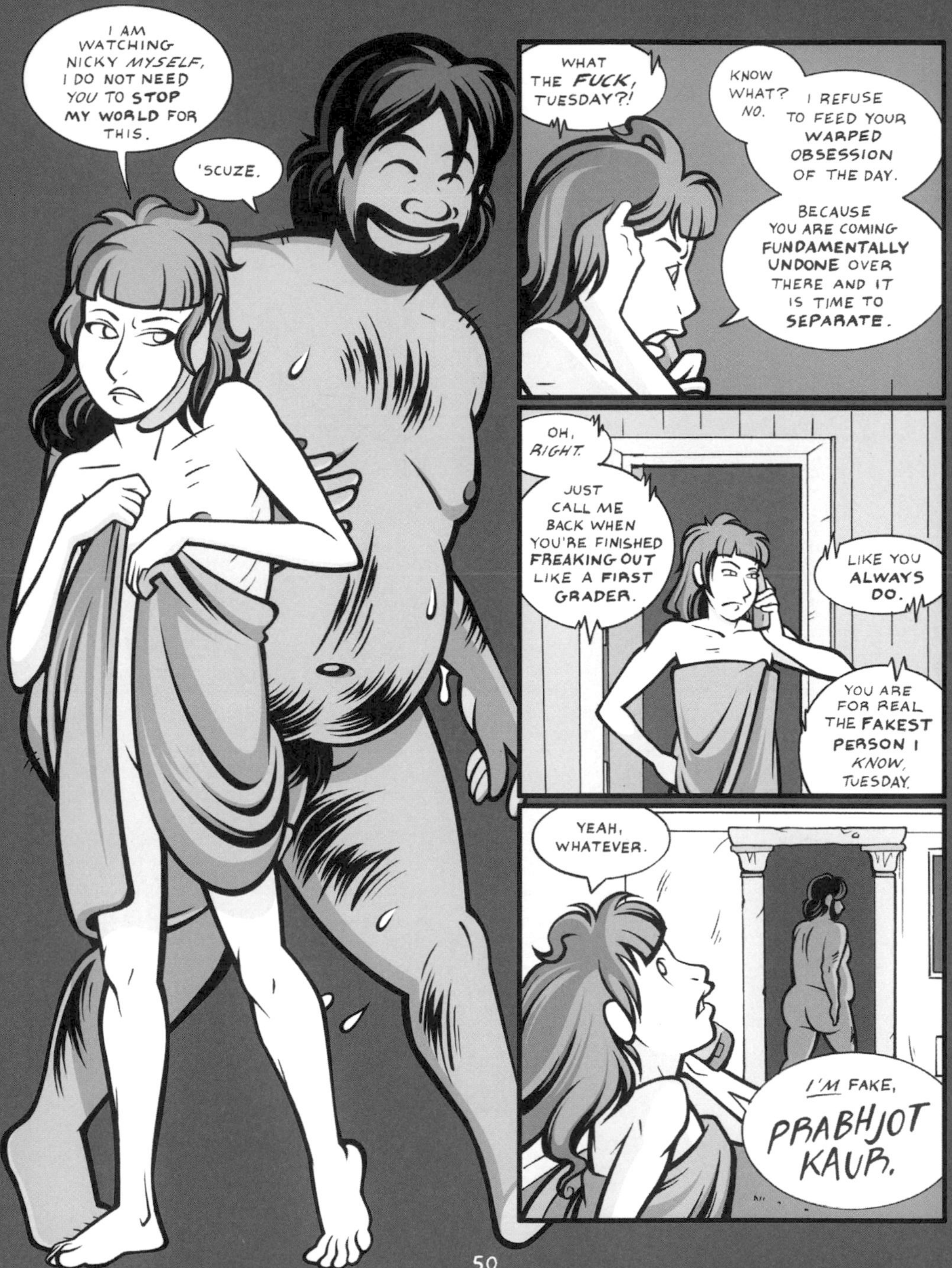

I AM WATCHING NICKY *MYSELF*, I DO NOT NEED *YOU* TO **STOP MY WORLD** FOR THIS.
'SCUZE.
WHAT THE ***FUCK***, TUESDAY?!
KNOW WHAT? *NO.*
I REFUSE TO FEED YOUR **WARPED OBSESSION** OF THE DAY.
BECAUSE YOU ARE COMING **FUNDAMENTALLY UNDONE** OVER THERE AND IT IS TIME TO **SEPARATE**.
OH, *RIGHT.*
JUST CALL ME BACK WHEN YOU'RE FINISHED **FREAKING OUT** LIKE A **FIRST GRADER**.
LIKE YOU **ALWAYS DO**.
YOU ARE FOR REAL THE **FAKEST PERSON I** *KNOW*, TUESDAY.
YEAH, WHATEVER.
I'M FAKE,
PRABHJOT KAUR.

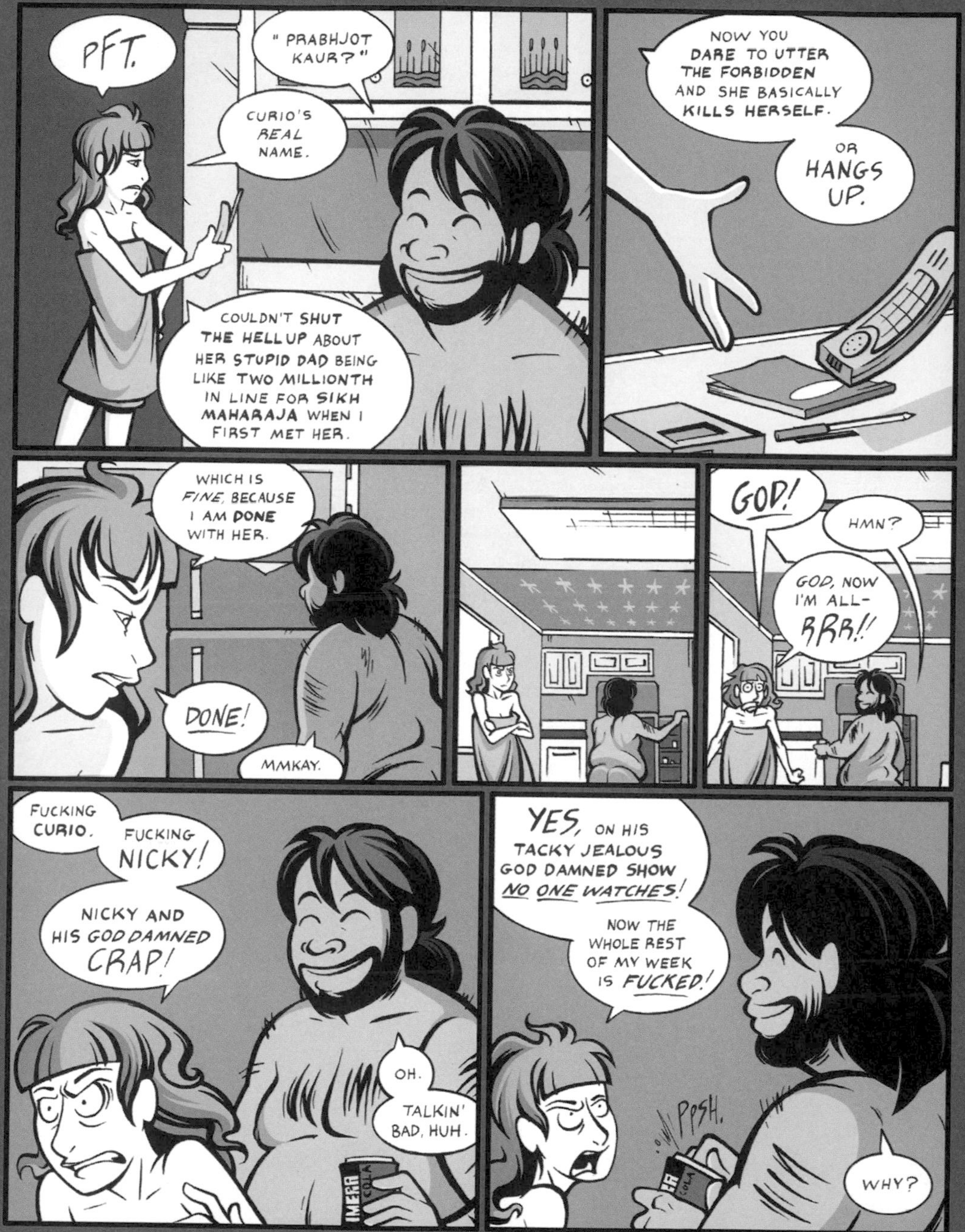
PFT.
" PRABHJOT KAUR?"
CURIO'S REAL NAME.
COULDN'T SHUT THE HELL UP ABOUT HER STUPID DAD BEING LIKE TWO MILLIONTH IN LINE FOR SIKH MAHARAJA WHEN I FIRST MET HER.
NOW YOU DARE TO UTTER THE FORBIDDEN AND SHE BASICALLY KILLS HERSELF.
OR HANGS UP.
WHICH IS FINE, BECAUSE I AM DONE WITH HER.
DONE!
MMKAY.
GOD!
HMN?
GOD, NOW I'M ALL-RRR!!
FUCKING CURIO.
FUCKING NICKY!
NICKY AND HIS GOD DAMNED CRAP!
OH.
TALKIN' BAD, HUH.
YES, ON HIS TACKY JEALOUS GOD DAMNED SHOW NO ONE WATCHES!
NOW THE WHOLE REST OF MY WEEK IS FUCKED!
PPSH.
WHY?

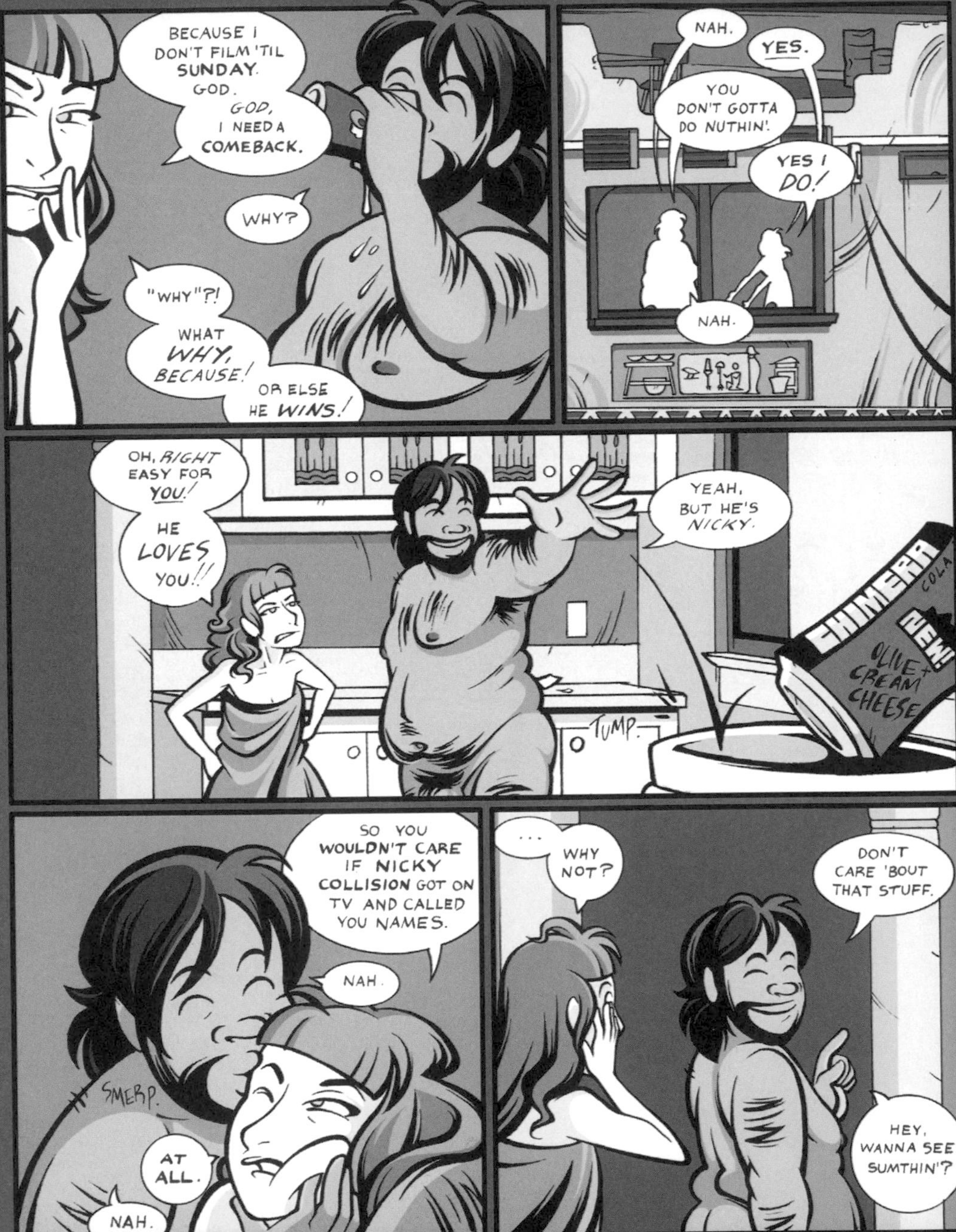
BECAUSE I DON'T FILM 'TIL SUNDAY.
GOD.
GOD, I NEED A COMEBACK.
WHY?
"WHY"?!
WHAT WHY, BECAUSE!
OR ELSE HE WINS!
NAH.
YES.
YOU DON'T GOTTA DO NUTHIN'.
YES I DO!
NAH.
OH, RIGHT EASY FOR YOU!
HE LOVES YOU!!
YEAH, BUT HE'S NICKY.
CHIMERA COLA
NEW!
OLIVE + CREAM CHEESE
TUMP.
SO YOU WOULDN'T CARE IF NICKY COLLISION GOT ON TV AND CALLED YOU NAMES.
NAH.
SMERP.
AT ALL.
NAH.
...
WHY NOT?
DON'T CARE 'BOUT THAT STUFF.
HEY, WANNA SEE SUMTHIN'?

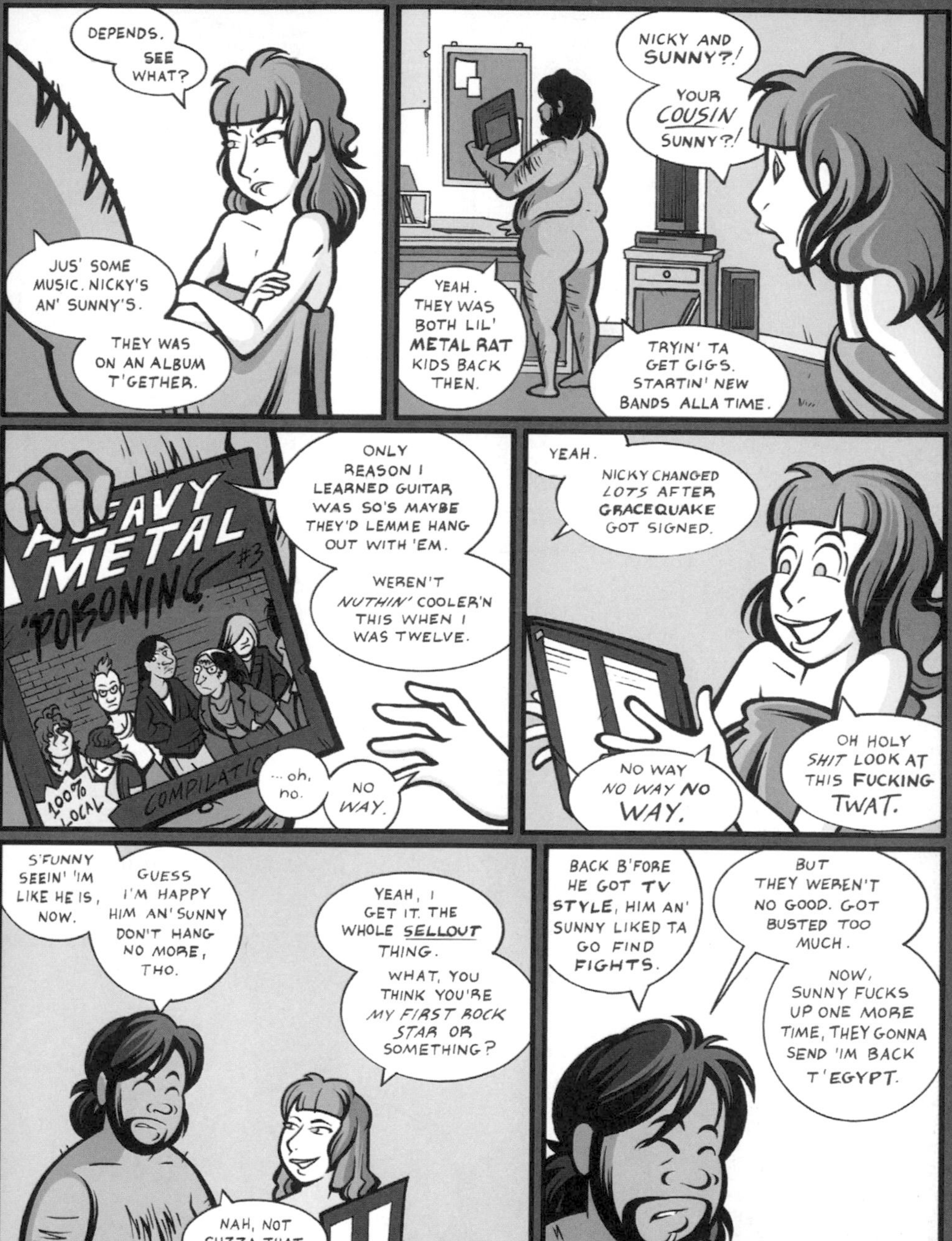
DEPENDS.
SEE WHAT?
JUS' SOME MUSIC. NICKY'S AN' SUNNY'S.
THEY WAS ON AN ALBUM T'GETHER.
NICKY AND SUNNY?!
YOUR COUSIN SUNNY?!
YEAH. THEY WAS BOTH LIL' METAL RAT KIDS BACK THEN.
TRYIN' TA GET GIGS. STARTIN' NEW BANDS ALLA TIME.
HEAVY METAL POISONING #3
COMPILATION
100% LOCAL
ONLY REASON I LEARNED GUITAR WAS SO'S MAYBE THEY'D LEMME HANG OUT WITH 'EM.
WEREN'T NUTHIN' COOLER'N THIS WHEN I WAS TWELVE.
...oh, no.
NO WAY.
YEAH.
NICKY CHANGED LOTS AFTER GRACEQUAKE GOT SIGNED.
NO WAY NO WAY NO WAY.
OH HOLY SHIT LOOK AT THIS FUCKING TWAT.
S'FUNNY SEEIN' 'IM LIKE HE IS, NOW.
GUESS I'M HAPPY HIM AN' SUNNY DON'T HANG NO MORE, THO.
YEAH, I GET IT. THE WHOLE SELLOUT THING.
WHAT, YOU THINK YOU'RE MY FIRST ROCK STAR OR SOMETHING?
NAH, NOT CUZZA THAT.
BACK B'FORE HE GOT TV STYLE, HIM AN' SUNNY LIKED TA GO FIND FIGHTS.
BUT THEY WEREN'T NO GOOD. GOT BUSTED TOO MUCH.
NOW, SUNNY FUCKS UP ONE MORE TIME, THEY GONNA SEND 'IM BACK T'EGYPT.

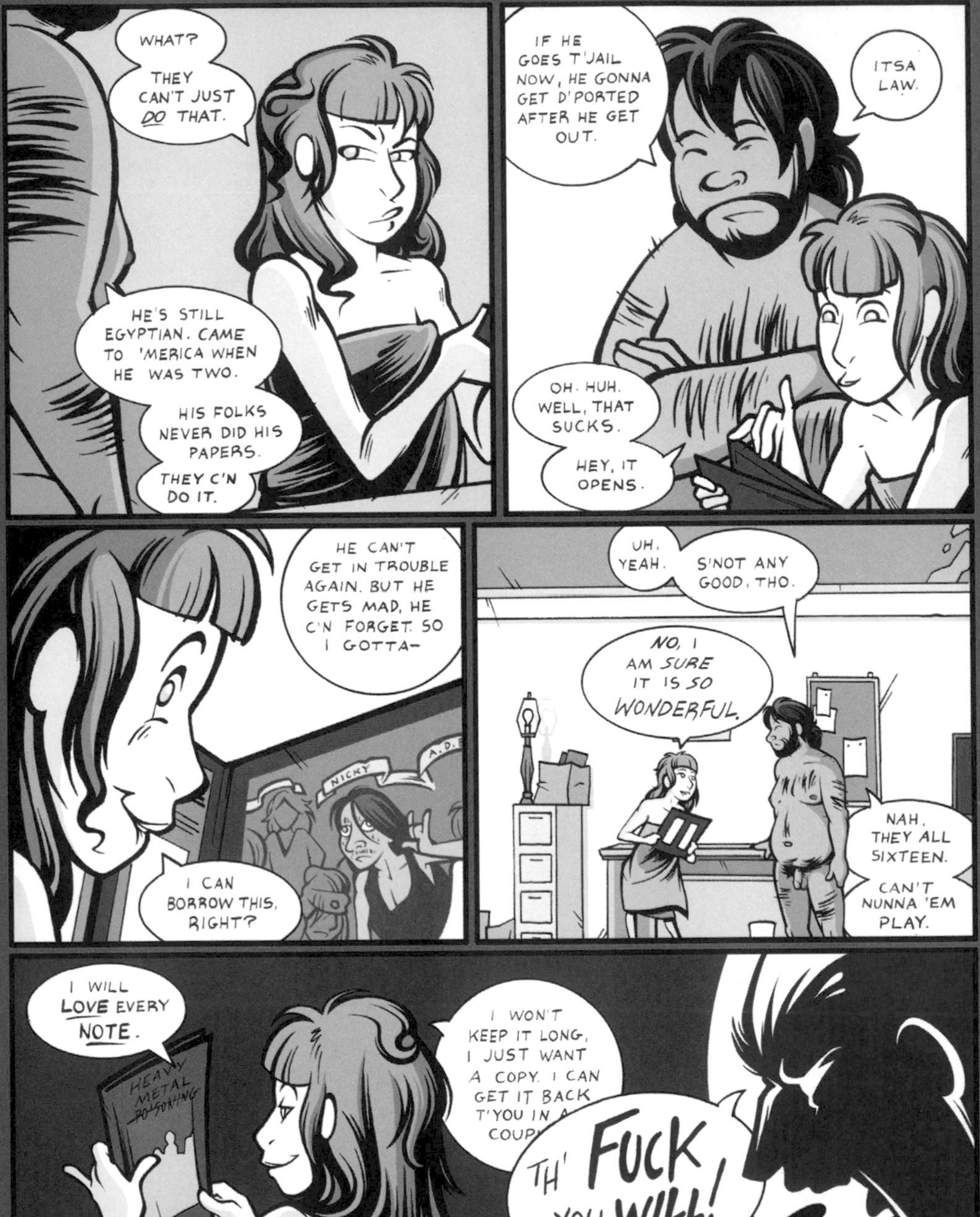
WHAT?
THEY CAN'T JUST DO THAT.
HE'S STILL EGYPTIAN. CAME TO 'MERICA WHEN HE WAS TWO.
HIS FOLKS NEVER DID HIS PAPERS.
THEY C'N DO IT.
IF HE GOES T'JAIL NOW, HE GONNA GET D'PORTED AFTER HE GET OUT.
ITSA LAW.
OH. HUH. WELL, THAT SUCKS.
HEY, IT OPENS.
HE CAN'T GET IN TROUBLE AGAIN. BUT HE GETS MAD, HE C'N FORGET. SO I GOTTA—
NICKY
I CAN BORROW THIS, RIGHT?
UH. YEAH.
S'NOT ANY GOOD, THO.
NO, I AM SURE IT IS SO WONDERFUL.
NAH. THEY ALL SIXTEEN.
CAN'T NUNNA 'EM PLAY.
I WILL LOVE EVERY NOTE.
HEAVY METAL POISONING
I WON'T KEEP IT LONG, I JUST WANT A COPY. I CAN GET IT BACK T'YOU IN A
TH' FUCK YOU WILL!

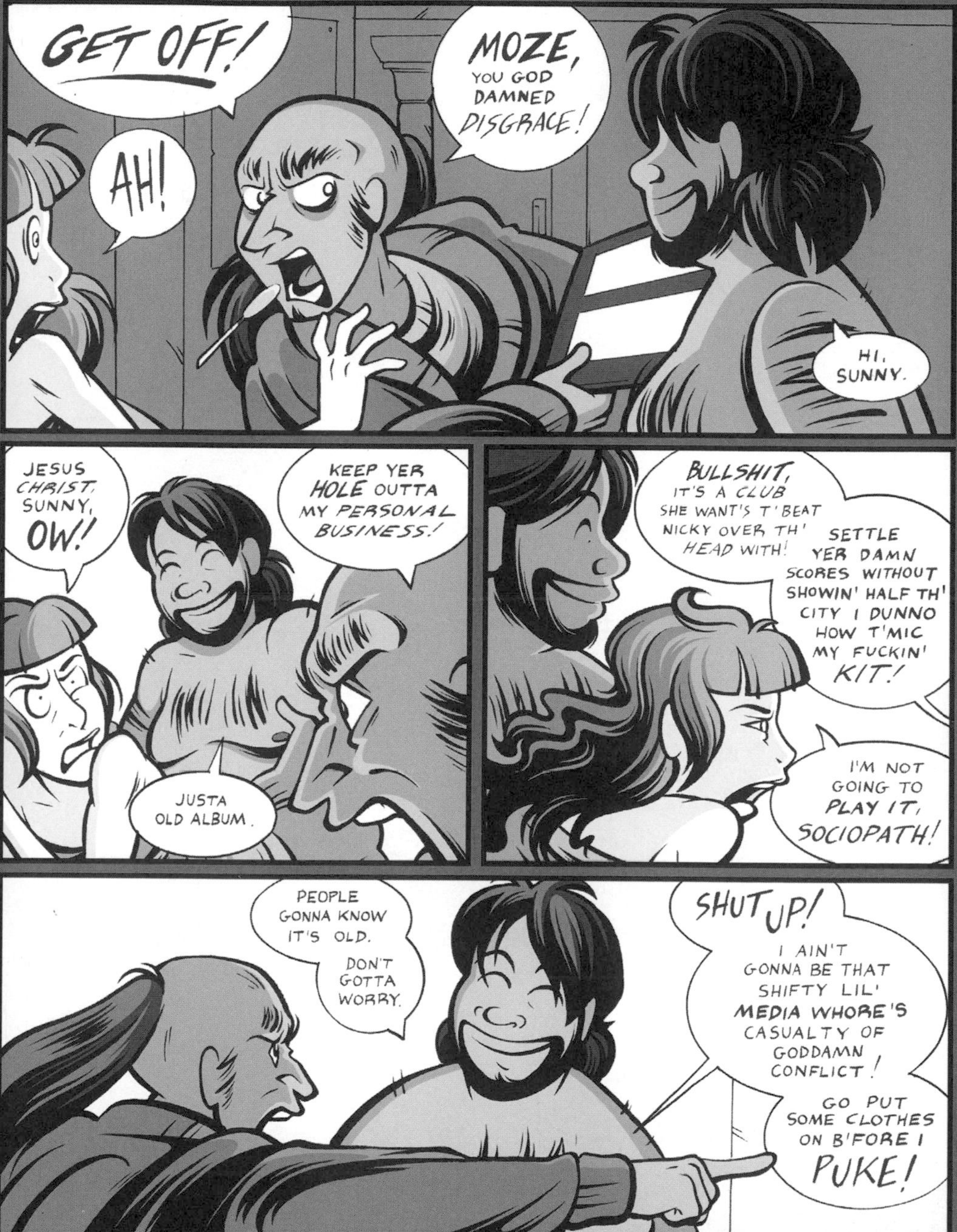
GET OFF!
AH!
MOZE, YOU GOD DAMNED DISGRACE!
HI, SUNNY.
JESUS CHRIST, SUNNY, OW!
KEEP YER HOLE OUTTA MY PERSONAL BUSINESS!
JUSTA OLD ALBUM.
BULLSHIT, IT'S A CLUB SHE WANT'S T' BEAT NICKY OVER TH' HEAD WITH!
SETTLE YER DAMN SCORES WITHOUT SHOWIN' HALF TH' CITY I DUNNO HOW T'MIC MY FUCKIN' KIT!
I'M NOT GOING TO PLAY IT, SOCIOPATH!
PEOPLE GONNA KNOW IT'S OLD.
DON'T GOTTA WORRY.
SHUT UP!
I AIN'T GONNA BE THAT SHIFTY LIL' MEDIA WHORE'S CASUALTY OF GODDAMN CONFLICT!
GO PUT SOME CLOTHES ON B'FORE I PUKE!

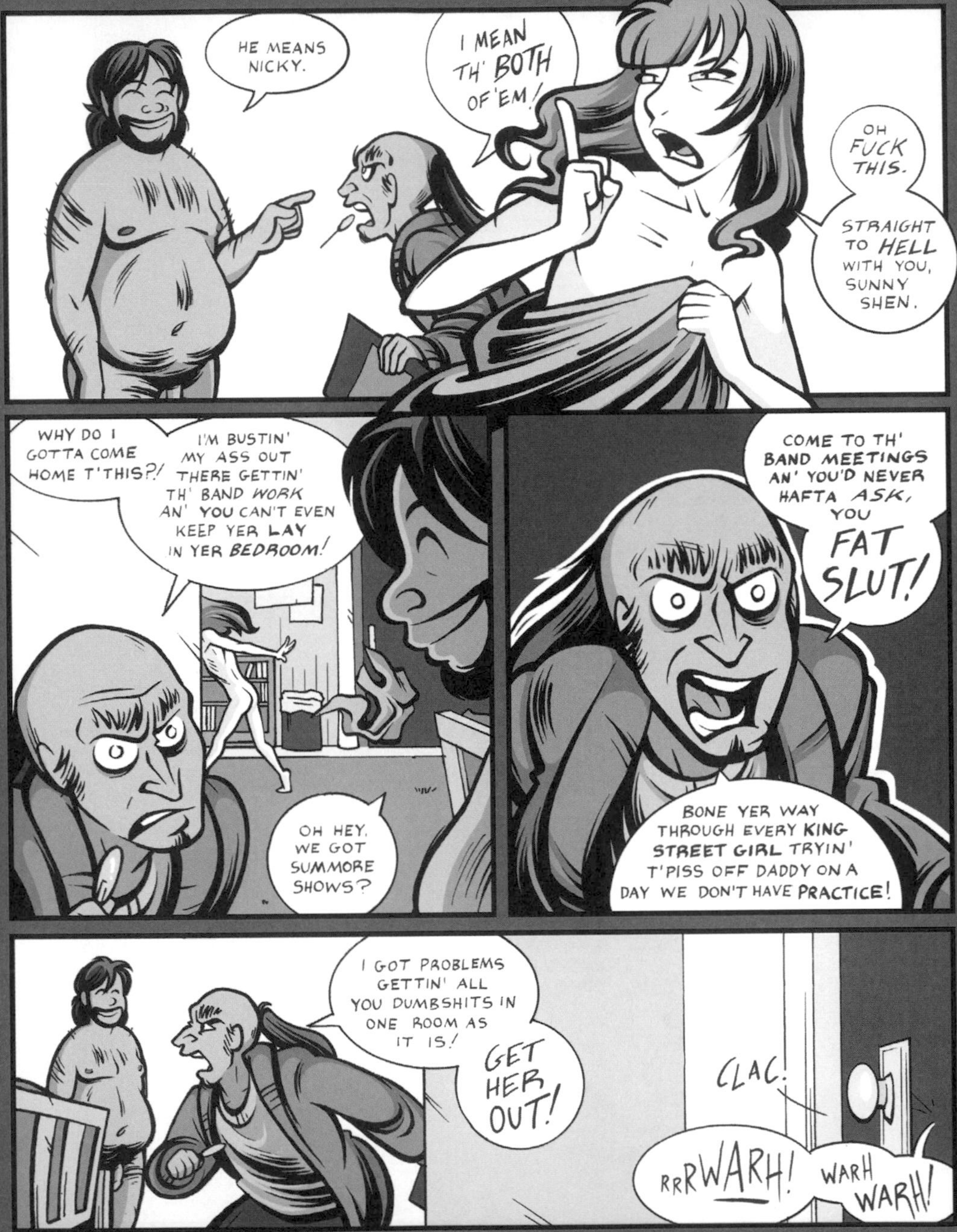
HE MEANS NICKY.
I MEAN TH' BOTH OF 'EM!
OH FUCK THIS.
STRAIGHT TO HELL WITH YOU, SUNNY SHEN.
WHY DO I GOTTA COME HOME T'THIS?!
I'M BUSTIN' MY ASS OUT THERE GETTIN' TH' BAND WORK AN' YOU CAN'T EVEN KEEP YER LAY IN YER BEDROOM!
OH HEY. WE GOT SUMMORE SHOWS?
COME TO TH' BAND MEETINGS AN' YOU'D NEVER HAFTA ASK, YOU FAT SLUT!
BONE YER WAY THROUGH EVERY KING STREET GIRL TRYIN' T'PISS OFF DADDY ON A DAY WE DON'T HAVE PRACTICE!
I GOT PROBLEMS GETTIN' ALL YOU DUMBSHITS IN ONE ROOM AS IT IS!
GET HER OUT!
CLAC
RRRWARH! WARH WARH!

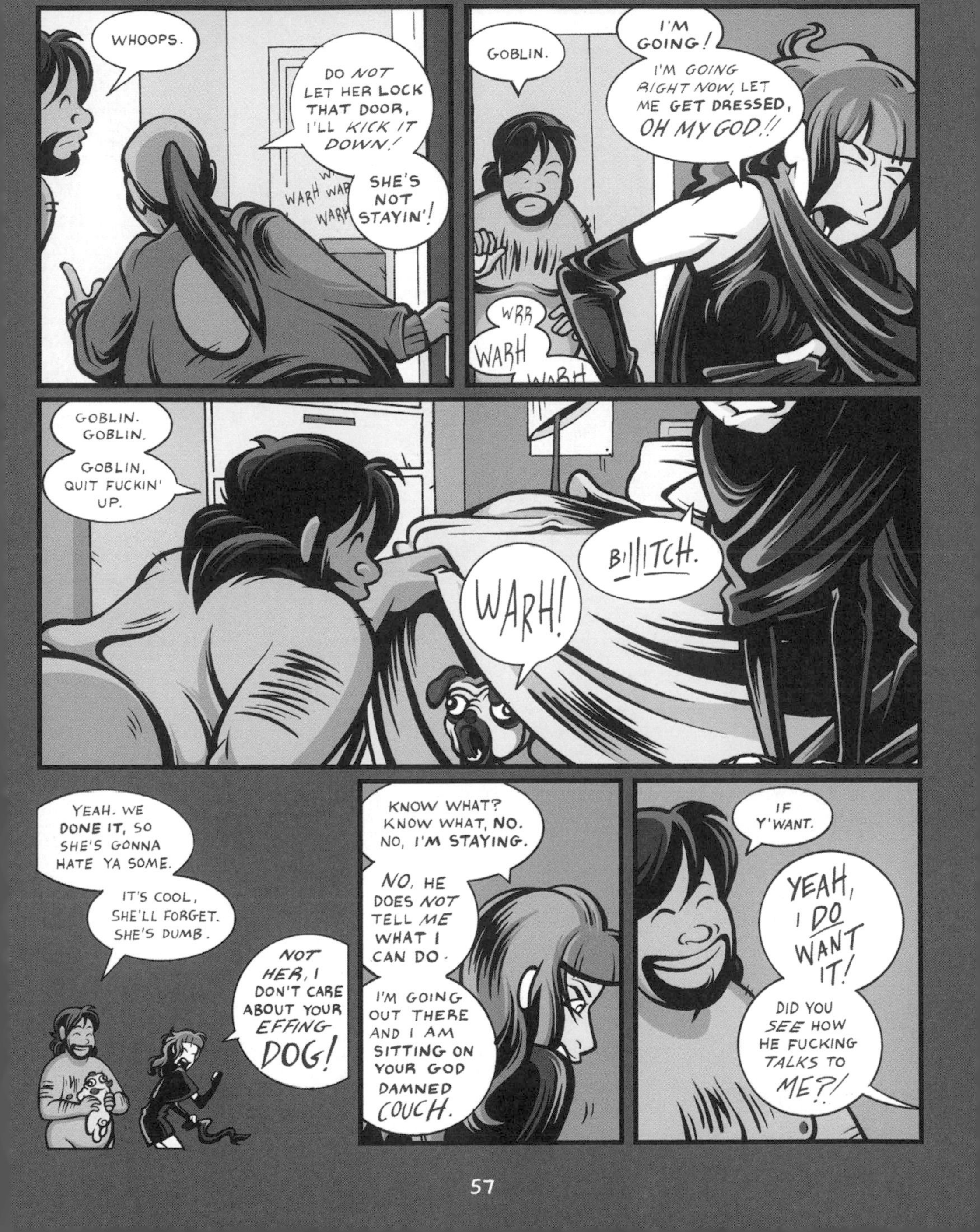
WHOOPS.
DO NOT LET HER LOCK THAT DOOR, I'LL KICK IT DOWN!
SHE'S NOT STAYIN'!
WARH WARH WARH
GOBLIN.
I'M GOING!
I'M GOING RIGHT NOW, LET ME GET DRESSED, OH MY GOD!!
WRR
WARH
GOBLIN. GOBLIN.
GOBLIN, QUIT FUCKIN' UP.
WARH!
BIIITCH.
YEAH. WE DONE IT, SO SHE'S GONNA HATE YA SOME.
IT'S COOL, SHE'LL FORGET. SHE'S DUMB.
NOT HER, I DON'T CARE ABOUT YOUR EFFING DOG!
KNOW WHAT? KNOW WHAT, NO. NO, I'M STAYING.
NO, HE DOES NOT TELL ME WHAT I CAN DO.
I'M GOING OUT THERE AND I AM SITTING ON YOUR GOD DAMNED COUCH.
IF Y'WANT.
YEAH, I DO WANT IT!
DID YOU SEE HOW HE FUCKING TALKS TO ME?!

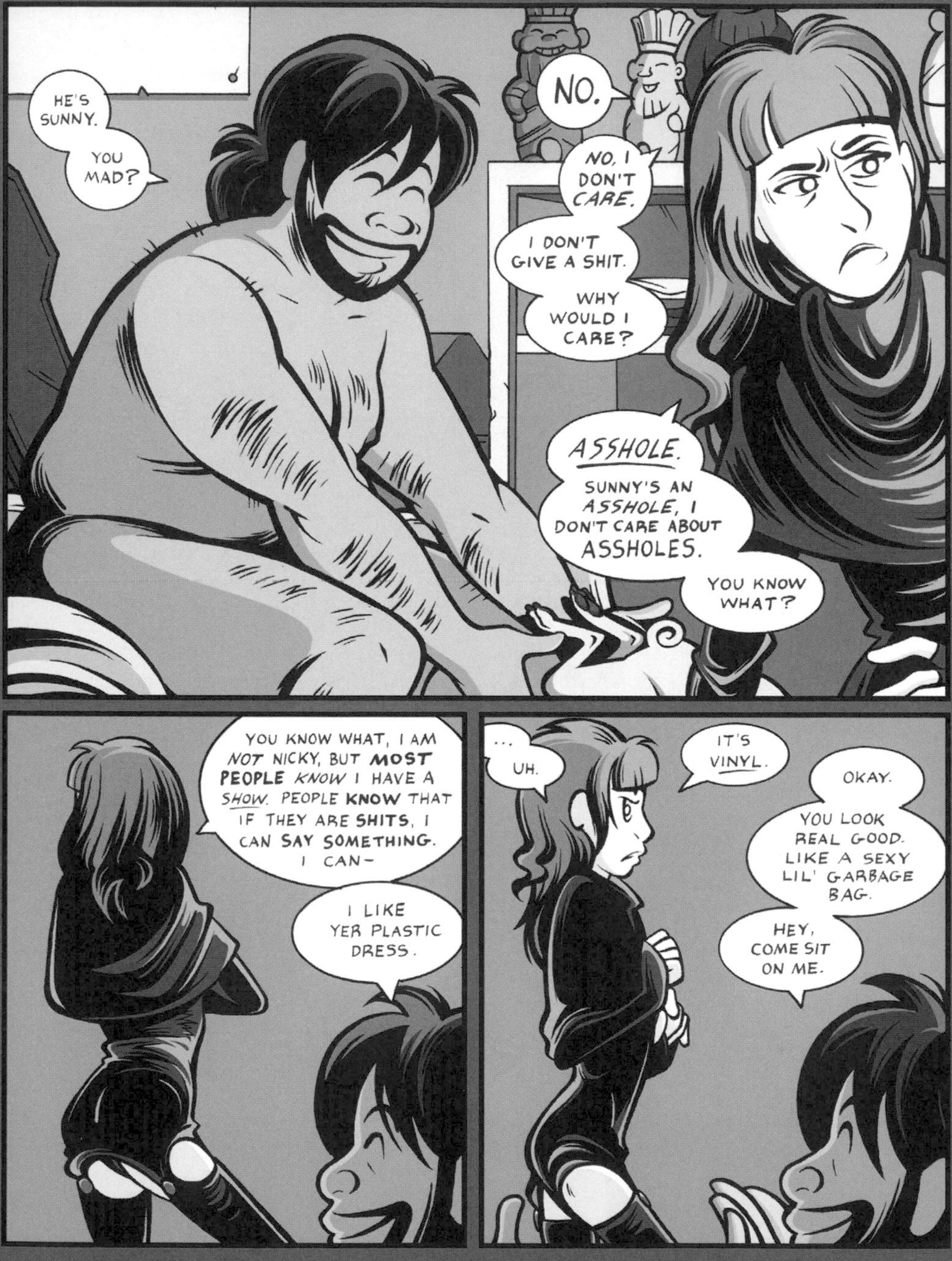
HE'S SUNNY.
YOU MAD?
NO.
NO, I DON'T CARE.
I DON'T GIVE A SHIT.
WHY WOULD I CARE?
ASSHOLE.
SUNNY'S AN ASSHOLE, I DON'T CARE ABOUT ASSHOLES.
YOU KNOW WHAT?
YOU KNOW WHAT, I AM NOT NICKY, BUT MOST PEOPLE KNOW I HAVE A SHOW. PEOPLE KNOW THAT IF THEY ARE SHITS, I CAN SAY SOMETHING. I CAN-
I LIKE YER PLASTIC DRESS.
... UH.
IT'S VINYL.
OKAY.
YOU LOOK REAL GOOD. LIKE A SEXY LIL' GARBAGE BAG.
HEY, COME SIT ON ME.

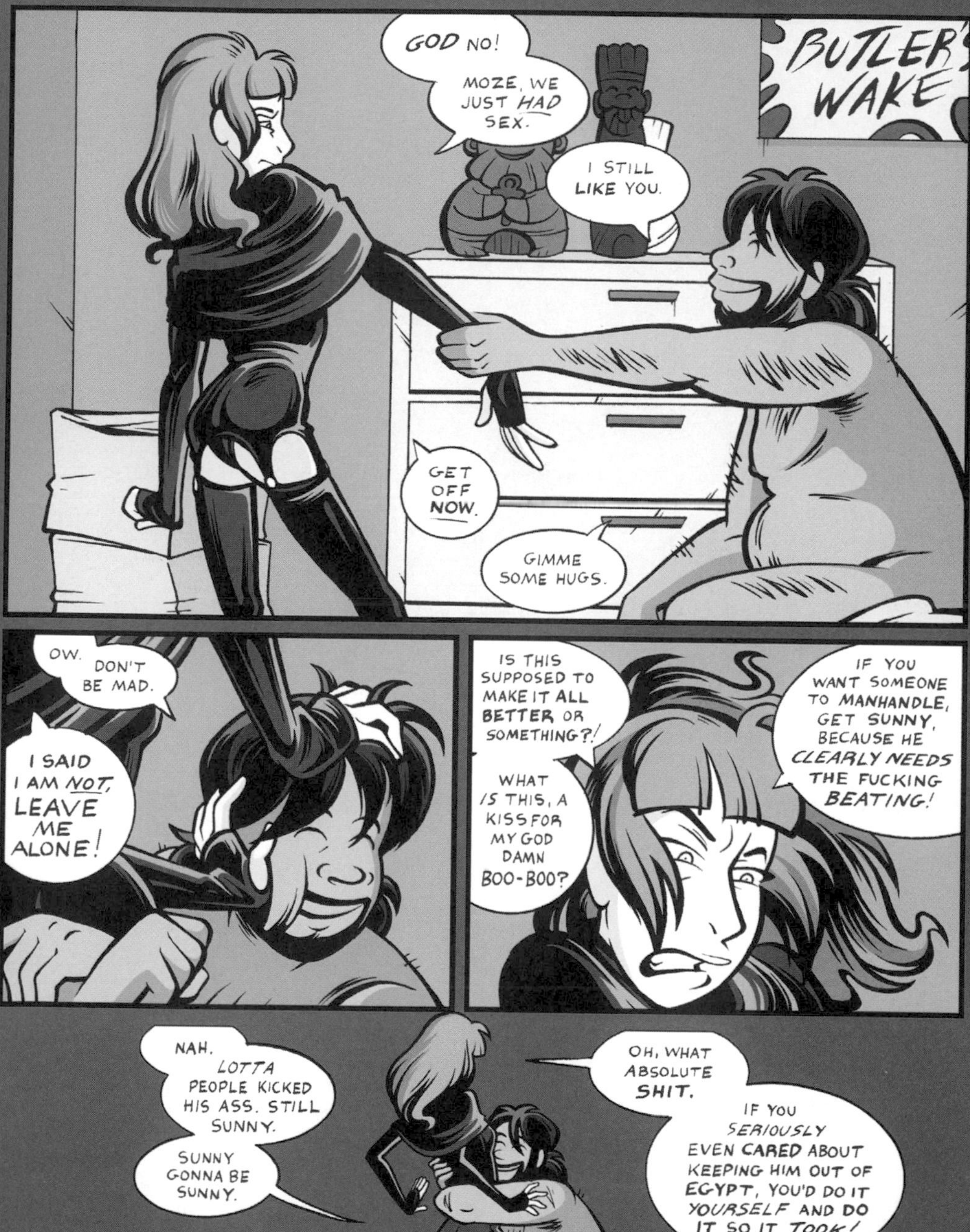
BUTLER'S WAKE
GOD NO!
MOZE, WE JUST HAD SEX.
I STILL LIKE YOU.
GET OFF NOW.
GIMME SOME HUGS.
OW. DON'T BE MAD.
I SAID I AM NOT, LEAVE ME ALONE!
IS THIS SUPPOSED TO MAKE IT ALL BETTER OR SOMETHING?!
WHAT IS THIS, A KISS FOR MY GOD DAMN BOO-BOO?
IF YOU WANT SOMEONE TO MANHANDLE, GET SUNNY, BECAUSE HE CLEARLY NEEDS THE FUCKING BEATING!
NAH. LOTTA PEOPLE KICKED HIS ASS. STILL SUNNY.
SUNNY GONNA BE SUNNY.
OH, WHAT ABSOLUTE SHIT.
IF YOU SERIOUSLY EVEN CARED ABOUT KEEPING HIM OUT OF EGYPT, YOU'D DO IT YOURSELF AND DO IT SO IT TOOK!

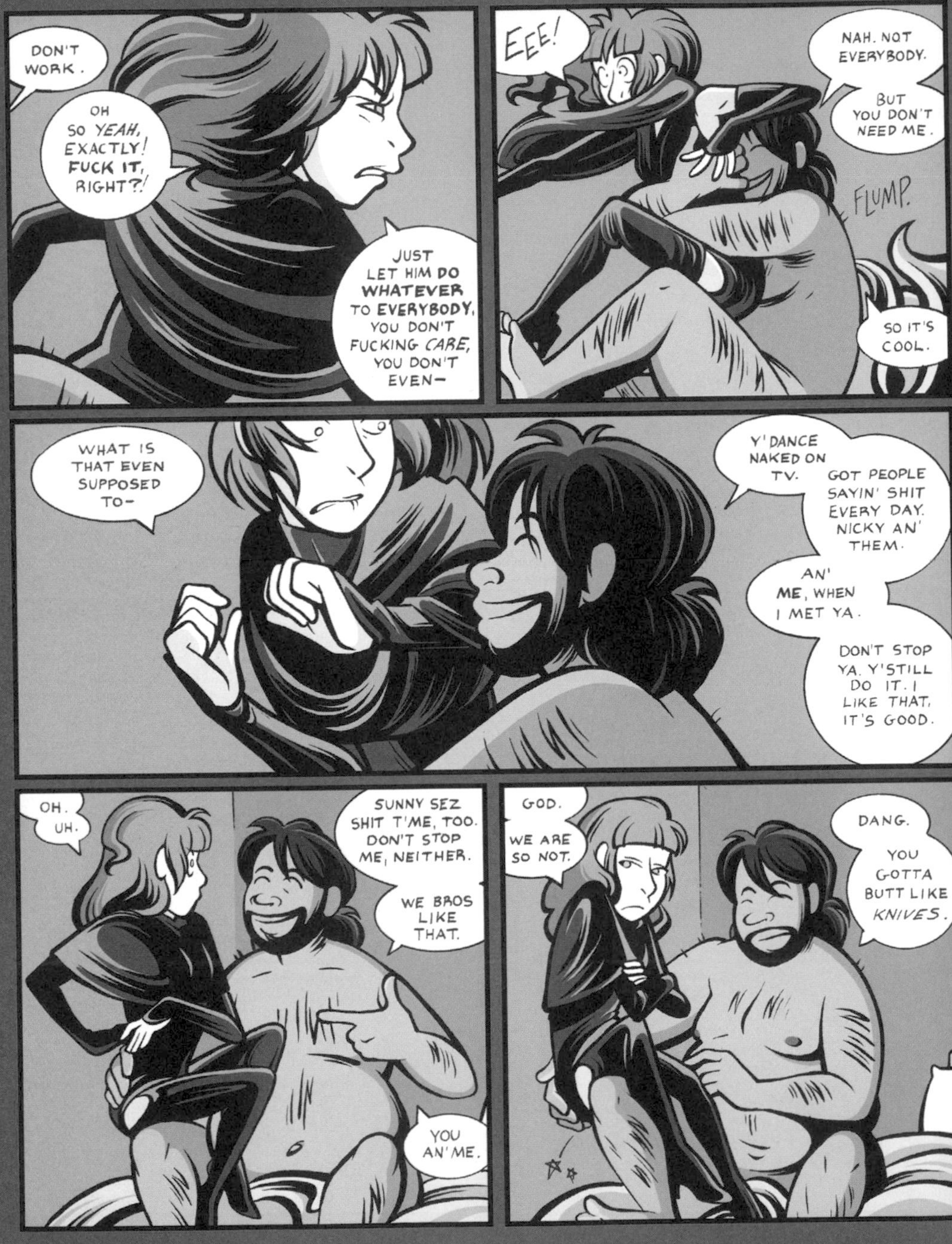
DON'T WORK.
OH SO YEAH, EXACTLY! FUCK IT, RIGHT?!
JUST LET HIM DO WHATEVER TO EVERYBODY, YOU DON'T FUCKING CARE, YOU DON'T EVEN—
EEE!
NAH. NOT EVERYBODY.
BUT YOU DON'T NEED ME.
FLUMP.
SO IT'S COOL.
WHAT IS THAT EVEN SUPPOSED TO-
Y'DANCE NAKED ON TV.
GOT PEOPLE SAYIN' SHIT EVERY DAY. NICKY AN' THEM.
AN' ME, WHEN I MET YA.
DON'T STOP YA. Y'STILL DO IT. I LIKE THAT. IT'S GOOD.
OH. UH.
SUNNY SEZ SHIT T'ME, TOO. DON'T STOP ME, NEITHER.
WE BROS LIKE THAT.
YOU AN'ME.
GOD.
WE ARE SO NOT.
DANG.
YOU GOTTA BUTT LIKE KNIVES.

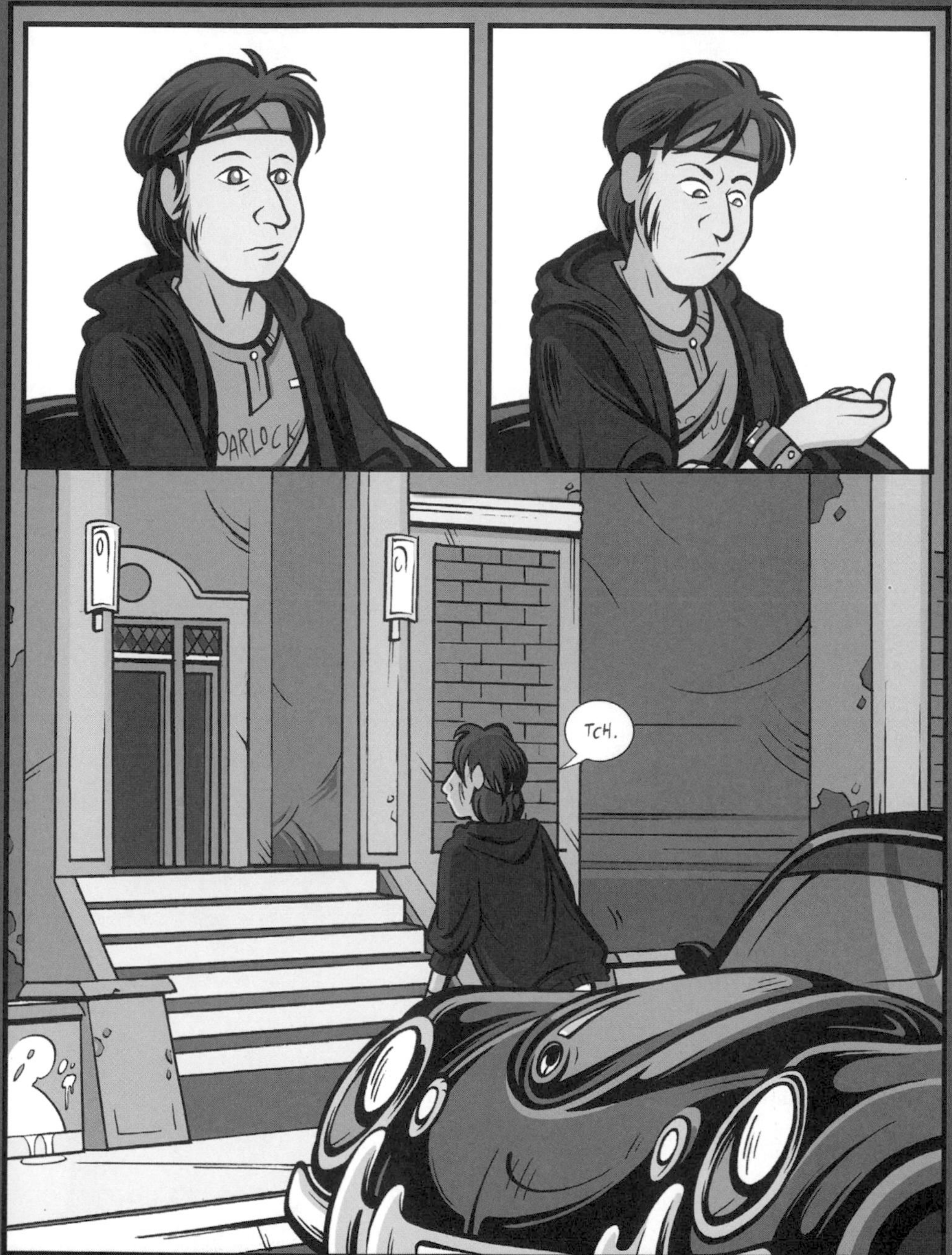
OARLOCK
TCH.

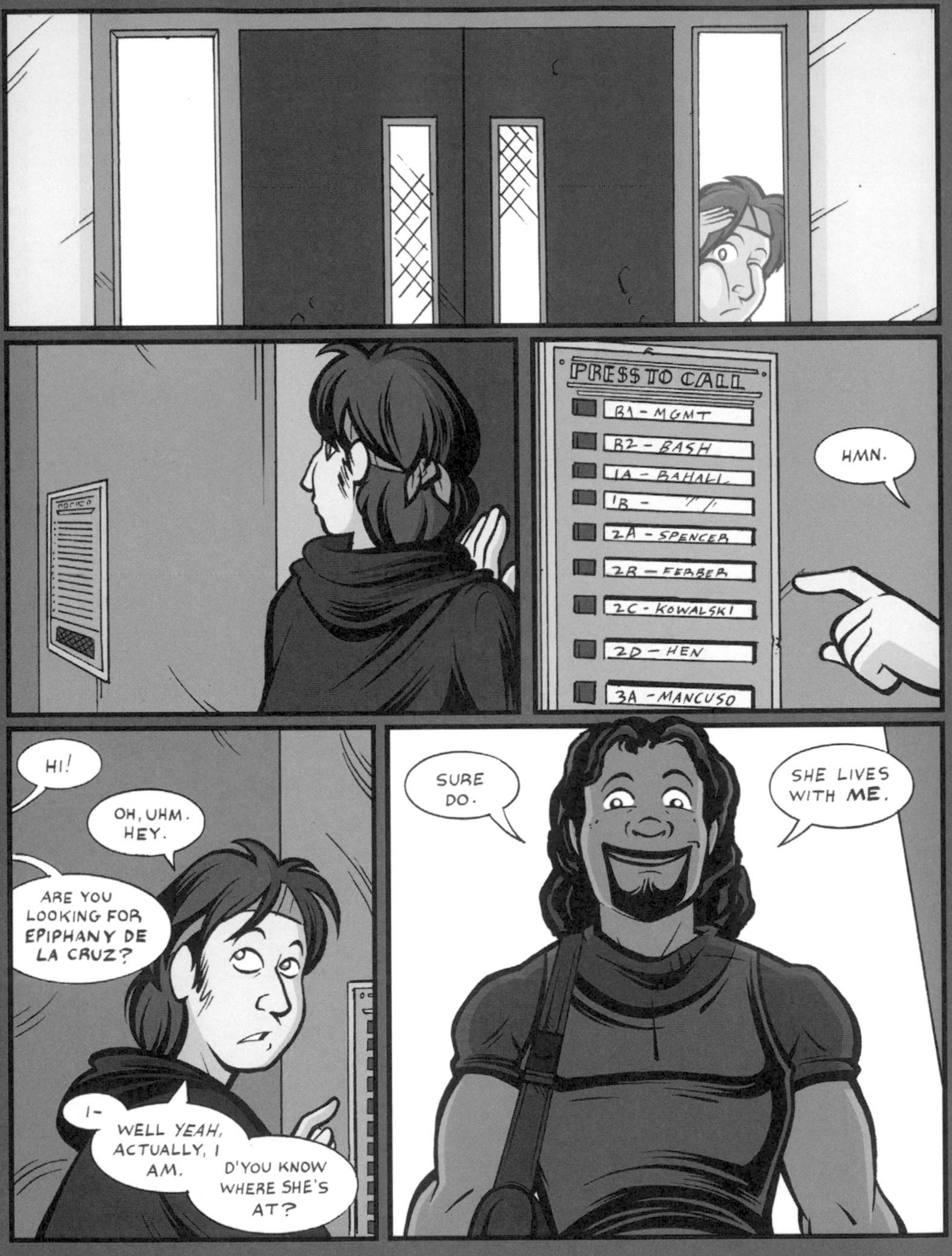
PRESS TO CALL
B1 - MGMT
B2 - BASH
1A - BAHALL
1B -
2A - SPENCER
2B - FERBER
2C - KOWALSKI
2D - HEN
3A - MANCUSO
HMN.
HI!
OH, UHM. HEY.
ARE YOU LOOKING FOR EPIPHANY DE LA CRUZ?
I-
WELL YEAH, ACTUALLY, I AM.
D'YOU KNOW WHERE SHE'S AT?
SURE DO.
SHE LIVES WITH ME.

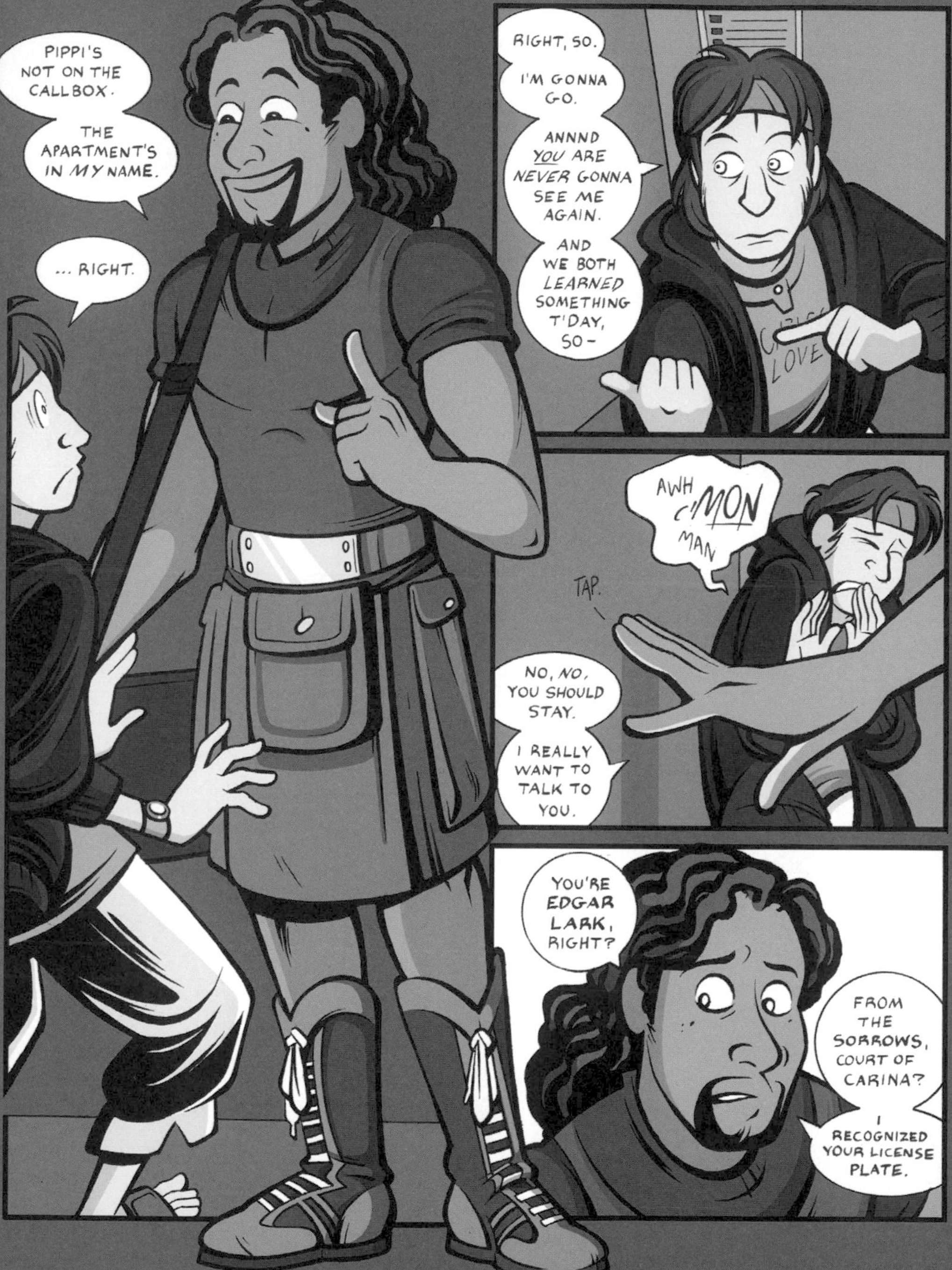
PIPPI'S NOT ON THE CALLBOX.
THE APARTMENT'S IN *MY* NAME.
... RIGHT.
RIGHT, SO.
I'M GONNA GO.
ANNND *YOU* ARE *NEVER* GONNA SEE ME AGAIN.
AND WE BOTH *LEARNED* SOMETHING T'DAY, SO-
AWH C'*MON* MAN
TAP.
NO, *NO*, YOU SHOULD STAY.
I REALLY WANT TO TALK TO YOU.
YOU'RE **EDGAR LARK**, RIGHT?
FROM THE SORROWS, COURT OF CARINA?
I RECOGNIZED YOUR LICENSE PLATE.

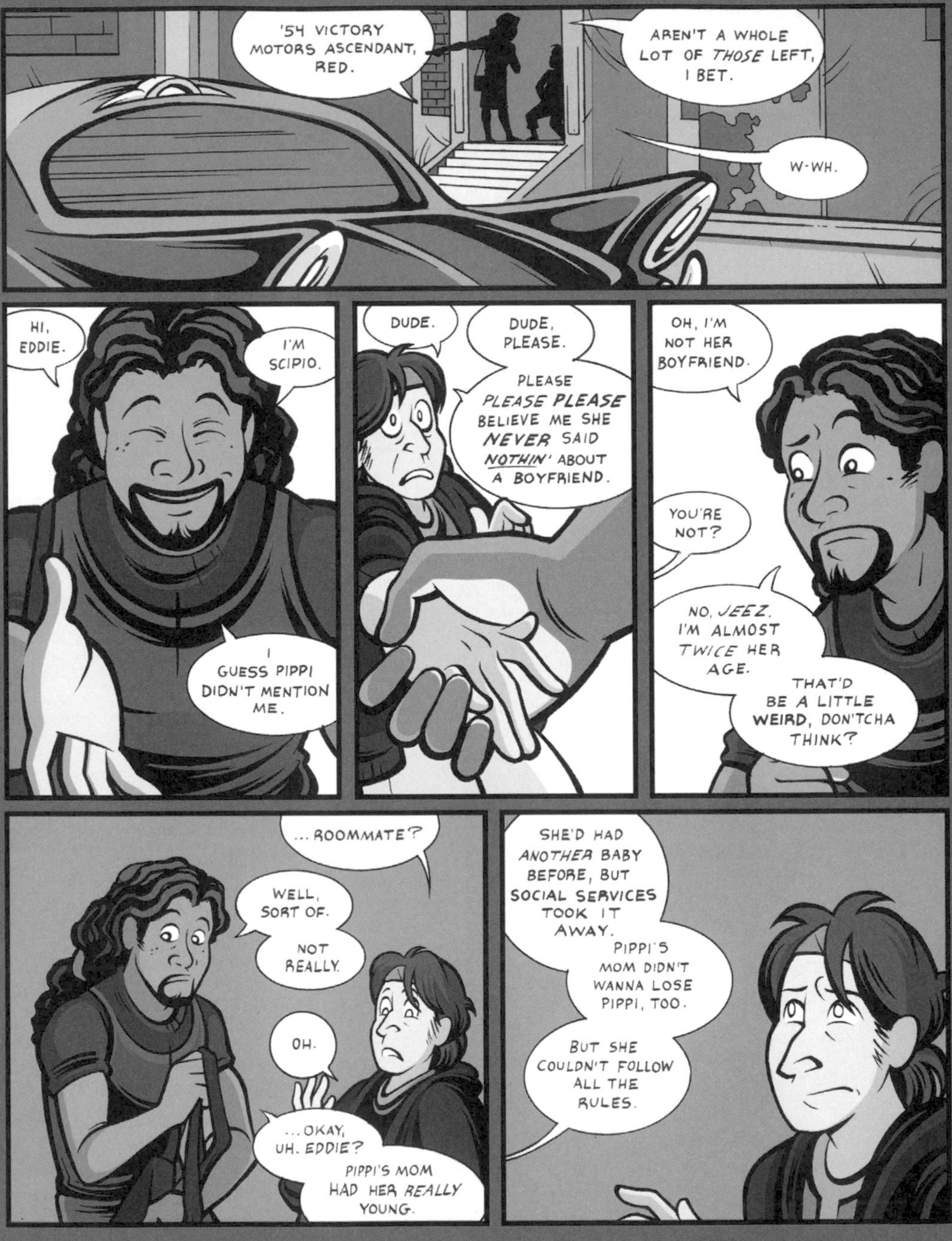
'54 VICTORY MOTORS ASCENDANT, RED.
AREN'T A WHOLE LOT OF *THOSE* LEFT, I BET.
W-WH.
HI, EDDIE.
I'M SCIPIO.
I GUESS PIPPI DIDN'T MENTION ME.
DUDE.
DUDE, PLEASE.
PLEASE *PLEASE* ***PLEASE*** BELIEVE ME SHE ***NEVER*** SAID *NOTHIN'* ABOUT A BOYFRIEND.
OH, I'M NOT HER BOYFRIEND.
YOU'RE NOT?
NO, *JEEZ*. I'M ALMOST *TWICE* HER AGE.
THAT'D BE A LITTLE **WEIRD**, DON'TCHA THINK?
...ROOMMATE?
WELL, SORT OF.
NOT REALLY.
OH.
...OKAY, UH. EDDIE?
PIPPI'S MOM HAD HER *REALLY* YOUNG.
SHE'D HAD *ANOTHER* BABY BEFORE, BUT **SOCIAL SERVICES** TOOK IT AWAY.
PIPPI'S MOM DIDN'T WANNA LOSE PIPPI, TOO.
BUT SHE COULDN'T FOLLOW ALL THE RULES.

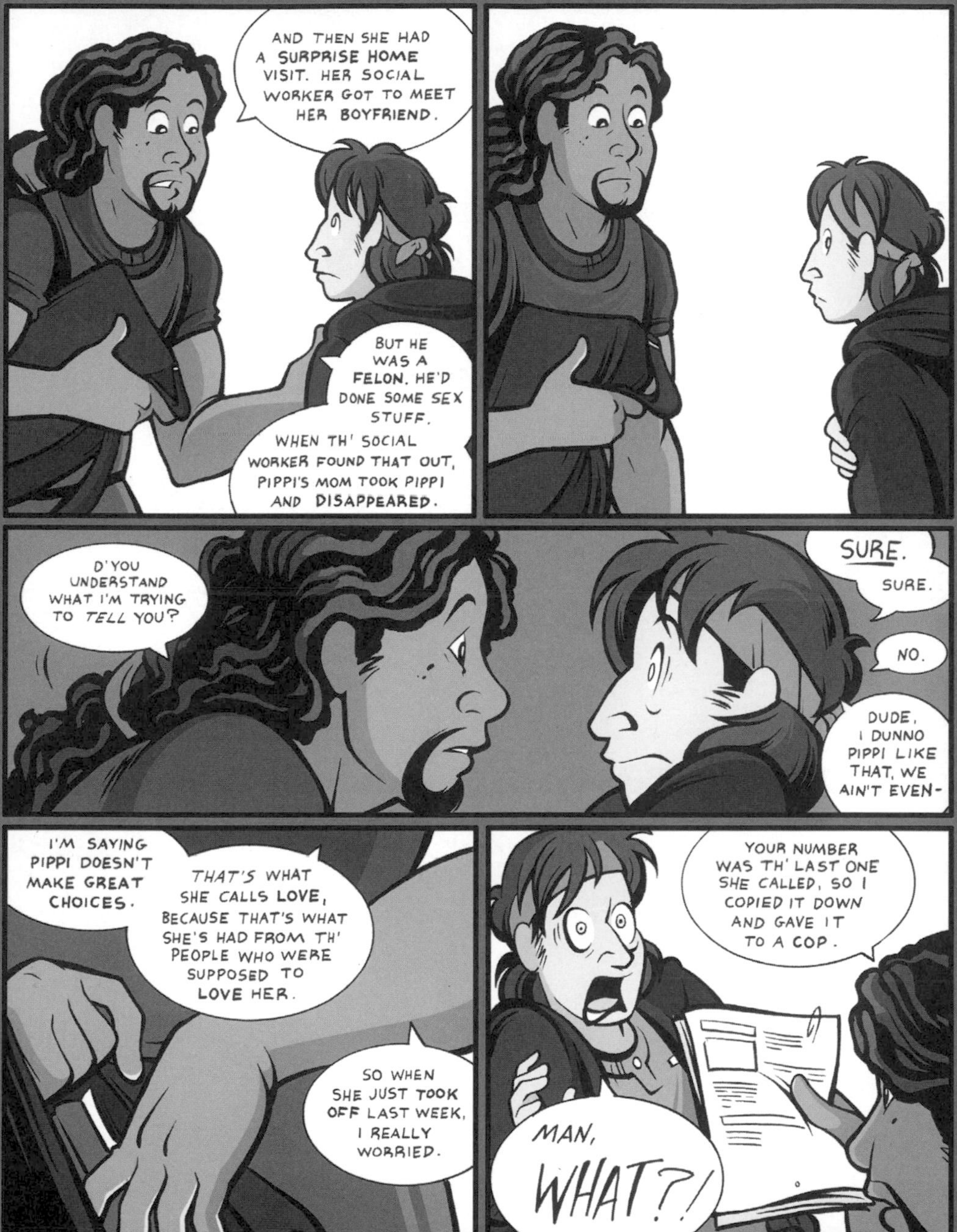
AND THEN SHE HAD A SURPRISE HOME VISIT. HER SOCIAL WORKER GOT TO MEET HER BOYFRIEND.
BUT HE WAS A FELON. HE'D DONE SOME SEX STUFF.
WHEN TH' SOCIAL WORKER FOUND THAT OUT, PIPPI'S MOM TOOK PIPPI AND DISAPPEARED.
D'YOU UNDERSTAND WHAT I'M TRYING TO TELL YOU?
SURE.
SURE.
NO.
DUDE, I DUNNO PIPPI LIKE THAT, WE AIN'T EVEN-
I'M SAYING PIPPI DOESN'T MAKE GREAT CHOICES.
THAT'S WHAT SHE CALLS LOVE, BECAUSE THAT'S WHAT SHE'S HAD FROM TH' PEOPLE WHO WERE SUPPOSED TO LOVE HER.
SO WHEN SHE JUST TOOK OFF LAST WEEK, I REALLY WORRIED.
YOUR NUMBER WAS TH' LAST ONE SHE CALLED, SO I COPIED IT DOWN AND GAVE IT TO A COP.
MAN, WHAT?!

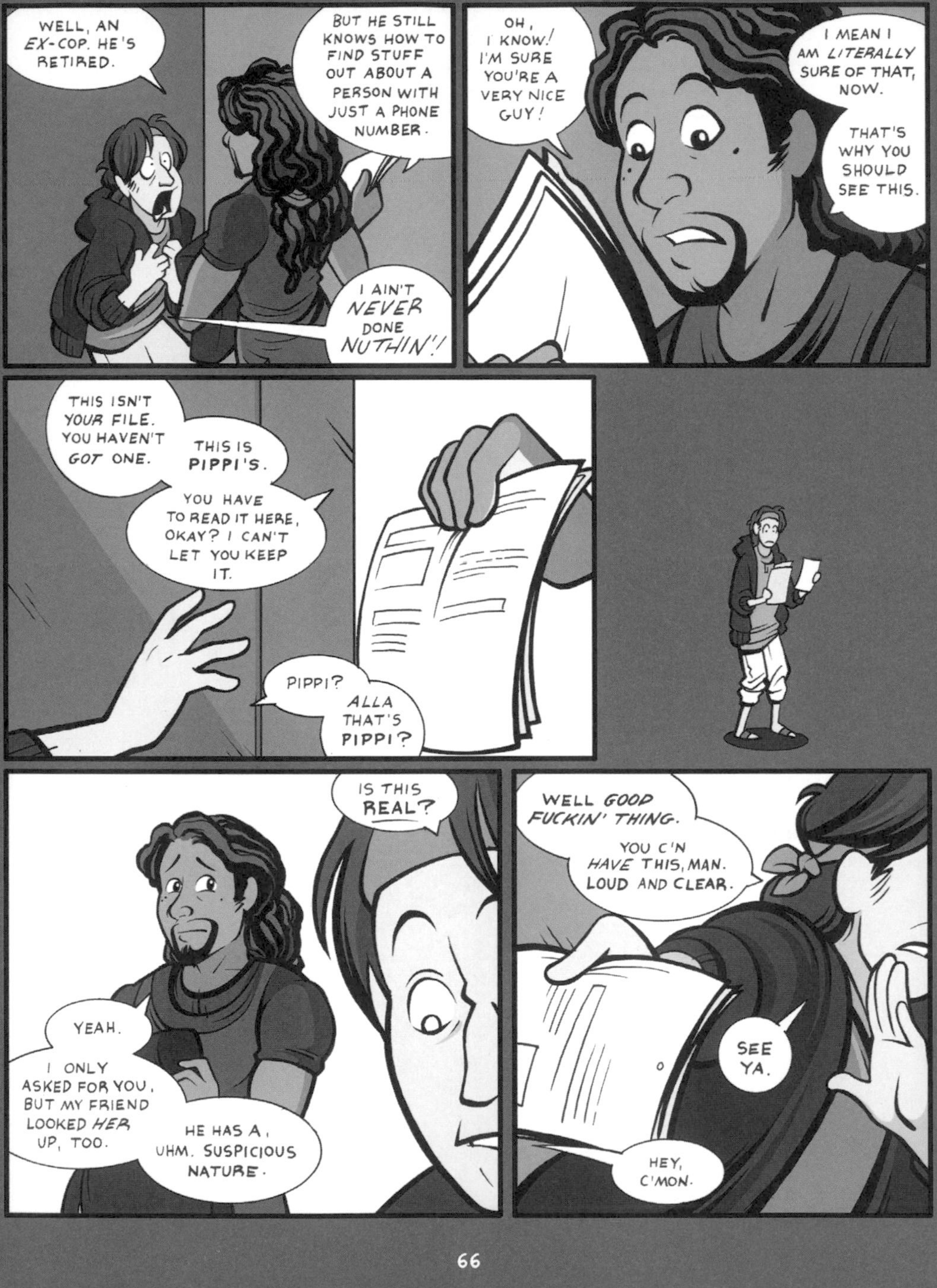
WELL, AN *EX*-COP. HE'S RETIRED.
BUT HE STILL KNOWS HOW TO FIND STUFF OUT ABOUT A PERSON WITH JUST A PHONE NUMBER.
I AIN'T *NEVER* DONE *NUTHIN'!*
OH, I KNOW! I'M SURE YOU'RE A VERY NICE GUY!
I MEAN I AM *LITERALLY* SURE OF THAT, NOW.
THAT'S WHY YOU SHOULD SEE THIS.
THIS ISN'T *YOUR* FILE. YOU HAVEN'T *GOT* ONE.
THIS IS PIPPI'S.
YOU HAVE TO READ IT HERE, OKAY? I CAN'T LET YOU KEEP IT.
PIPPI?
ALLA THAT'S PIPPI?
IS THIS REAL?
YEAH.
I ONLY ASKED FOR YOU, BUT MY FRIEND LOOKED *HER* UP, TOO.
HE HAS A, UHM. SUSPICIOUS NATURE.
WELL *GOOD FUCKIN' THING.*
YOU C'N *HAVE* THIS, MAN. LOUD AND CLEAR.
SEE YA.
HEY, C'MON.

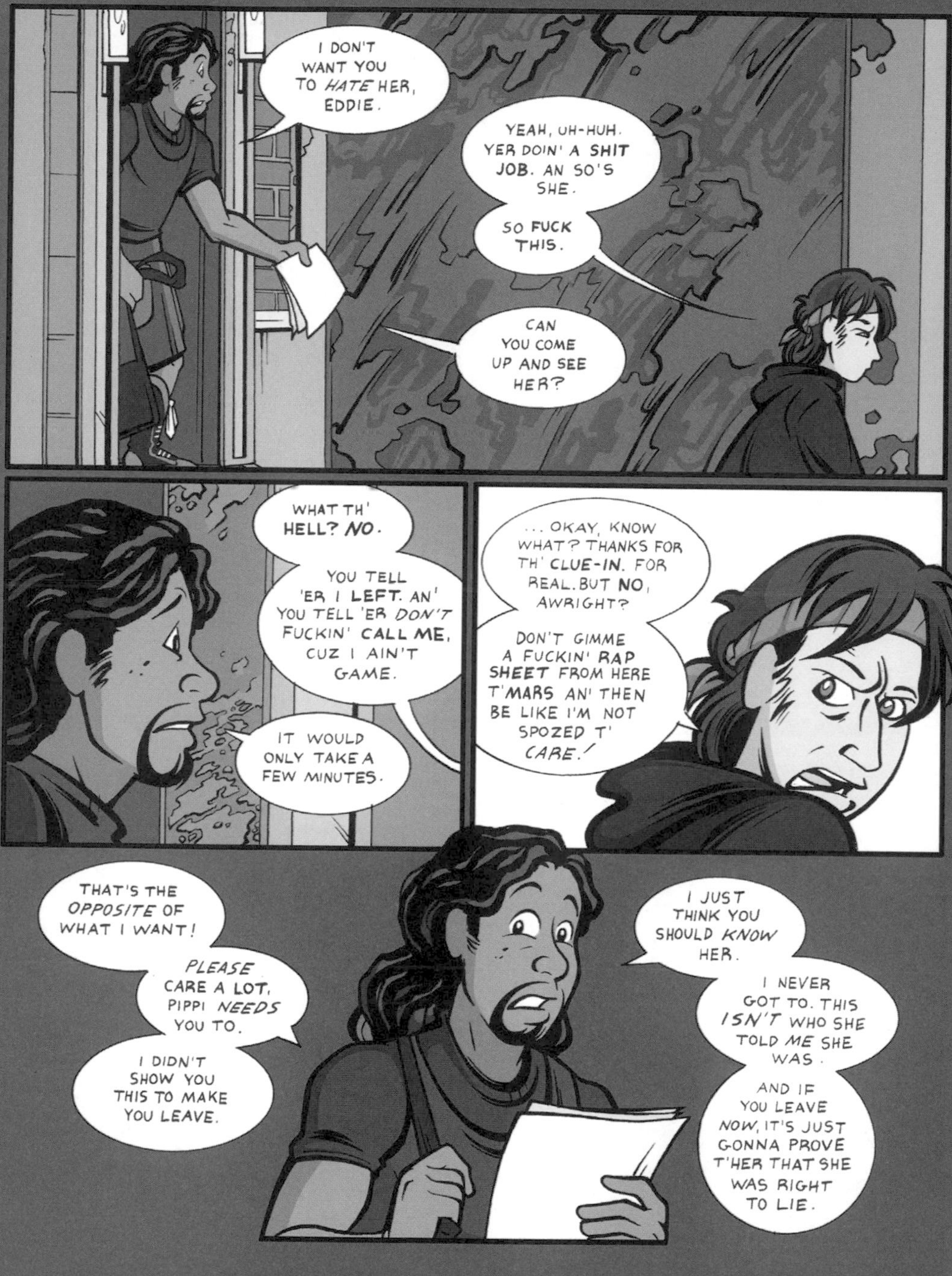
I DON'T WANT YOU TO HATE HER, EDDIE.
YEAH, UH-HUH. YER DOIN' A SHIT JOB. AN SO'S SHE.
SO FUCK THIS.
CAN YOU COME UP AND SEE HER?
WHAT TH' HELL? NO.
YOU TELL 'ER I LEFT. AN' YOU TELL 'ER DON'T FUCKIN' CALL ME, CUZ I AIN'T GAME.
IT WOULD ONLY TAKE A FEW MINUTES.
...OKAY, KNOW WHAT? THANKS FOR TH' CLUE-IN. FOR REAL. BUT NO, AWRIGHT?
DON'T GIMME A FUCKIN' RAP SHEET FROM HERE T'MARS AN' THEN BE LIKE I'M NOT SPOZED T' CARE!
THAT'S THE OPPOSITE OF WHAT I WANT!
PLEASE CARE A LOT. PIPPI NEEDS YOU TO.
I DIDN'T SHOW YOU THIS TO MAKE YOU LEAVE.
I JUST THINK YOU SHOULD KNOW HER.
I NEVER GOT TO. THIS ISN'T WHO SHE TOLD ME SHE WAS.
AND IF YOU LEAVE NOW, IT'S JUST GONNA PROVE T'HER THAT SHE WAS RIGHT TO LIE.

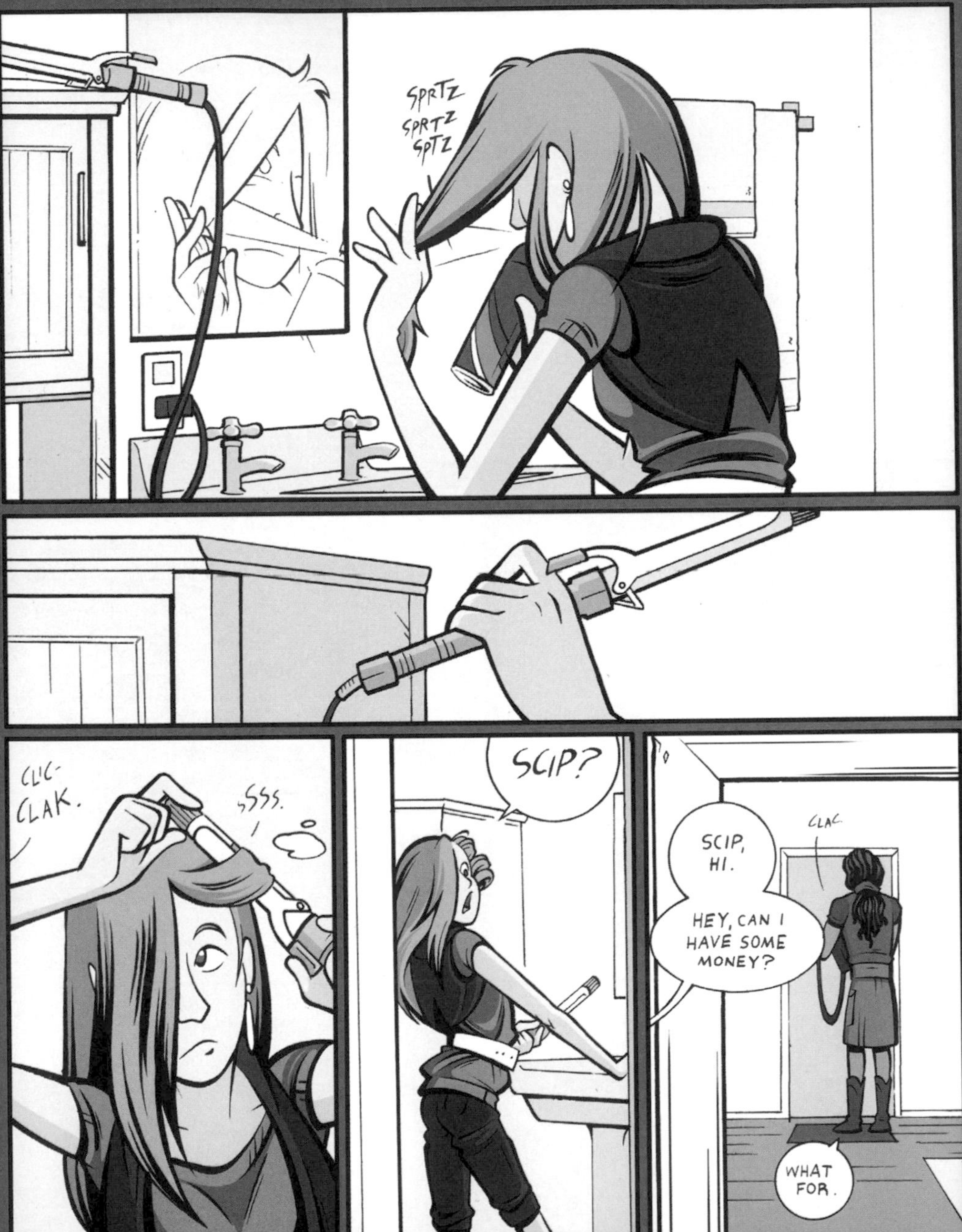
SPRTZ
SPRTZ
SPTZ
CLIC-
CLAK.
SSS.
SCIP?
SCIP,
HI.
HEY, CAN I
HAVE SOME
MONEY?
CLAC.
WHAT
FOR.

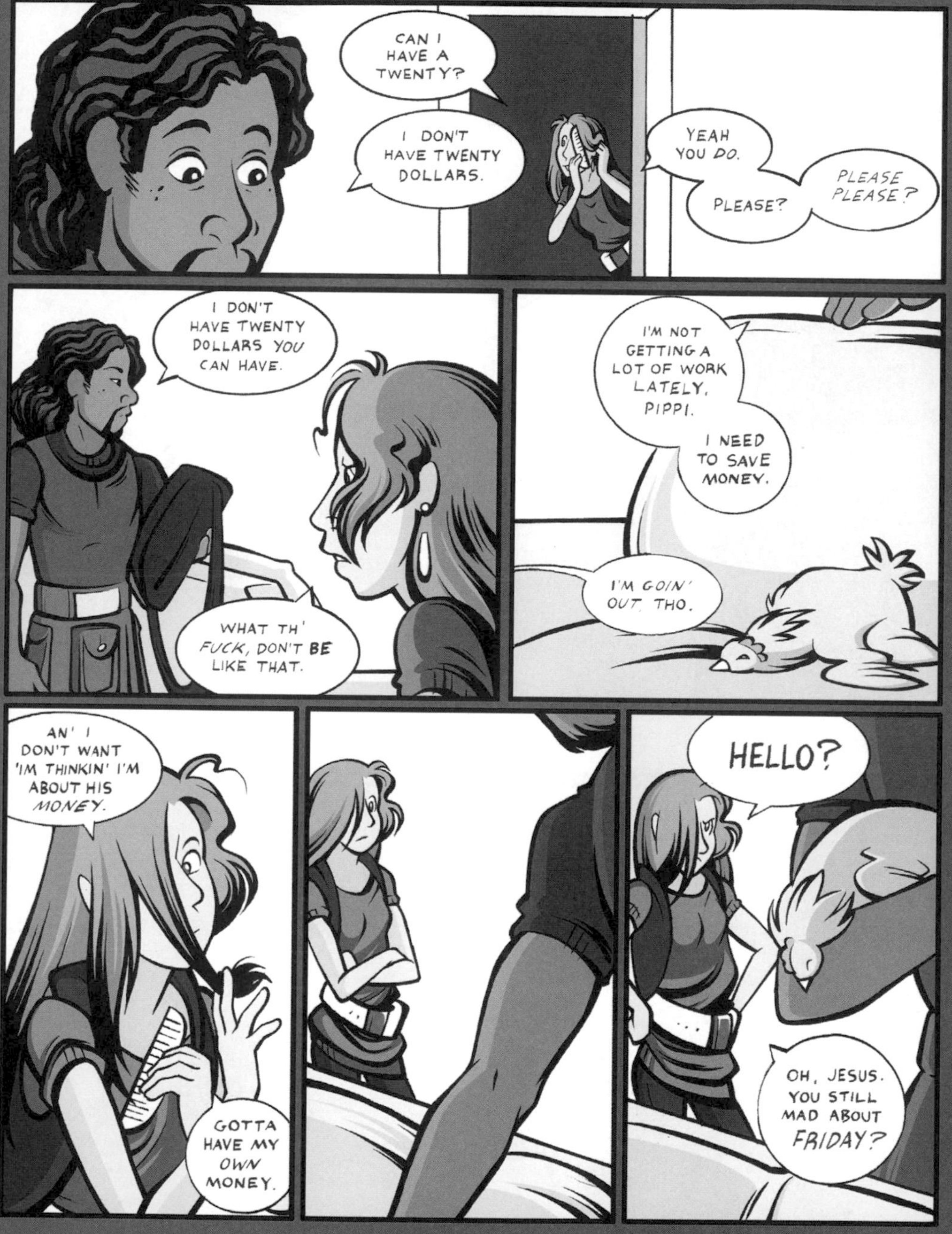
CAN I HAVE A TWENTY?
I DON'T HAVE TWENTY DOLLARS.
YEAH YOU DO.
PLEASE?
PLEASE PLEASE?
I DON'T HAVE TWENTY DOLLARS YOU CAN HAVE.
WHAT TH' FUCK, DON'T BE LIKE THAT.
I'M NOT GETTING A LOT OF WORK LATELY, PIPPI.
I NEED TO SAVE MONEY.
I'M GOIN' OUT, THO.
AN' I DON'T WANT 'IM THINKIN' I'M ABOUT HIS MONEY.
GOTTA HAVE MY OWN MONEY.
HELLO?
OH, JESUS. YOU STILL MAD ABOUT FRIDAY?

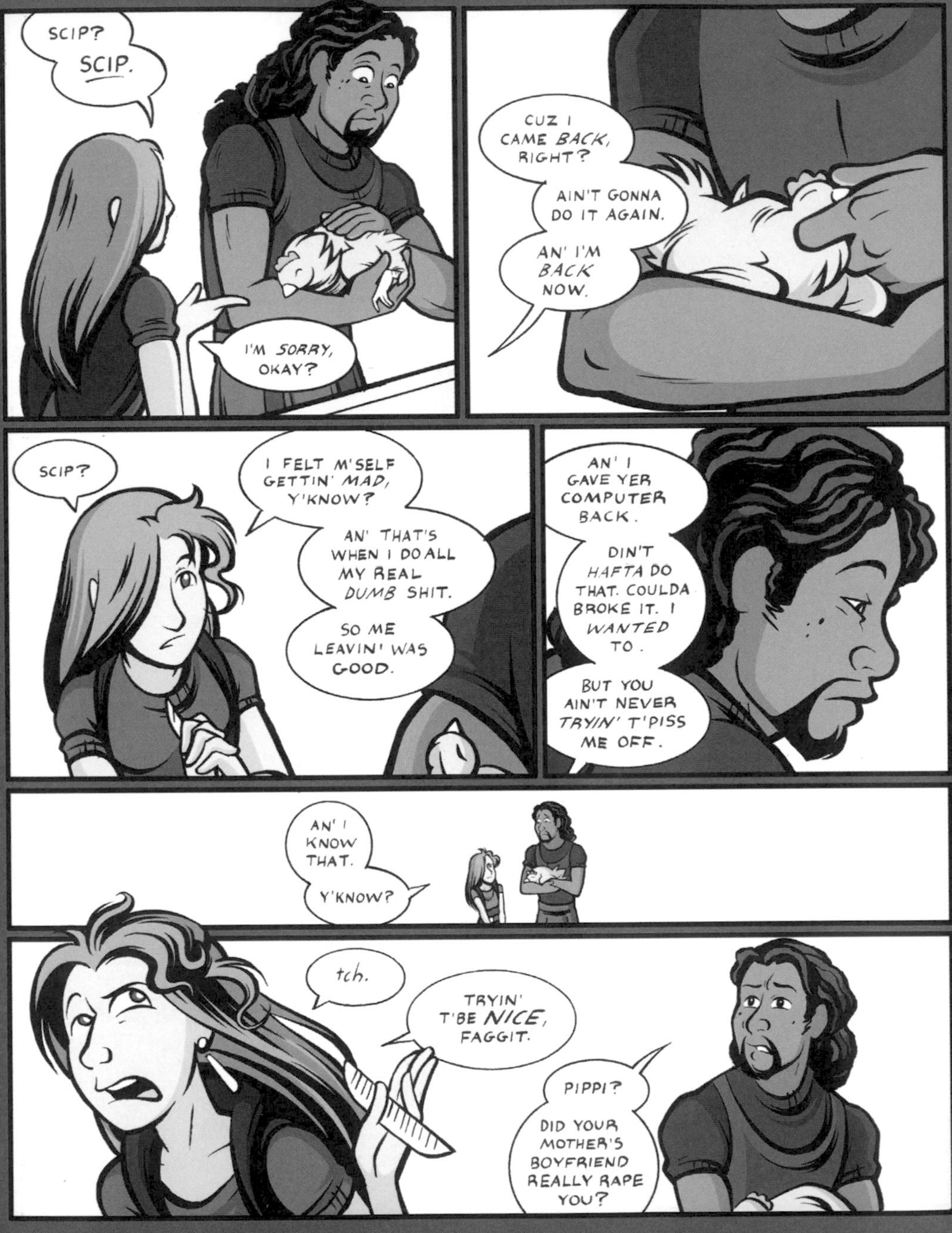
SCIP?
SCIP.
I'M SORRY, OKAY?
CUZ I CAME BACK, RIGHT?
AIN'T GONNA DO IT AGAIN.
AN' I'M BACK NOW.
SCIP?
I FELT M'SELF GETTIN' MAD, Y'KNOW?
AN' THAT'S WHEN I DO ALL MY REAL DUMB SHIT.
SO ME LEAVIN' WAS GOOD.
AN' I GAVE YER COMPUTER BACK.
DIN'T HAFTA DO THAT. COULDA BROKE IT. I WANTED TO.
BUT YOU AIN'T NEVER TRYIN' T'PISS ME OFF.
AN' I KNOW THAT.
Y'KNOW?
tch.
TRYIN' T'BE NICE, FAGGIT.
PIPPI?
DID YOUR MOTHER'S BOYFRIEND REALLY RAPE YOU?

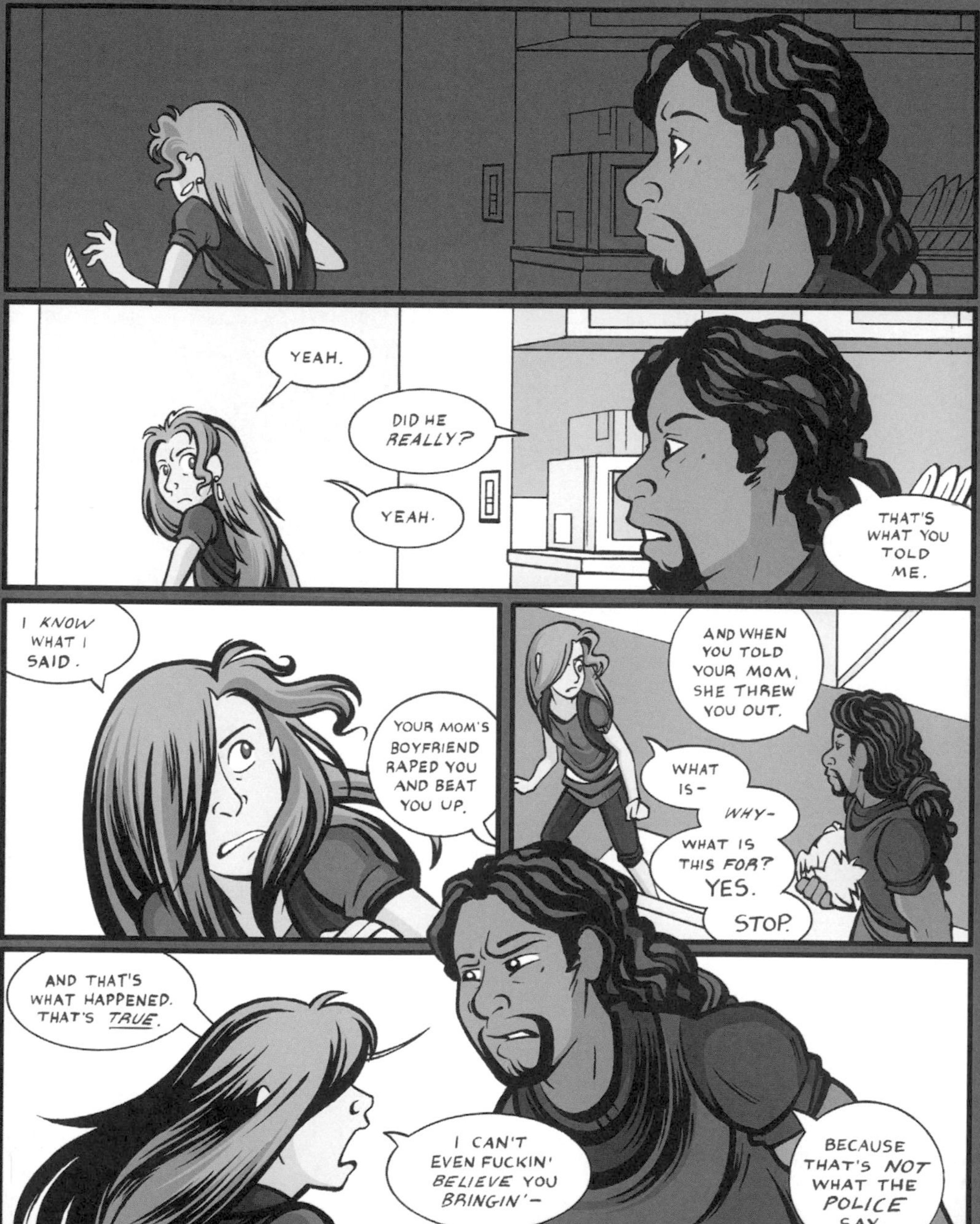
YEAH.
DID HE REALLY?
YEAH.
THAT'S WHAT YOU TOLD ME.
I KNOW WHAT I SAID.
YOUR MOM'S BOYFRIEND RAPED YOU AND BEAT YOU UP.
AND WHEN YOU TOLD YOUR MOM, SHE THREW YOU OUT.
WHAT IS- WHY- WHAT IS THIS FOR?
YES.
STOP.
AND THAT'S WHAT HAPPENED. THAT'S TRUE.
I CAN'T EVEN FUCKIN' BELIEVE YOU BRINGIN'-
BECAUSE THAT'S NOT WHAT THE POLICE SAY.

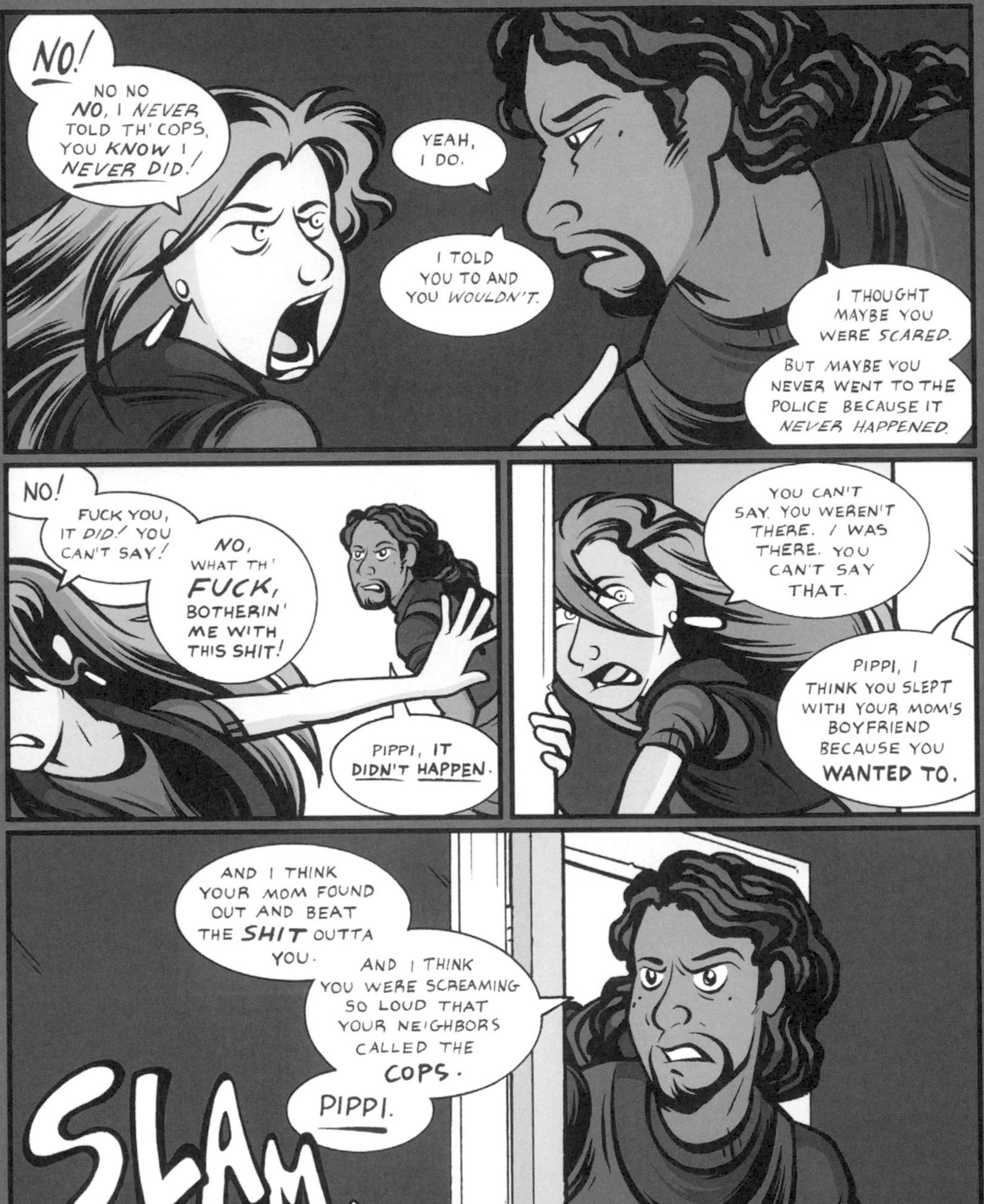
NO!
NO NO NO, I NEVER TOLD TH' COPS, YOU KNOW I NEVER DID!
YEAH, I DO.
I TOLD YOU TO AND YOU WOULDN'T.
I THOUGHT MAYBE YOU WERE SCARED.
BUT MAYBE YOU NEVER WENT TO THE POLICE BECAUSE IT NEVER HAPPENED.
NO!
FUCK YOU, IT DID! YOU CAN'T SAY!
NO, WHAT TH' FUCK, BOTHERIN' ME WITH THIS SHIT!
PIPPI, IT DIDN'T HAPPEN.
YOU CAN'T SAY. YOU WEREN'T THERE. I WAS THERE. YOU CAN'T SAY THAT.
PIPPI, I THINK YOU SLEPT WITH YOUR MOM'S BOYFRIEND BECAUSE YOU WANTED TO.
AND I THINK YOUR MOM FOUND OUT AND BEAT THE SHIT OUTTA YOU.
AND I THINK YOU WERE SCREAMING SO LOUD THAT YOUR NEIGHBORS CALLED THE COPS.
PIPPI.
SLAM.

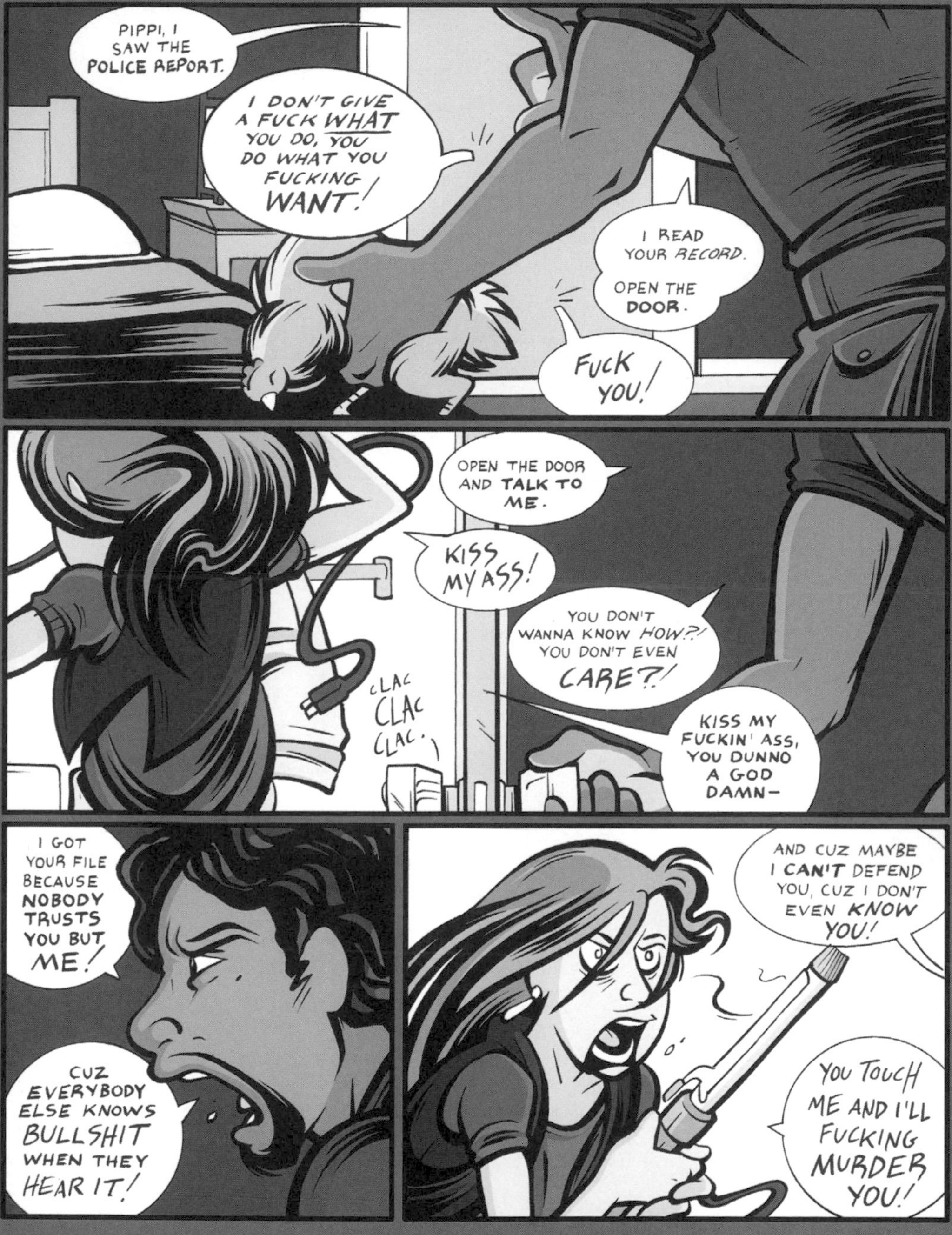
PIPPI, I SAW THE POLICE REPORT.
I DON'T GIVE A FUCK WHAT YOU DO, YOU DO WHAT YOU FUCKING WANT!
I READ YOUR RECORD.
OPEN THE DOOR.
FUCK YOU!
OPEN THE DOOR AND TALK TO ME.
KISS MY ASS!
YOU DON'T WANNA KNOW HOW?! YOU DON'T EVEN CARE?!
CLAC CLAC CLAC.
KISS MY FUCKIN' ASS, YOU DUNNO A GOD DAMN–
I GOT YOUR FILE BECAUSE NOBODY TRUSTS YOU BUT ME!
CUZ EVERYBODY ELSE KNOWS BULLSHIT WHEN THEY HEAR IT!
AND CUZ MAYBE I CAN'T DEFEND YOU, CUZ I DON'T EVEN KNOW YOU!
YOU TOUCH ME AND I'LL FUCKING MURDER YOU!

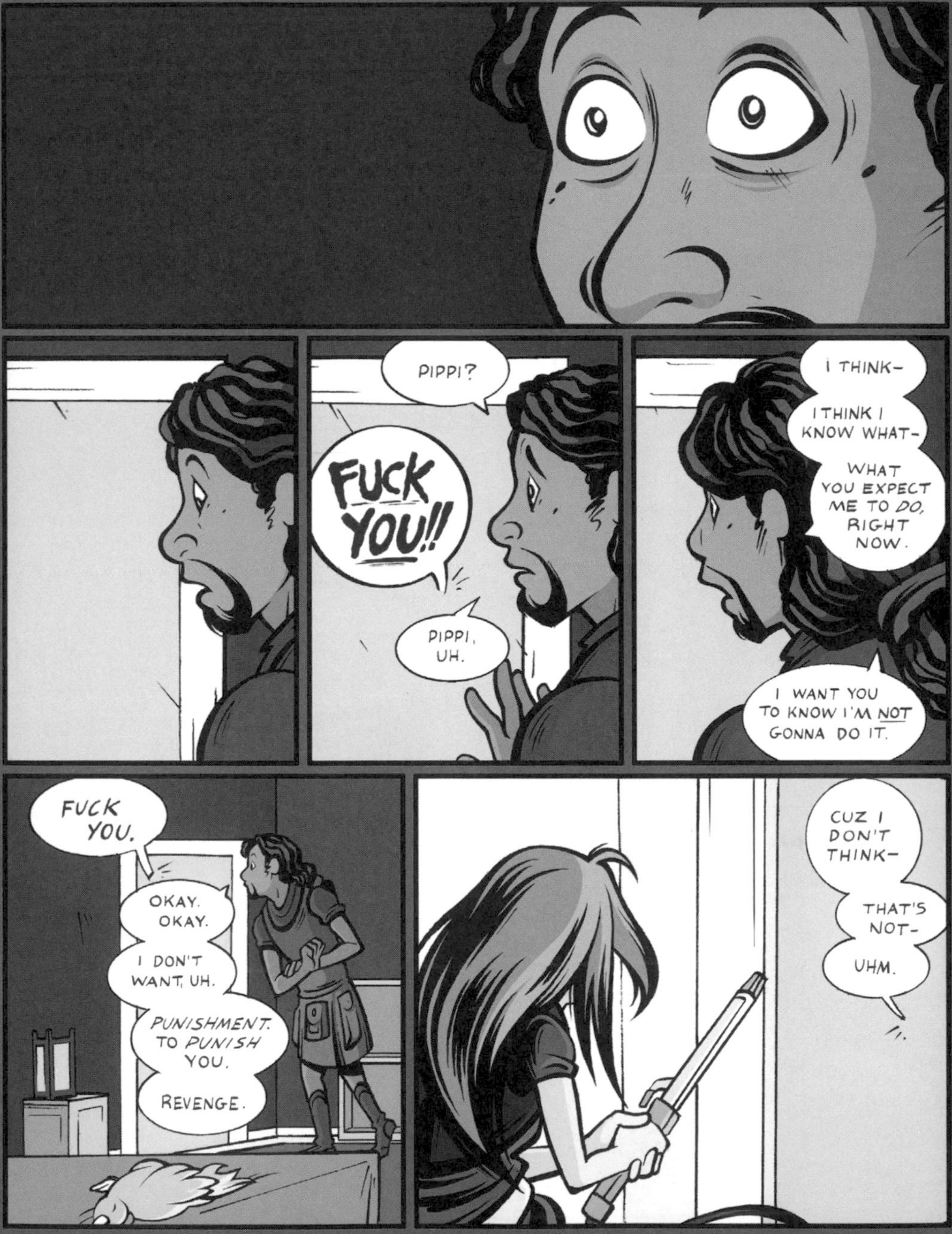
PIPPI?
FUCK YOU!!
PIPPI, UH.
I THINK-
I THINK I KNOW WHAT-
WHAT YOU EXPECT ME TO DO, RIGHT NOW.
I WANT YOU TO KNOW I'M NOT GONNA DO IT.
FUCK YOU.
OKAY. OKAY.
I DON'T WANT, UH.
PUNISHMENT. TO PUNISH YOU.
REVENGE.
CUZ I DON'T THINK-
THAT'S NOT-
UHM.

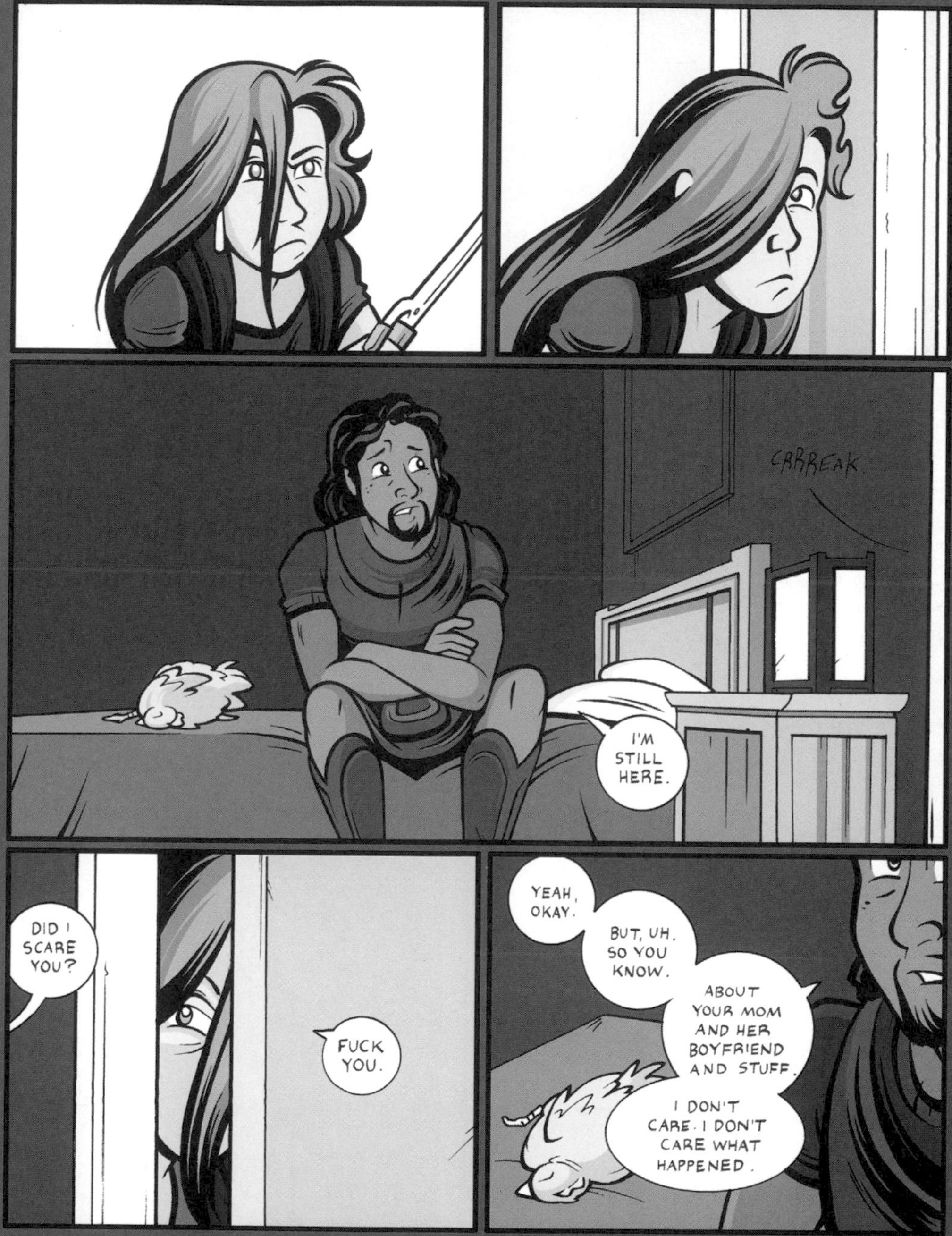
CRRREAK.
I'M STILL HERE.
DID I SCARE YOU?
FUCK YOU.
YEAH, OKAY.
BUT, UH. SO YOU KNOW.
ABOUT YOUR MOM AND HER BOYFRIEND AND STUFF.
I DON'T CARE. I DON'T CARE WHAT HAPPENED.

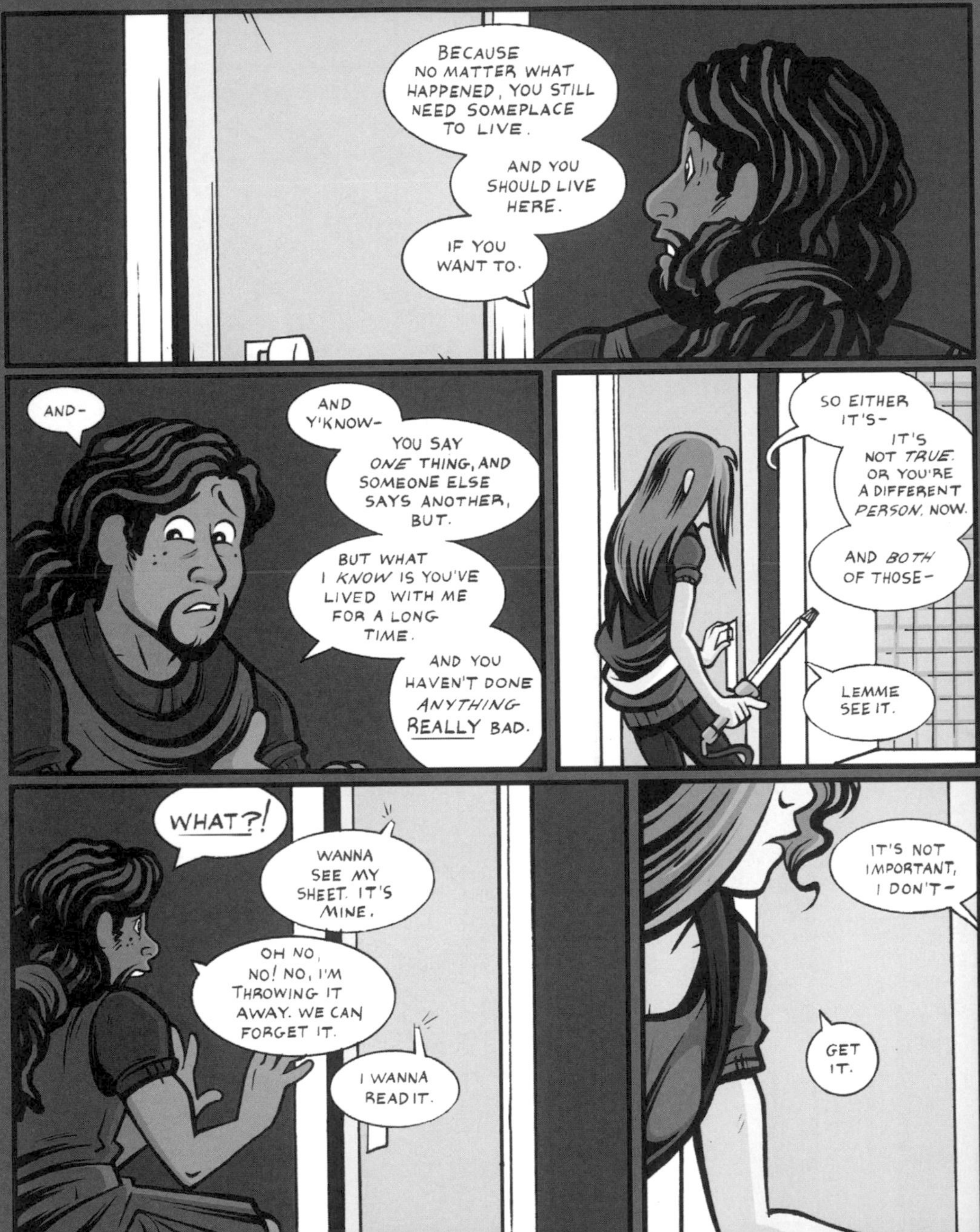
BECAUSE NO MATTER WHAT HAPPENED, YOU STILL NEED SOMEPLACE TO LIVE.
AND YOU SHOULD LIVE HERE.
IF YOU WANT TO.
AND-
AND Y'KNOW-
YOU SAY ONE THING, AND SOMEONE ELSE SAYS ANOTHER, BUT.
BUT WHAT I KNOW IS YOU'VE LIVED WITH ME FOR A LONG TIME.
AND YOU HAVEN'T DONE ANYTHING REALLY BAD.
SO EITHER IT'S-
IT'S NOT TRUE. OR YOU'RE A DIFFERENT PERSON. NOW.
AND BOTH OF THOSE-
LEMME SEE IT.
WHAT?!
WANNA SEE MY SHEET. IT'S MINE.
OH NO, NO! NO, I'M THROWING IT AWAY. WE CAN FORGET IT.
I WANNA READ IT.
IT'S NOT IMPORTANT, I DON'T-
GET IT.

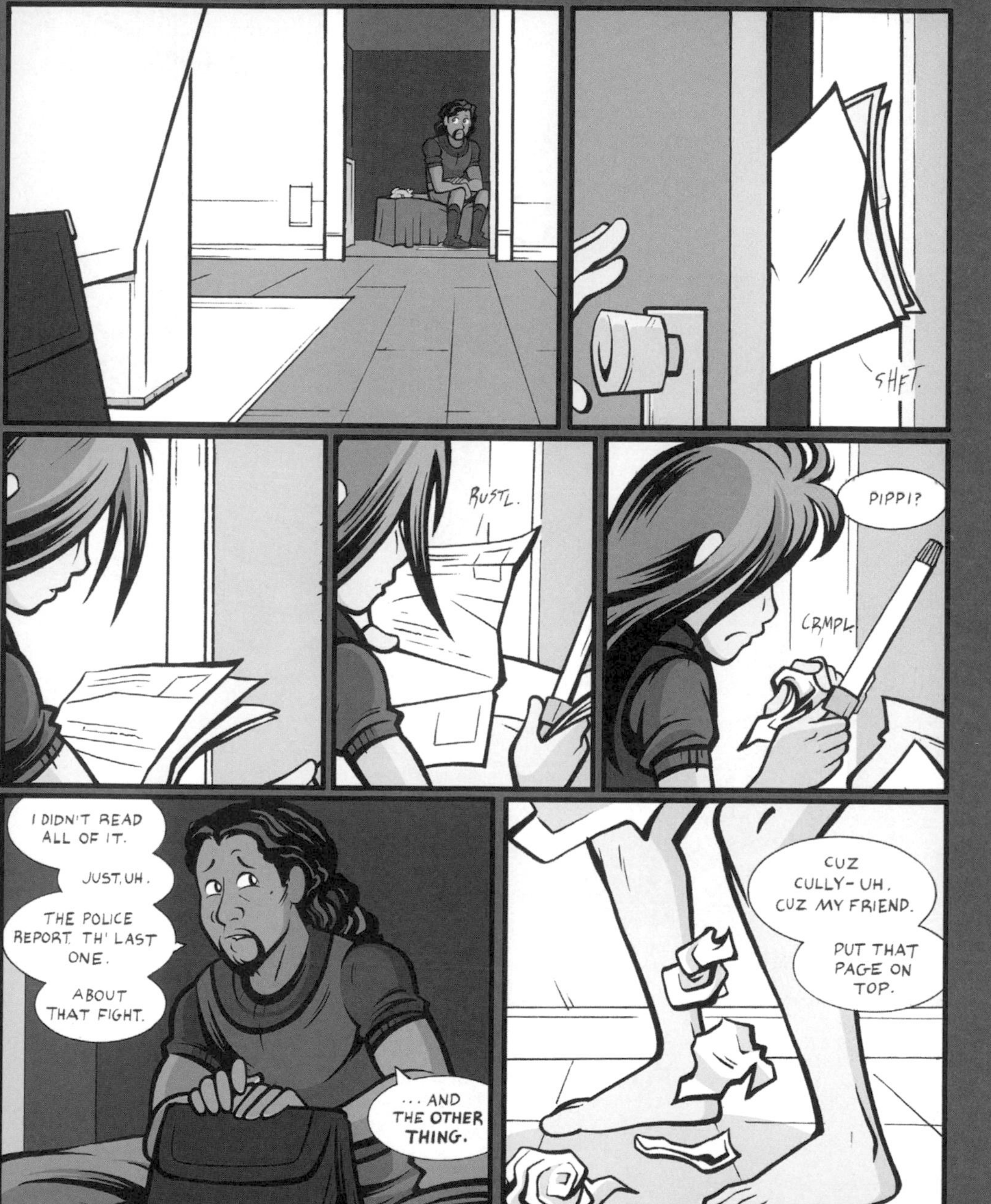
SHFT.
RUSTL.
PIPPI?
CRMPL.
I DIDN'T READ ALL OF IT.
JUST, UH.
THE POLICE REPORT. TH' LAST ONE.
ABOUT THAT FIGHT.
...AND THE OTHER THING.
CUZ CULLY- UH. CUZ MY FRIEND.
PUT THAT PAGE ON TOP.

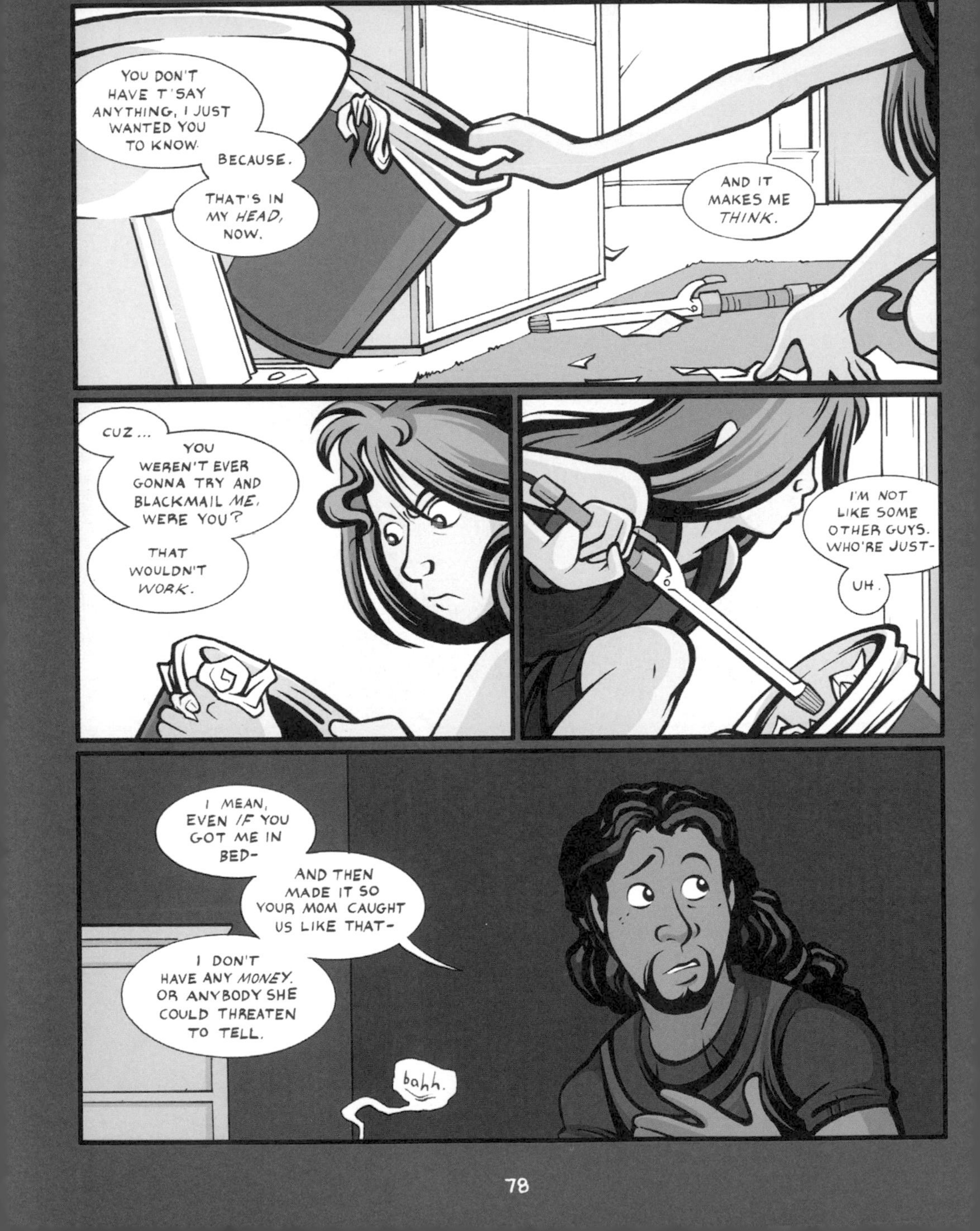
YOU DON'T HAVE T'SAY ANYTHING, I JUST WANTED YOU TO KNOW.
BECAUSE.
THAT'S IN MY HEAD, NOW.
AND IT MAKES ME THINK.
CUZ...
YOU WEREN'T EVER GONNA TRY AND BLACKMAIL ME, WERE YOU?
THAT WOULDN'T WORK.
I'M NOT LIKE SOME OTHER GUYS. WHO'RE JUST-
UH.
I MEAN, EVEN IF YOU GOT ME IN BED-
AND THEN MADE IT SO YOUR MOM CAUGHT US LIKE THAT-
I DON'T HAVE ANY MONEY. OR ANYBODY SHE COULD THREATEN TO TELL.
bahh.

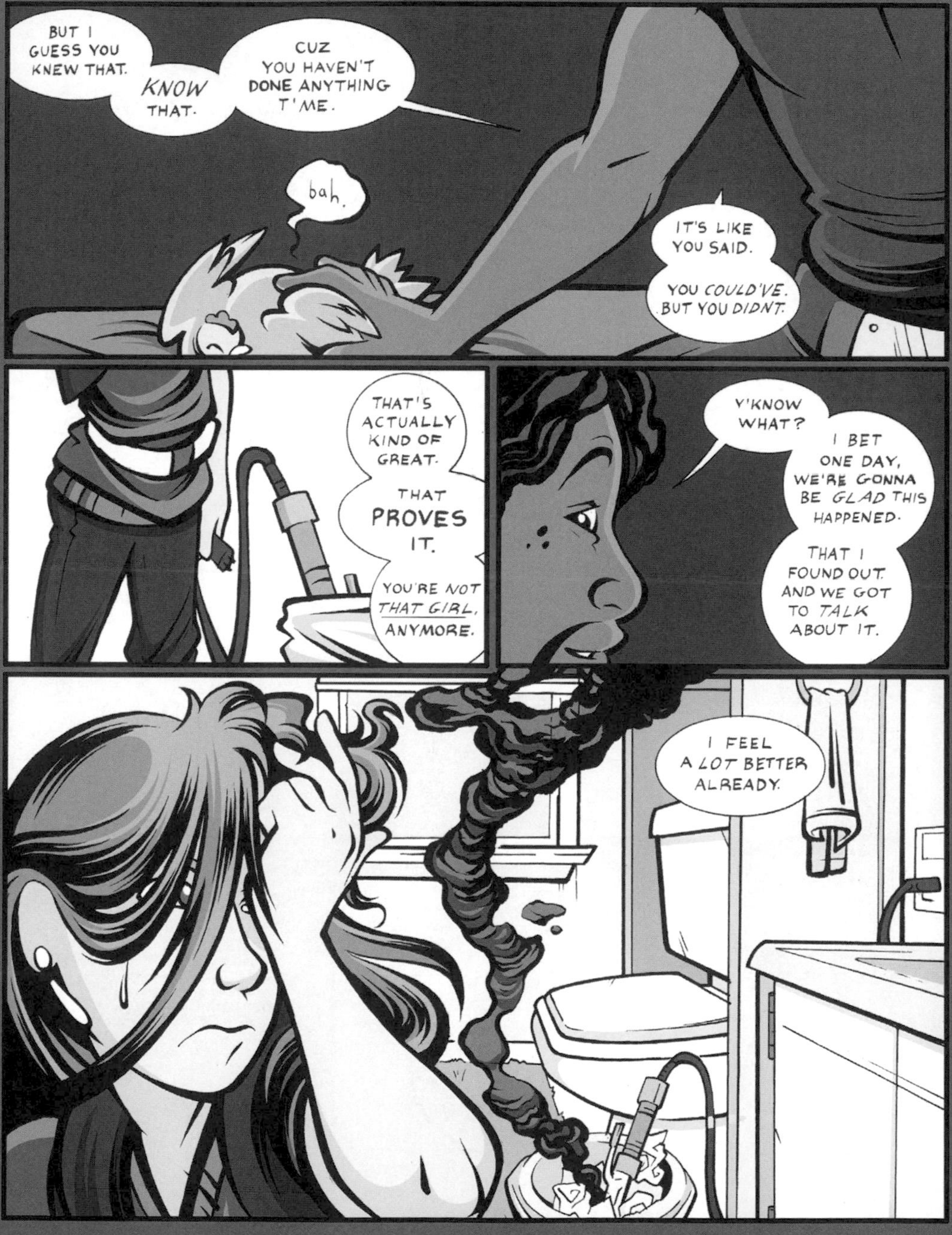
BUT I GUESS YOU KNEW THAT.
KNOW THAT.
CUZ YOU HAVEN'T DONE ANYTHING T'ME.
bah.
IT'S LIKE YOU SAID.
YOU COULD'VE. BUT YOU DIDNT.
THAT'S ACTUALLY KIND OF GREAT.
THAT PROVES IT.
YOU'RE NOT THAT GIRL, ANYMORE.
Y'KNOW WHAT?
I BET ONE DAY, WE'RE GONNA BE GLAD THIS HAPPENED.
THAT I FOUND OUT. AND WE GOT TO TALK ABOUT IT.
I FEEL A LOT BETTER ALREADY.

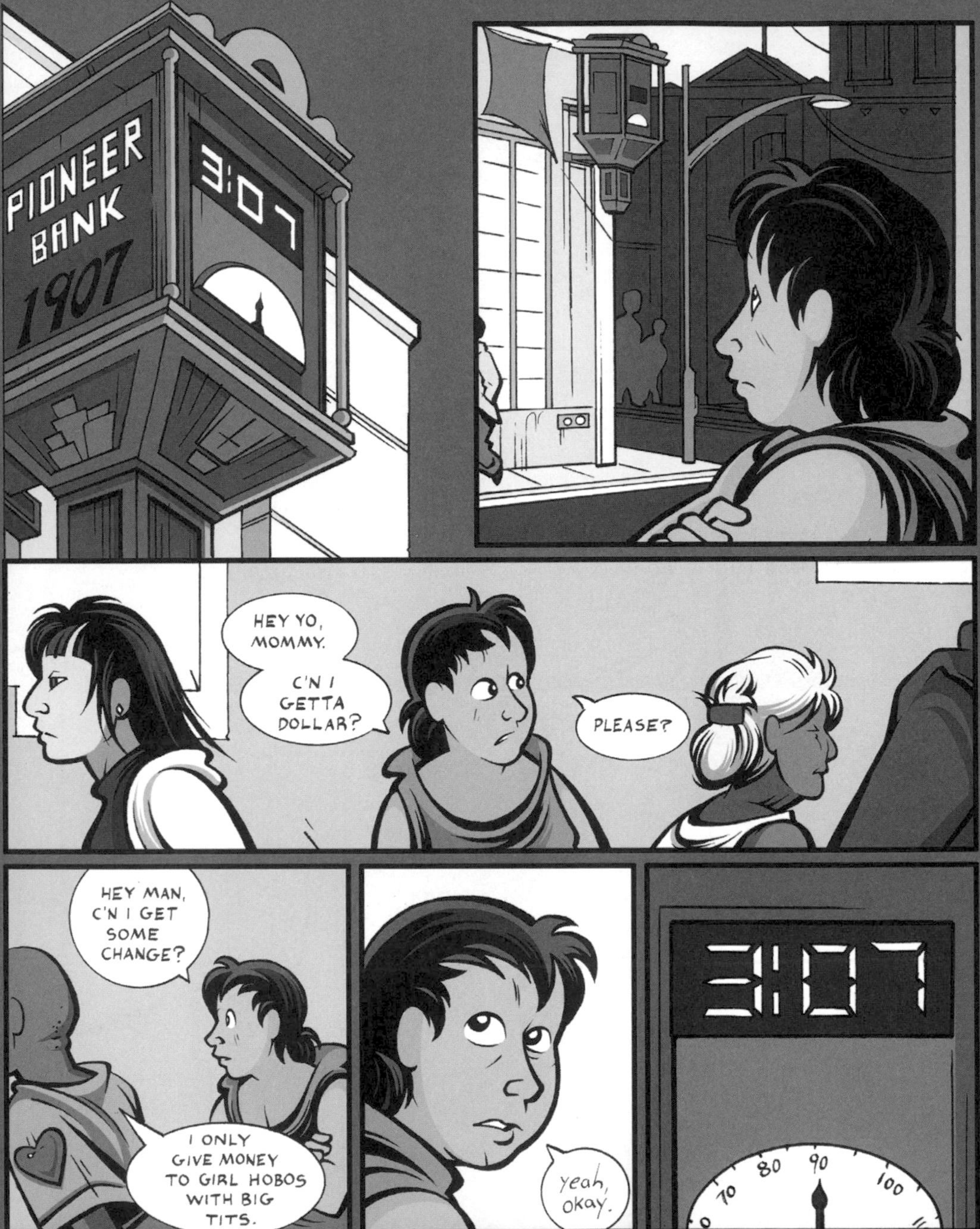
PIONEER BANK 1907
3:07
HEY YO, MOMMY.
C'N I GETTA DOLLAR?
PLEASE?
HEY MAN, C'N I GET SOME CHANGE?
I ONLY GIVE MONEY TO GIRL HOBOS WITH BIG TITS.
yeah, okay.
3:07
70 80 90 100

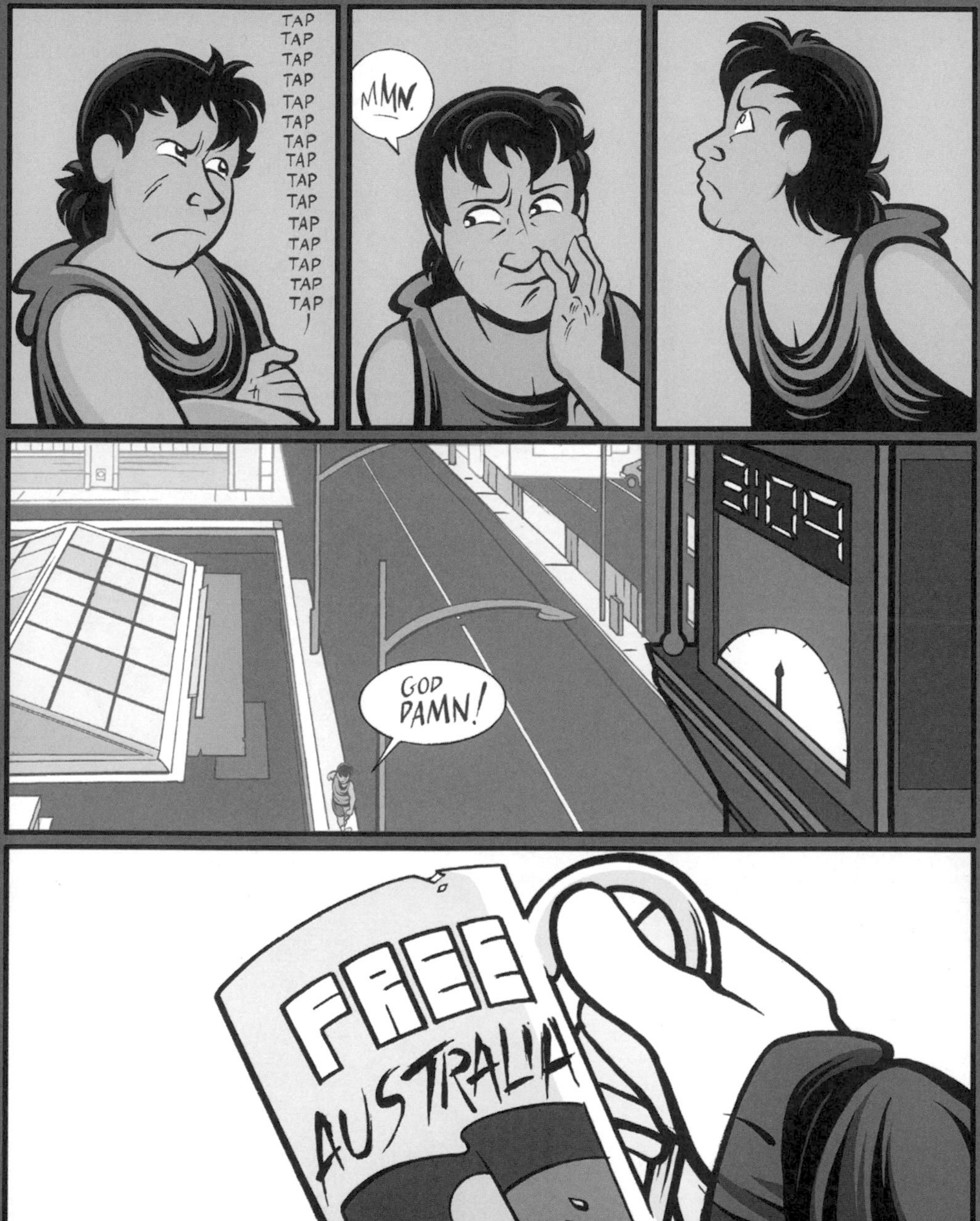
TAP TAP TAP TAP TAP TAP TAP TAP TAP TAP TAP TAP TAP TAP TAP
MMN.
3:04
GOD DAMN!
FREE AUSTRALIA

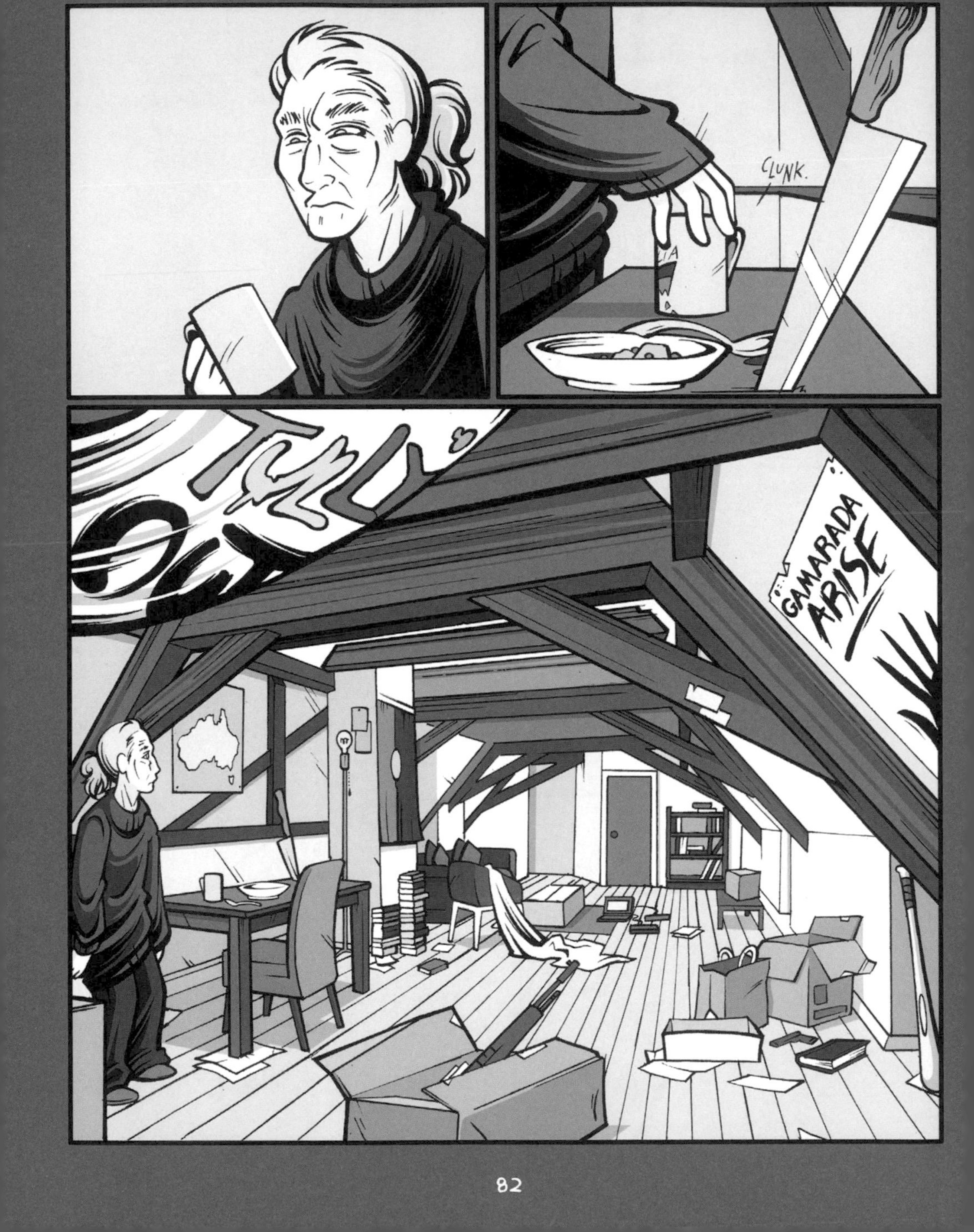
CLUNK.
GAMARADA ARISE

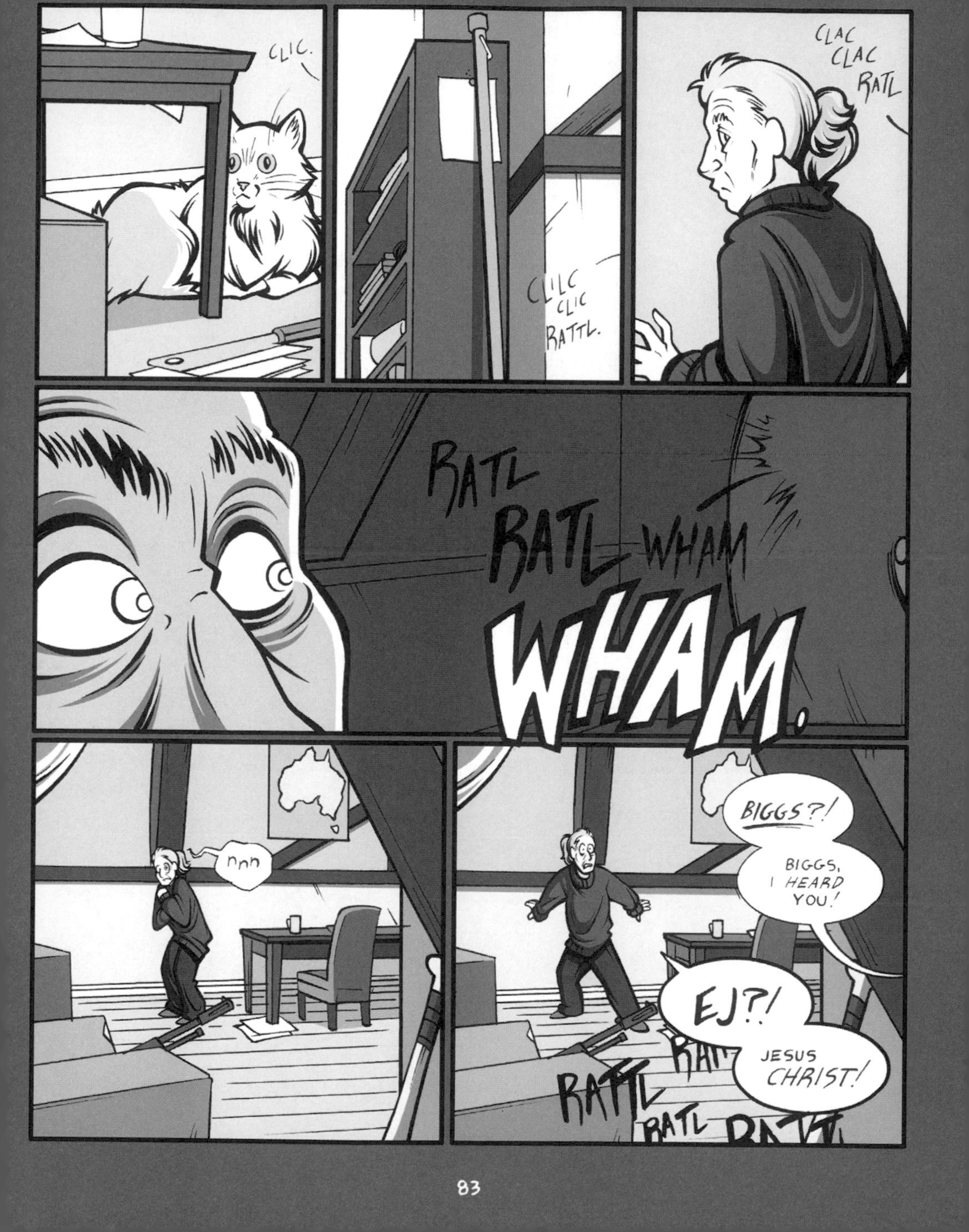
CLIC.
CLILC
CLIC
RATTL.
CLAC
CLAC
RATL
RATL
RATL WHAM
WHAM.
nnn
BIGGS?!
BIGGS, I HEARD YOU!
EJ?!
JESUS CHRIST!
RATTL
RATL

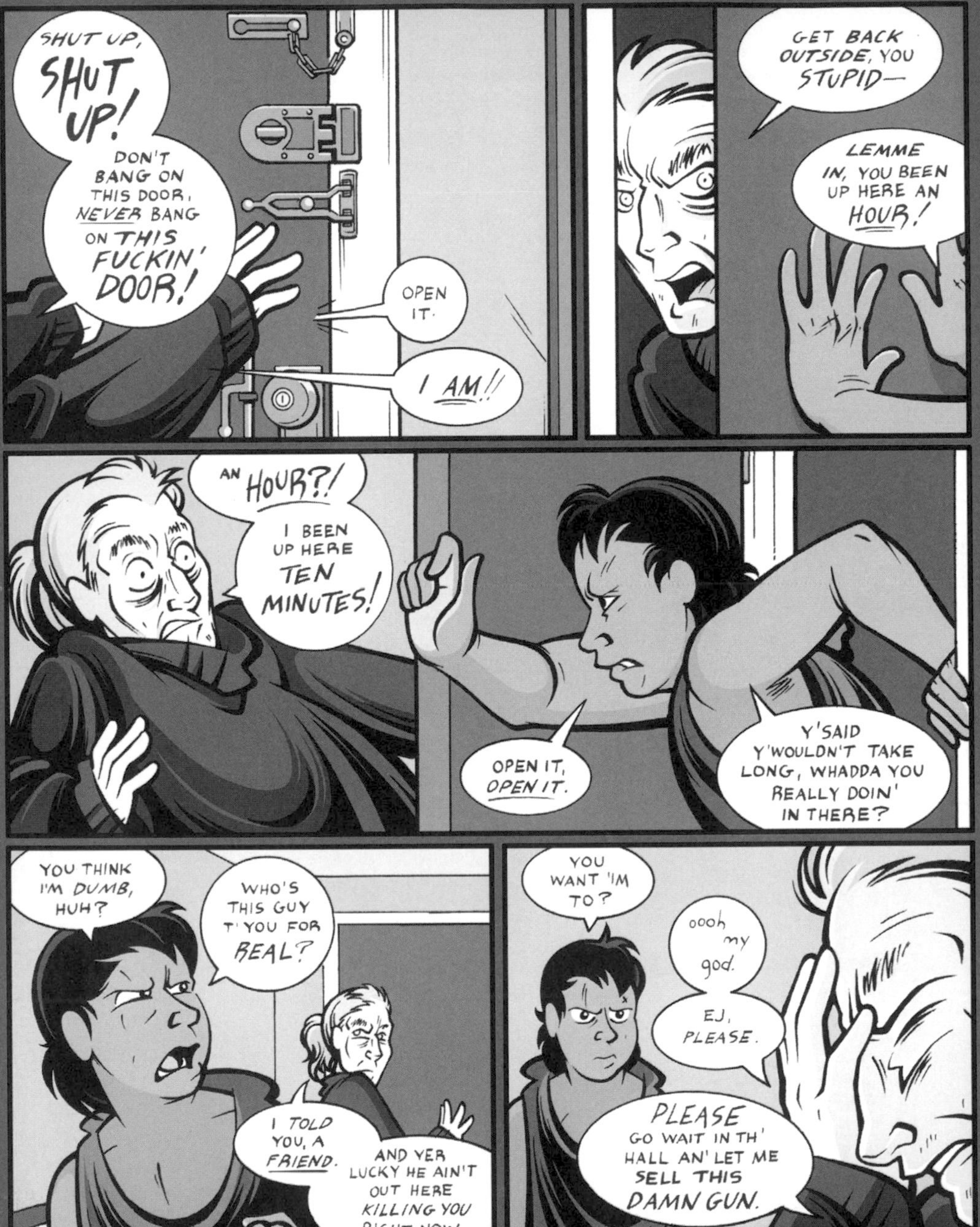
SHUT UP, SHUT UP!
DON'T BANG ON THIS DOOR, NEVER BANG ON THIS FUCKIN' DOOR!
OPEN IT.
I AM!!
GET BACK OUTSIDE, YOU STUPID—
LEMME IN, YOU BEEN UP HERE AN HOUR!
AN HOUR?!
I BEEN UP HERE TEN MINUTES!
OPEN IT, OPEN IT.
Y'SAID Y'WOULDN'T TAKE LONG, WHADDA YOU REALLY DOIN' IN THERE?
YOU THINK I'M DUMB, HUH?
WHO'S THIS GUY T' YOU FOR REAL?
I TOLD YOU, A FRIEND.
AND YER LUCKY HE AIN'T OUT HERE KILLING YOU RIGHT NOW.
YOU WANT 'IM TO?
oooh my god.
EJ, PLEASE.
PLEASE GO WAIT IN TH' HALL AN' LET ME SELL THIS DAMN GUN.

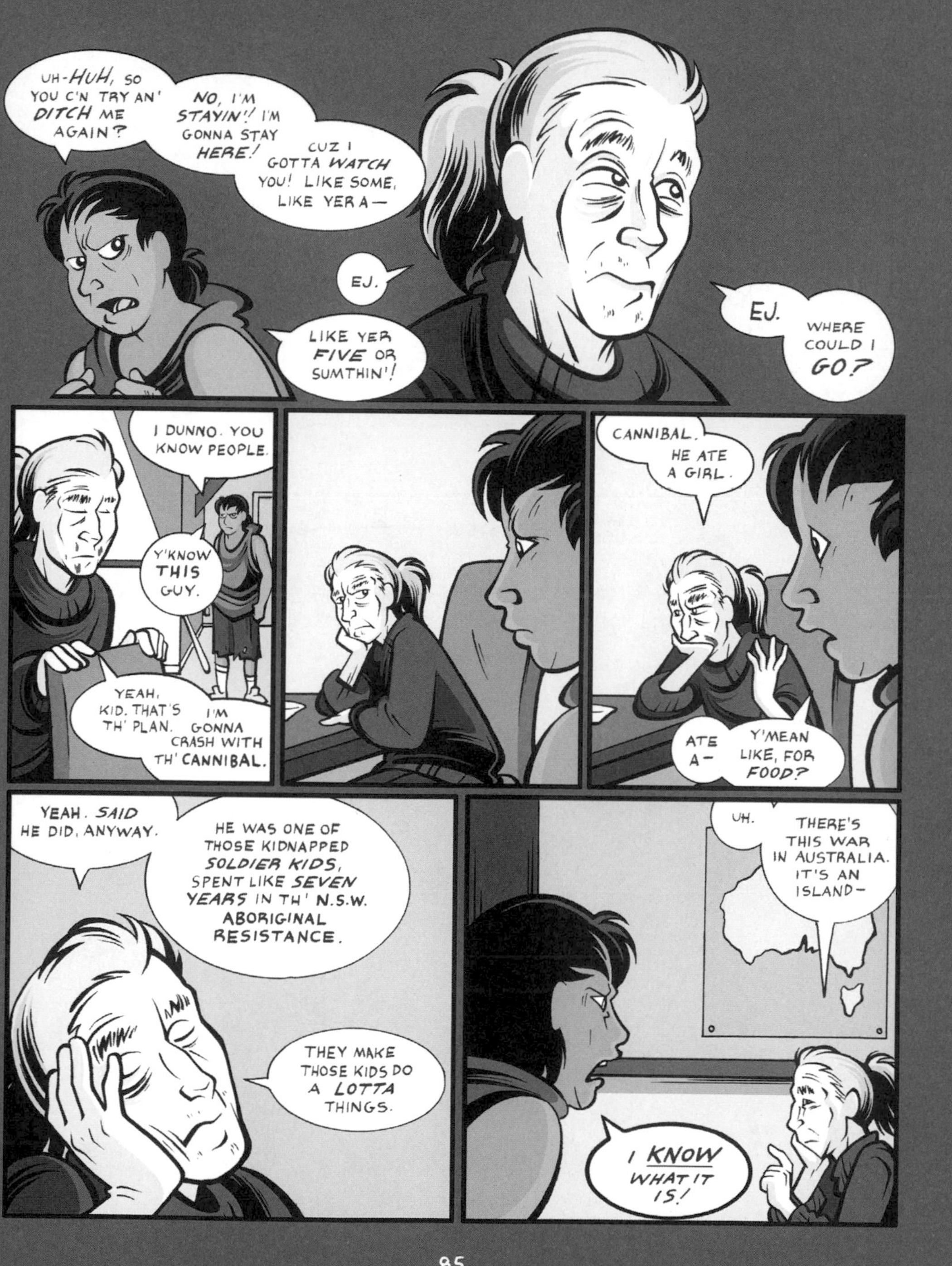
UH-HUH, SO YOU C'N TRY AN' DITCH ME AGAIN?
NO, I'M STAYIN'! I'M GONNA STAY HERE!
CUZ I GOTTA WATCH YOU! LIKE SOME, LIKE YER A—
EJ.
LIKE YER FIVE OR SUMTHIN'!
EJ.
WHERE COULD I GO?
I DUNNO. YOU KNOW PEOPLE.
Y'KNOW THIS GUY.
YEAH, KID. THAT'S TH' PLAN.
I'M GONNA CRASH WITH TH' CANNIBAL.
CANNIBAL.
HE ATE A GIRL.
ATE A—
Y'MEAN LIKE, FOR FOOD?
YEAH. SAID HE DID, ANYWAY.
HE WAS ONE OF THOSE KIDNAPPED SOLDIER KIDS, SPENT LIKE SEVEN YEARS IN TH' N.S.W. ABORIGINAL RESISTANCE.
THEY MAKE THOSE KIDS DO A LOTTA THINGS.
UH.
THERE'S THIS WAR IN AUSTRALIA. IT'S AN ISLAND—
I KNOW WHAT IT IS!

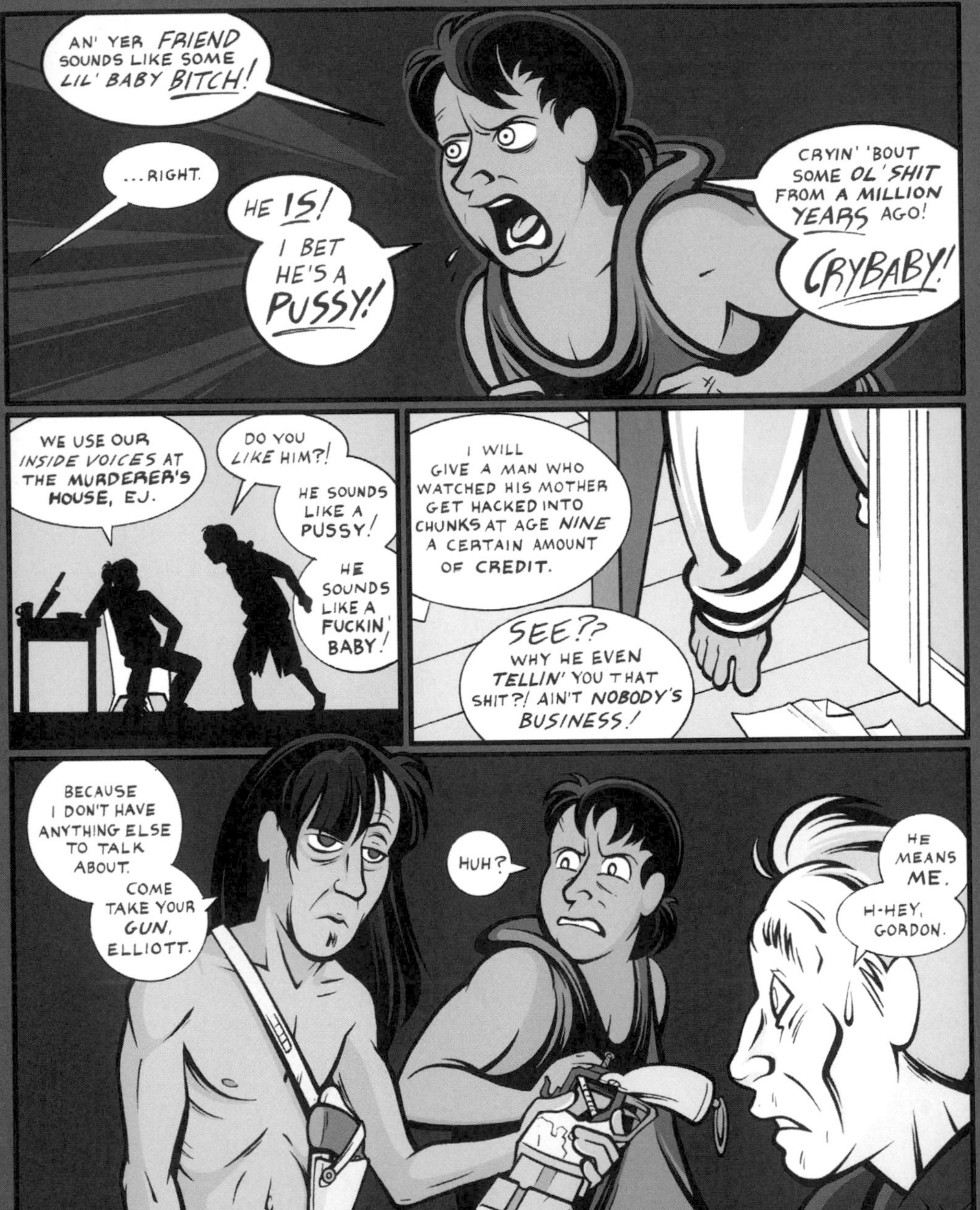
AN' YER FRIEND SOUNDS LIKE SOME LIL' BABY BITCH!
...RIGHT.
HE IS!
I BET HE'S A PUSSY!
CRYIN' 'BOUT SOME OL' SHIT FROM A MILLION YEARS AGO!
CRYBABY!
WE USE OUR INSIDE VOICES AT THE MURDERER'S HOUSE, EJ.
DO YOU LIKE HIM?!
HE SOUNDS LIKE A PUSSY!
HE SOUNDS LIKE A FUCKIN' BABY!
I WILL GIVE A MAN WHO WATCHED HIS MOTHER GET HACKED INTO CHUNKS AT AGE NINE A CERTAIN AMOUNT OF CREDIT.
SEE??
WHY HE EVEN TELLIN' YOU THAT SHIT?! AIN'T NOBODY'S BUSINESS!
BECAUSE I DON'T HAVE ANYTHING ELSE TO TALK ABOUT.
COME TAKE YOUR GUN, ELLIOTT.
HUH?
HE MEANS ME.
H-HEY, GORDON.

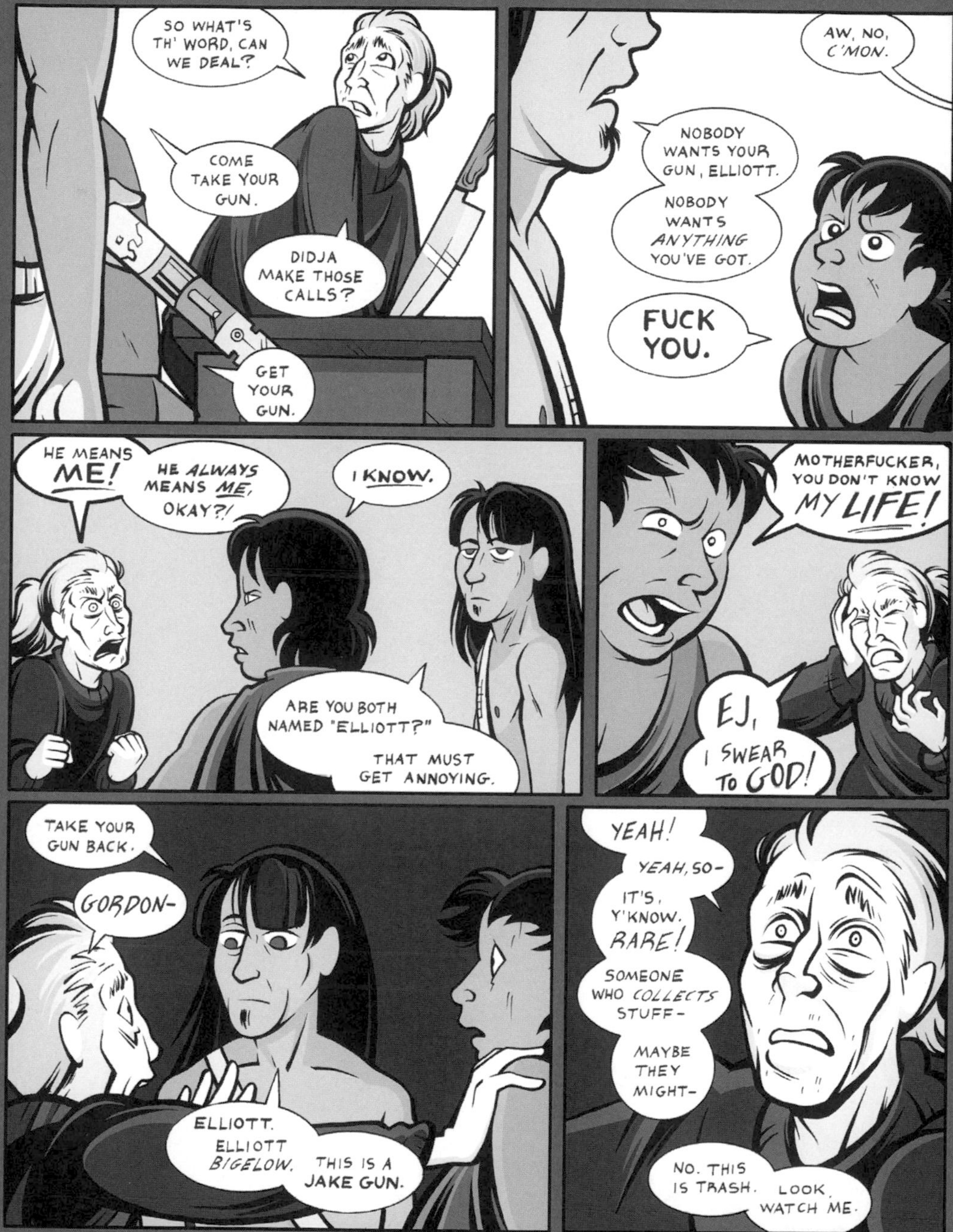
SO WHAT'S TH' WORD, CAN WE DEAL?
COME TAKE YOUR GUN.
DIDJA MAKE THOSE CALLS?
GET YOUR GUN.
AW, NO, C'MON.
NOBODY WANTS YOUR GUN, ELLIOTT.
NOBODY WANTS ANYTHING YOU'VE GOT.
FUCK YOU.
HE MEANS ME!
HE ALWAYS MEANS ME, OKAY?!
I KNOW.
ARE YOU BOTH NAMED "ELLIOTT?"
THAT MUST GET ANNOYING.
MOTHERFUCKER, YOU DON'T KNOW MY LIFE!
EJ, I SWEAR TO GOD!
TAKE YOUR GUN BACK.
GORDON-
ELLIOTT. ELLIOTT BIGELOW.
THIS IS A JAKE GUN.
YEAH!
YEAH, SO-
IT'S, Y'KNOW. RARE!
SOMEONE WHO COLLECTS STUFF-
MAYBE THEY MIGHT-
NO. THIS IS TRASH.
LOOK. WATCH ME.

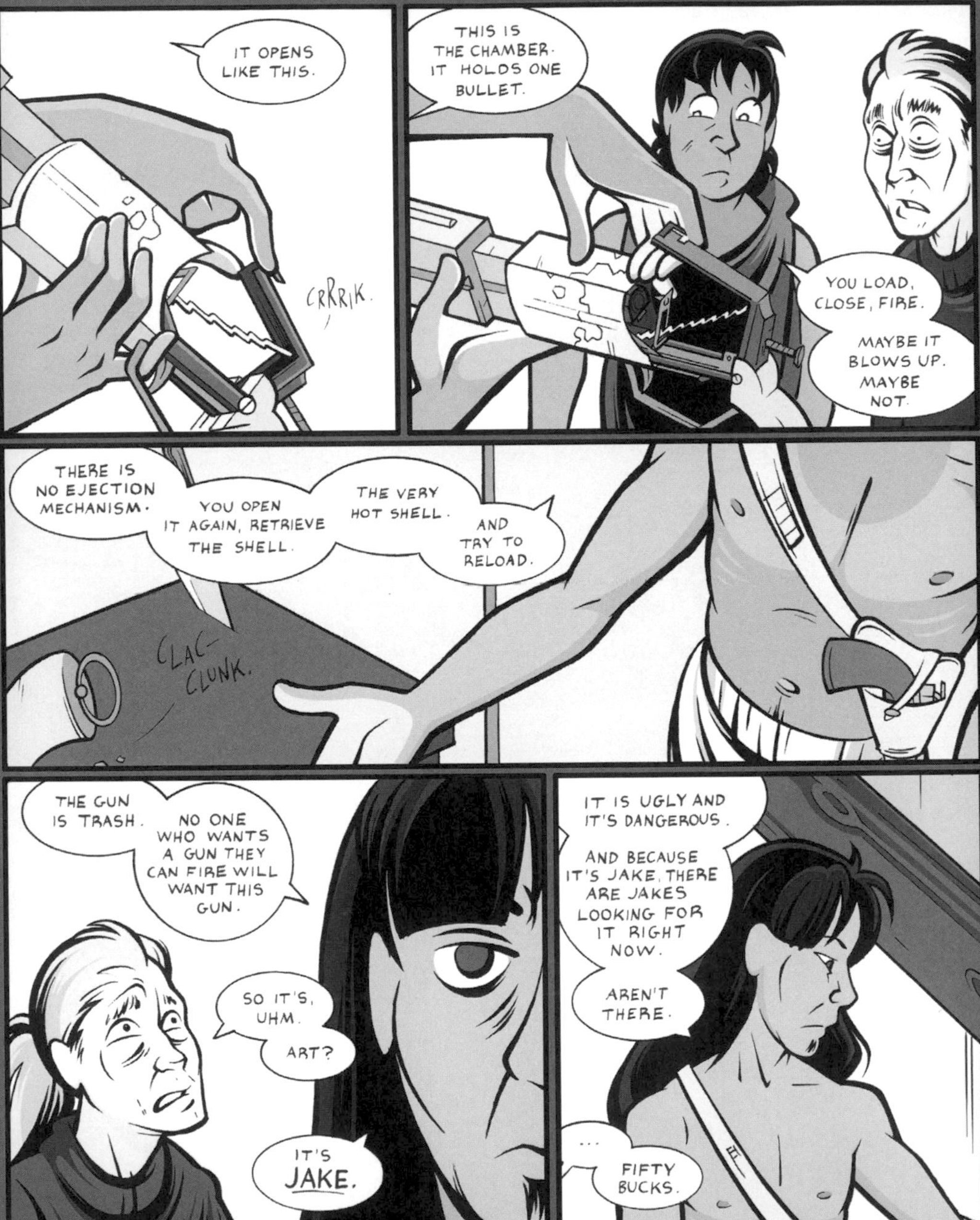
IT OPENS LIKE THIS.
CRRRIK.
THIS IS THE CHAMBER. IT HOLDS ONE BULLET.
YOU LOAD, CLOSE, FIRE.
MAYBE IT BLOWS UP. MAYBE NOT.
THERE IS NO EJECTION MECHANISM.
YOU OPEN IT AGAIN, RETRIEVE THE SHELL.
THE VERY HOT SHELL.
AND TRY TO RELOAD.
CLAC-CLUNK.
THE GUN IS TRASH.
NO ONE WHO WANTS A GUN THEY CAN FIRE WILL WANT THIS GUN.
SO IT'S, UHM.
ART?
IT'S JAKE.
IT IS UGLY AND IT'S DANGEROUS.
AND BECAUSE IT'S JAKE, THERE ARE JAKES LOOKING FOR IT RIGHT NOW.
AREN'T THERE.
...
FIFTY BUCKS.

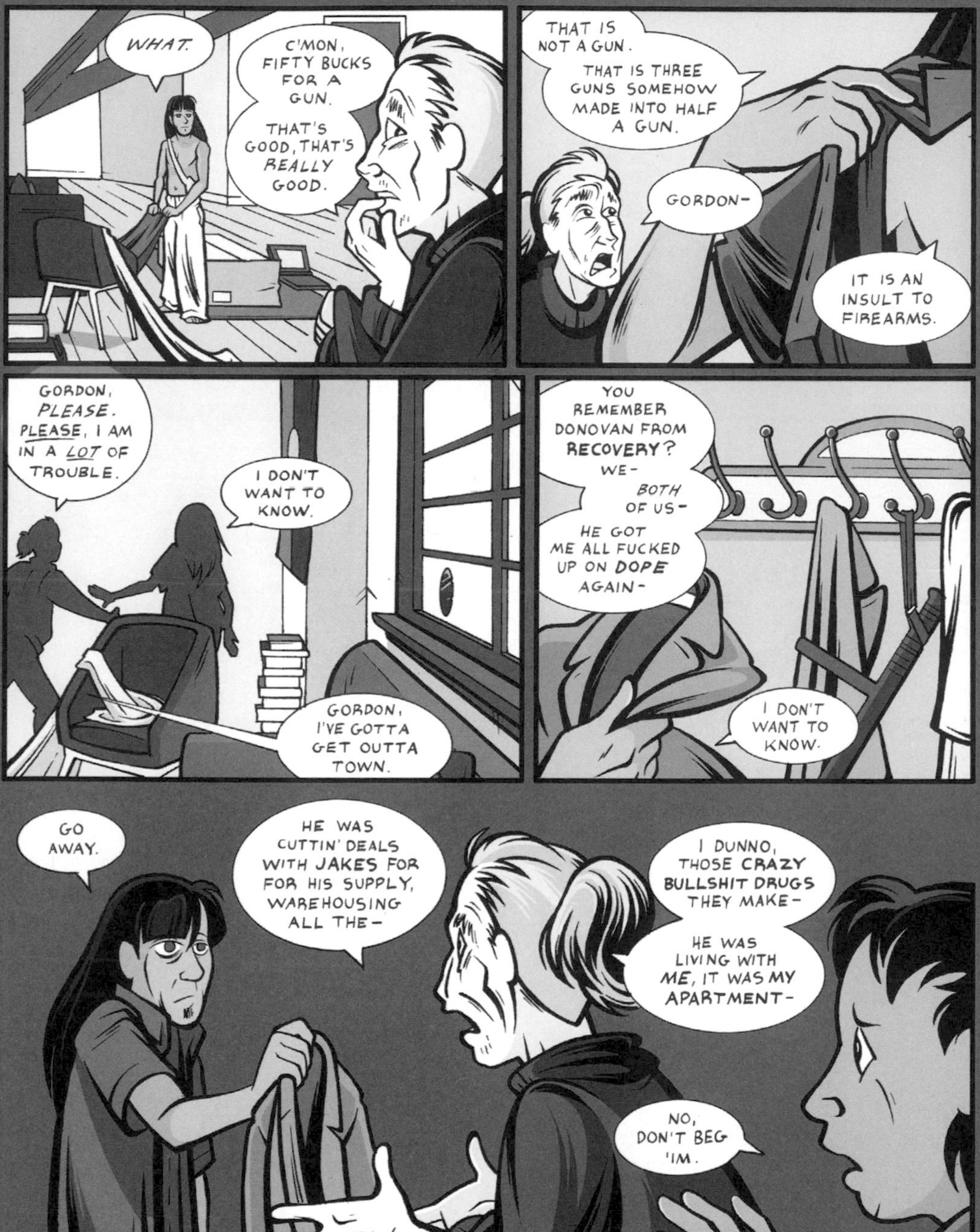
WHAT.
C'MON, FIFTY BUCKS FOR A GUN.
THAT'S GOOD, THAT'S REALLY GOOD.
THAT IS NOT A GUN.
THAT IS THREE GUNS SOMEHOW MADE INTO HALF A GUN.
GORDON-
IT IS AN INSULT TO FIREARMS.
GORDON, PLEASE. PLEASE, I AM IN A LOT OF TROUBLE.
I DON'T WANT TO KNOW.
GORDON, I'VE GOTTA GET OUTTA TOWN.
YOU REMEMBER DONOVAN FROM RECOVERY? WE-
BOTH OF US-
HE GOT ME ALL FUCKED UP ON DOPE AGAIN-
I DON'T WANT TO KNOW.
GO AWAY.
HE WAS CUTTIN' DEALS WITH JAKES FOR FOR HIS SUPPLY, WAREHOUSING ALL THE-
I DUNNO, THOSE CRAZY BULLSHIT DRUGS THEY MAKE-
HE WAS LIVING WITH ME, IT WAS MY APARTMENT-
NO, DON'T BEG 'IM.

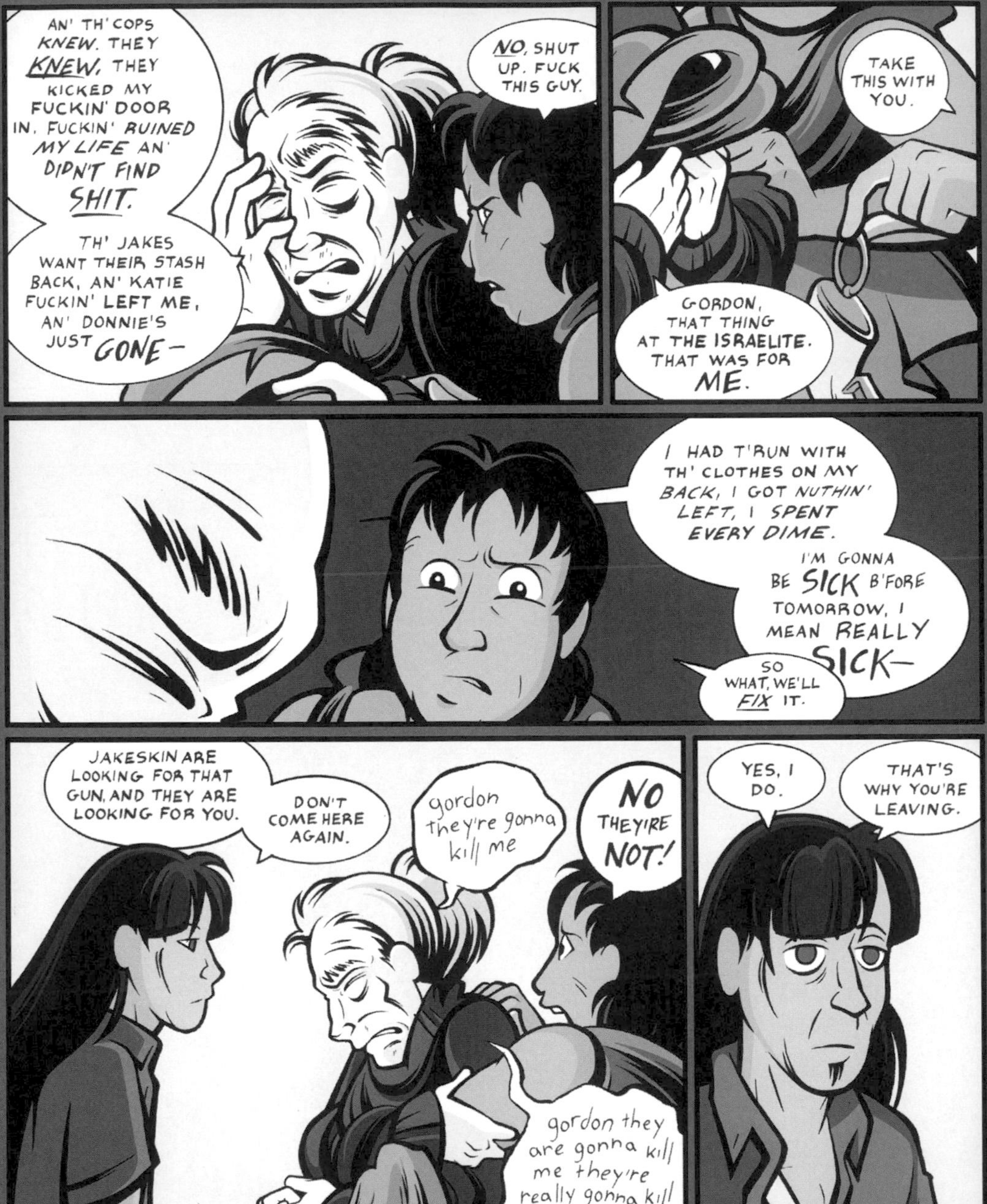

AN' TH' COPS KNEW. THEY KNEW, THEY KICKED MY FUCKIN' DOOR IN. FUCKIN' RUINED MY LIFE AN' DIDN'T FIND SHIT.
TH' JAKES WANT THEIR STASH BACK, AN' KATIE FUCKIN' LEFT ME, AN' DONNIE'S JUST GONE—
NO, SHUT UP. FUCK THIS GUY.
TAKE THIS WITH YOU.
GORDON, THAT THING AT THE ISRAELITE. THAT WAS FOR ME.
I HAD T'RUN WITH TH' CLOTHES ON MY BACK, I GOT NUTHIN' LEFT, I SPENT EVERY DIME.
I'M GONNA BE SICK B'FORE TOMORROW, I MEAN REALLY SICK—
SO WHAT, WE'LL FIX IT.
JAKESKIN ARE LOOKING FOR THAT GUN, AND THEY ARE LOOKING FOR YOU.
DON'T COME HERE AGAIN.
gordon they're gonna kill me
NO THEY'RE NOT!
gordon they are gonna kill me they're really gonna kill me please you don't know.
YES, I DO.
THAT'S WHY YOU'RE LEAVING.

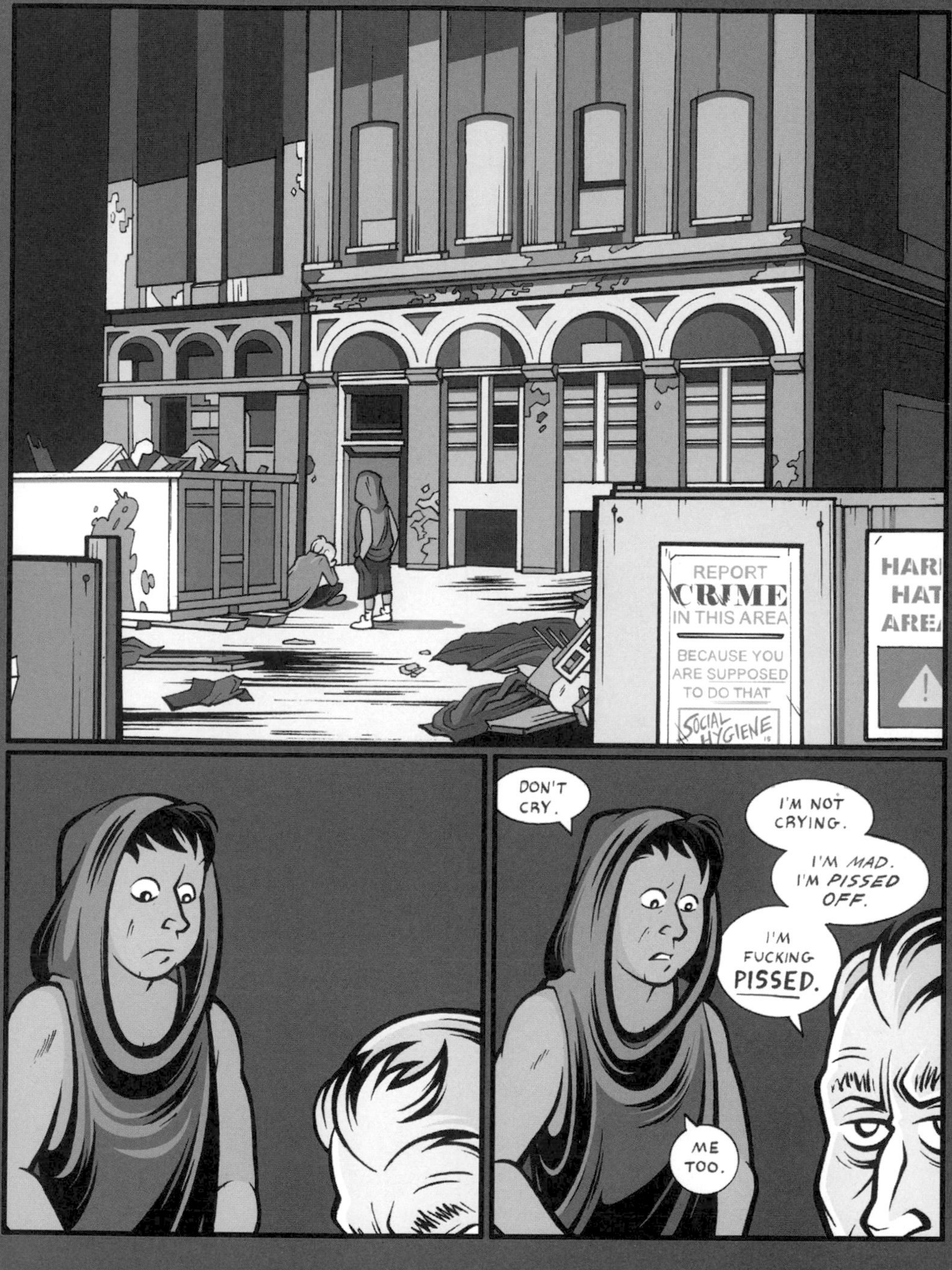
REPORT
CRIME
IN THIS AREA
BECAUSE YOU
ARE SUPPOSED
TO DO THAT
SOCIAL HYGIENE
DON'T CRY.
I'M NOT CRYING.
I'M MAD. I'M PISSED OFF.
I'M FUCKING PISSED.
ME TOO.

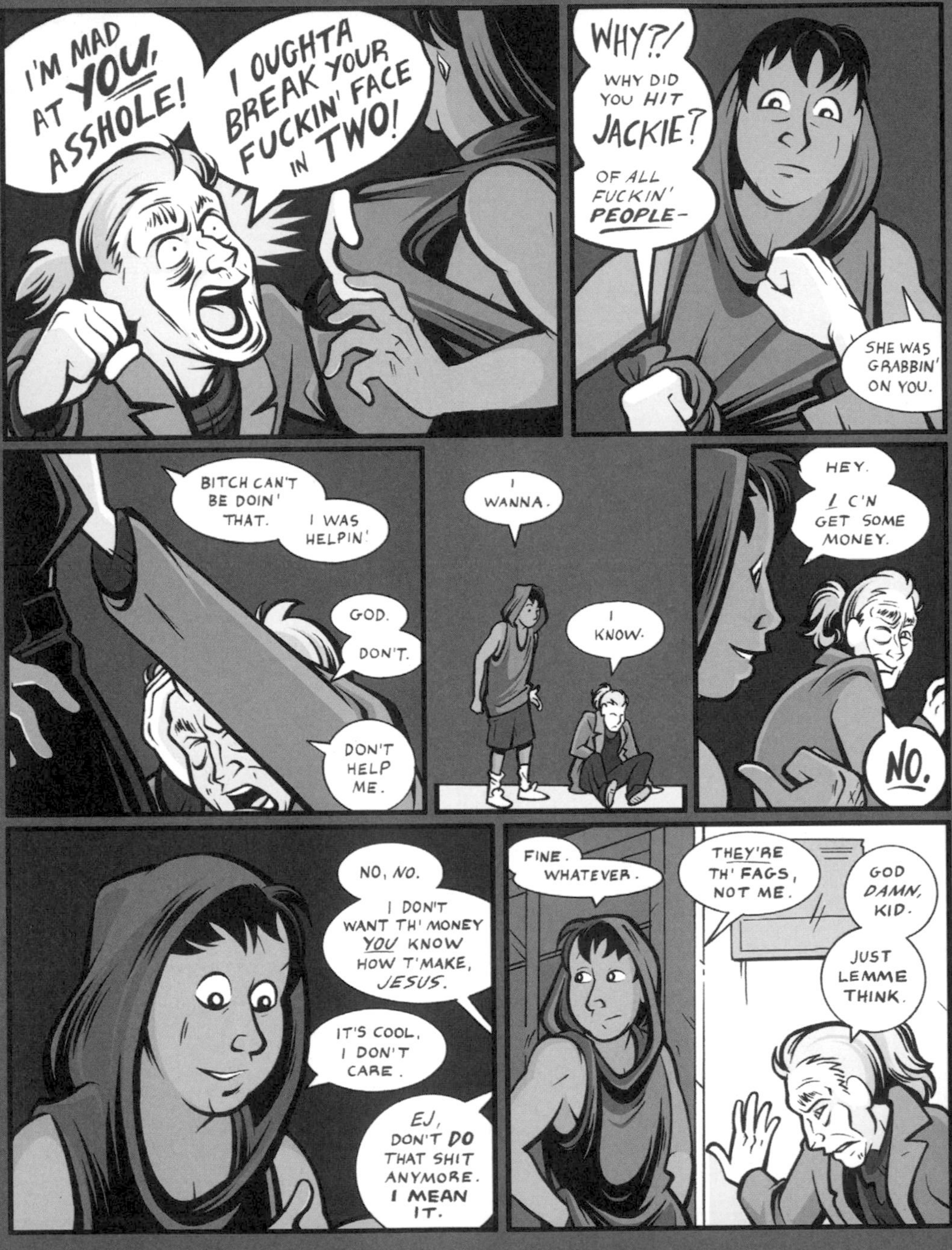
I'M MAD AT YOU, ASSHOLE!
I OUGHTA BREAK YOUR FUCKIN' FACE IN TWO!
WHY?!
WHY DID YOU HIT JACKIE?
OF ALL FUCKIN' PEOPLE-
SHE WAS GRABBIN' ON YOU.
BITCH CAN'T BE DOIN' THAT.
I WAS HELPIN'.
GOD.
DON'T.
DON'T HELP ME.
I WANNA.
I KNOW.
HEY.
I C'N GET SOME MONEY.
NO.
NO, NO.
I DON'T WANT TH' MONEY YOU KNOW HOW T'MAKE, JESUS.
IT'S COOL, I DON'T CARE.
EJ, DON'T DO THAT SHIT ANYMORE. I MEAN IT.
FINE. WHATEVER.
THEY'RE TH' FAGS, NOT ME.
GOD DAMN, KID.
JUST LEMME THINK.

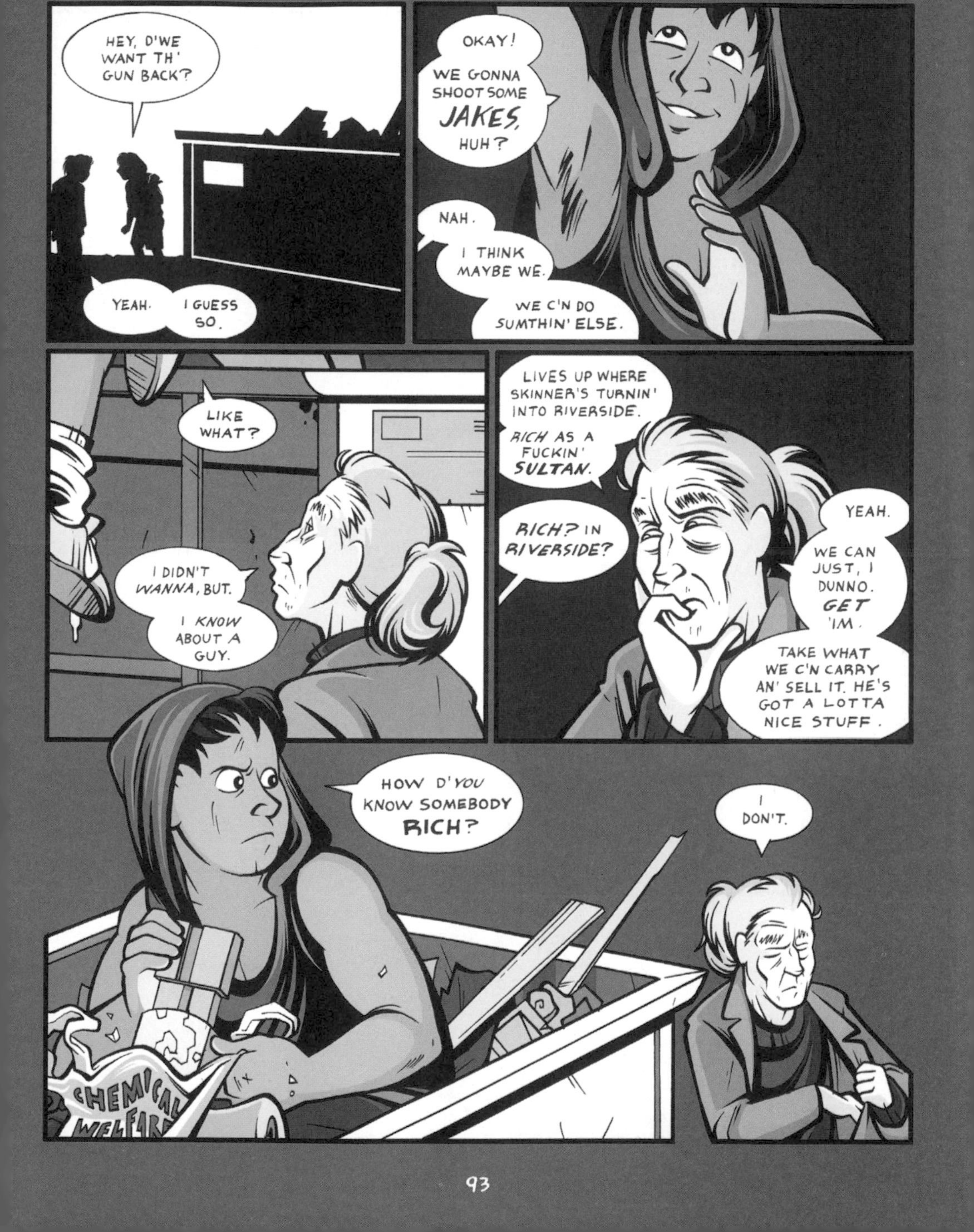
HEY, D'WE WANT TH' GUN BACK?
YEAH.
I GUESS SO.
OKAY!
WE GONNA SHOOT SOME JAKES, HUH?
NAH.
I THINK MAYBE WE.
WE C'N DO SUMTHIN' ELSE.
LIKE WHAT?
I DIDN'T WANNA, BUT.
I KNOW ABOUT A GUY.
LIVES UP WHERE SKINNER'S TURNIN' INTO RIVERSIDE.
RICH AS A FUCKIN' SULTAN.
RICH? IN RIVERSIDE?
YEAH.
WE CAN JUST, I DUNNO. GET 'IM.
TAKE WHAT WE C'N CARRY AN' SELL IT. HE'S GOT A LOTTA NICE STUFF.
HOW D'YOU KNOW SOMEBODY RICH?
I DON'T.
CHEMICAL WELFARE

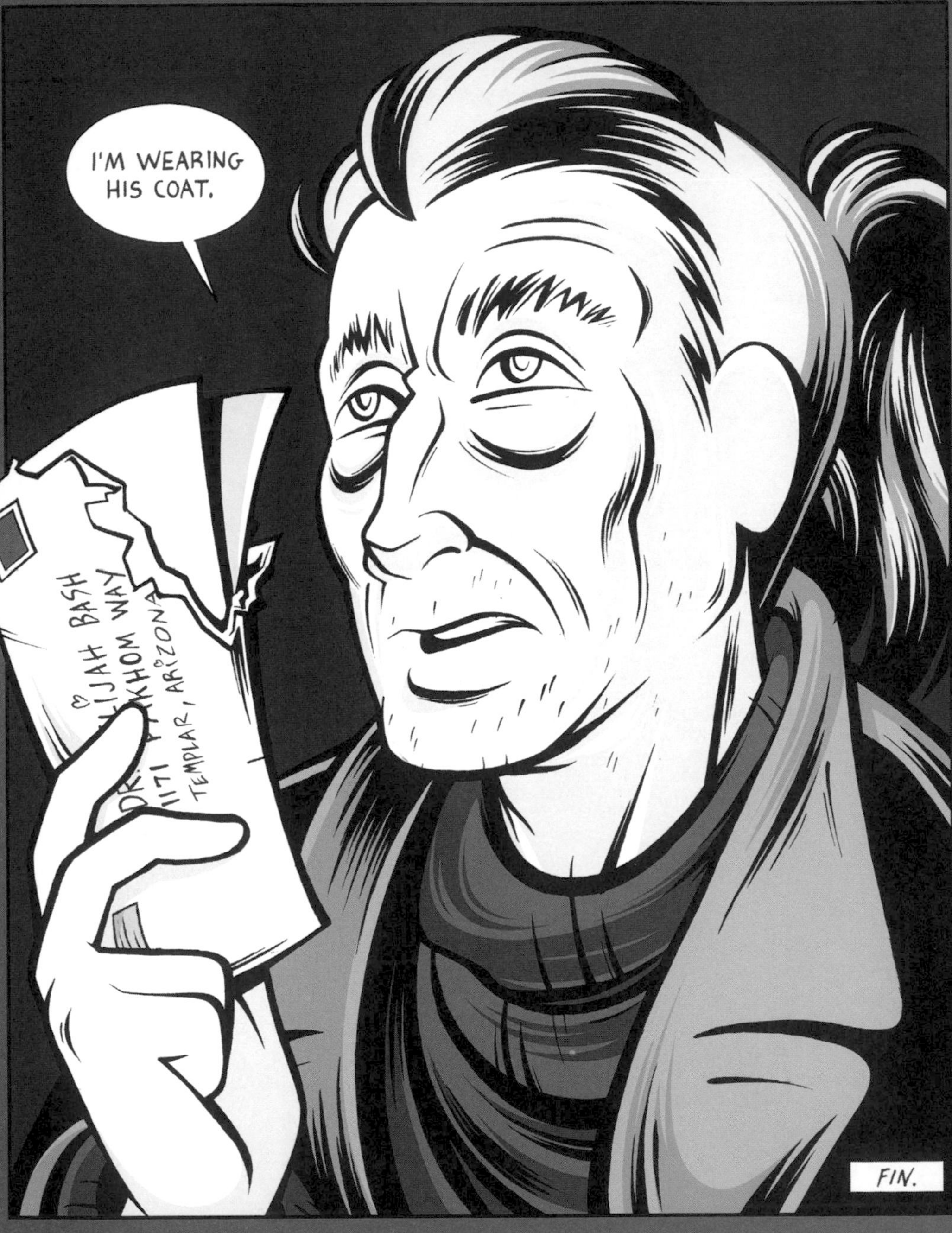
I'M WEARING HIS COAT.
TEMPLAR, ARIZONA
FIN.

TEMPLAR, ARIZONA.

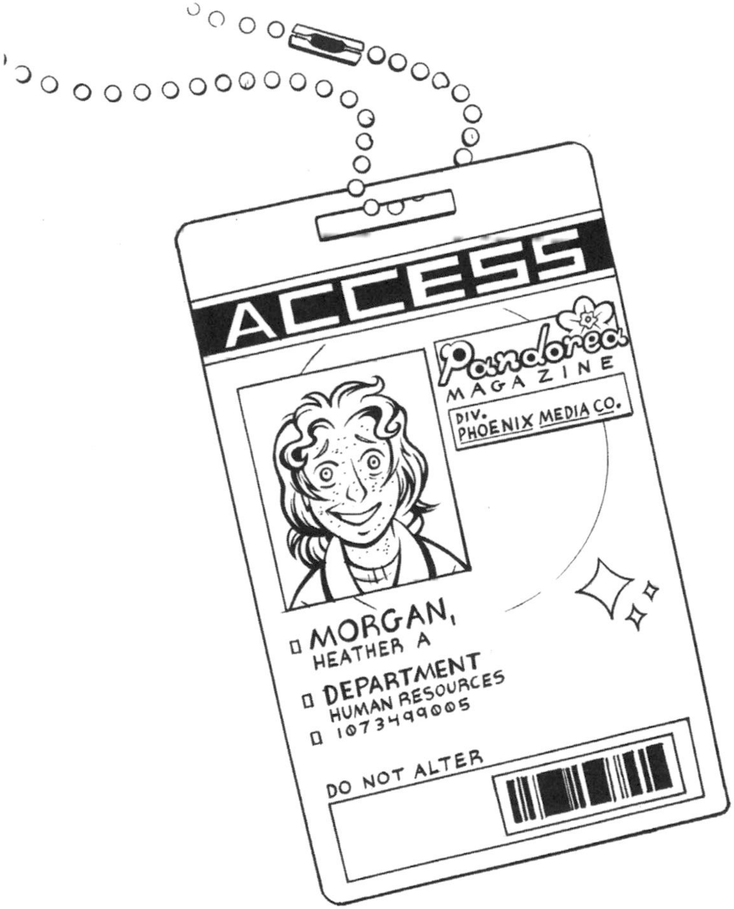
ACCESS
Pandorea
MAGAZINE
DIV.
PHOENIX MEDIA CO.
MORGAN,
HEATHER A
DEPARTMENT
HUMAN RESOURCES
1073499005
DO NOT ALTER

INTERMISSION:
EMPLOYEE APPRECIATION.

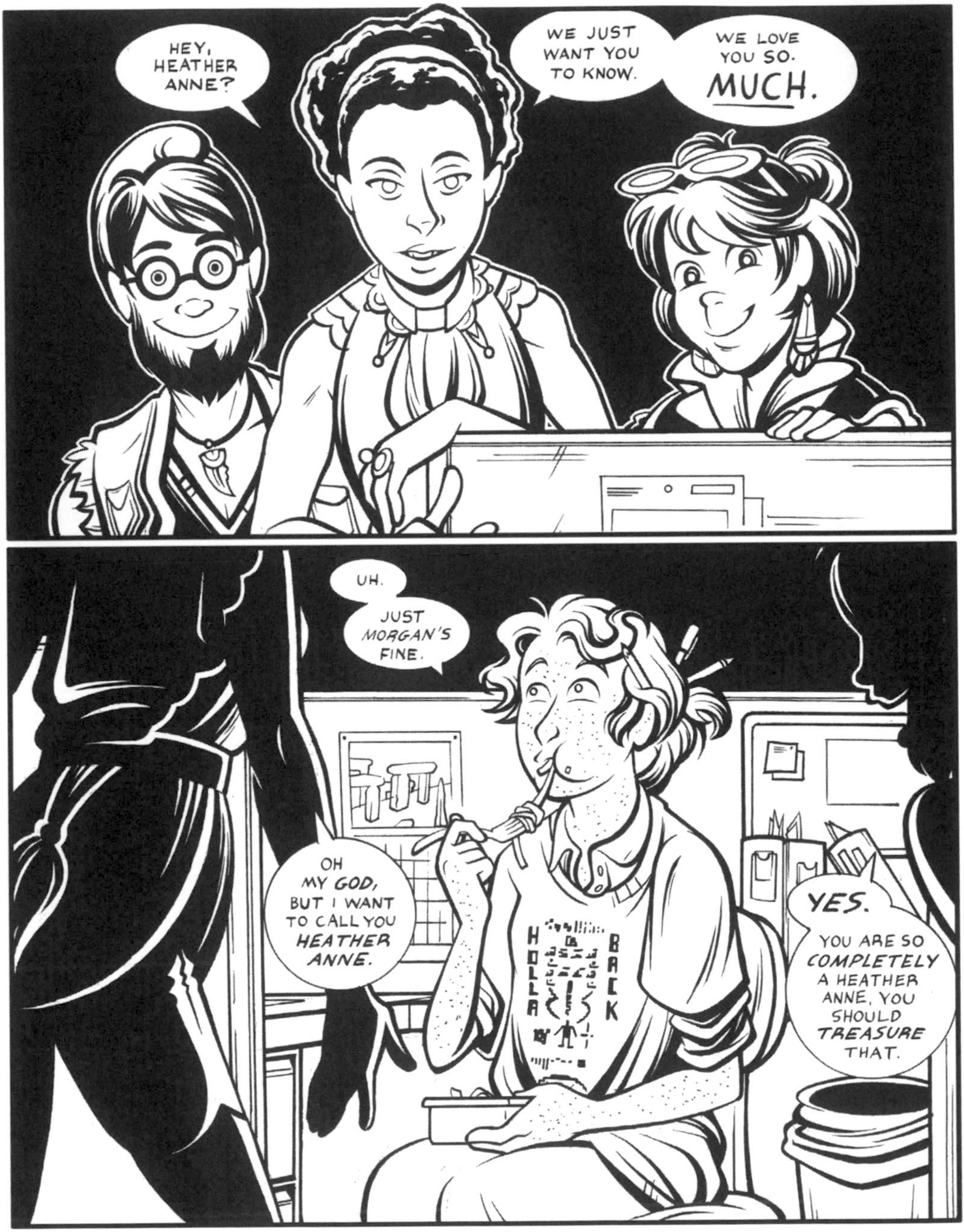
HEY, HEATHER ANNE?
WE JUST WANT YOU TO KNOW.
WE LOVE YOU SO. MUCH.
UH.
JUST MORGAN'S FINE.
OH MY GOD, BUT I WANT TO CALL YOU HEATHER ANNE.
HOLLA BACK
YES.
YOU ARE SO COMPLETELY A HEATHER ANNE, YOU SHOULD TREASURE THAT.

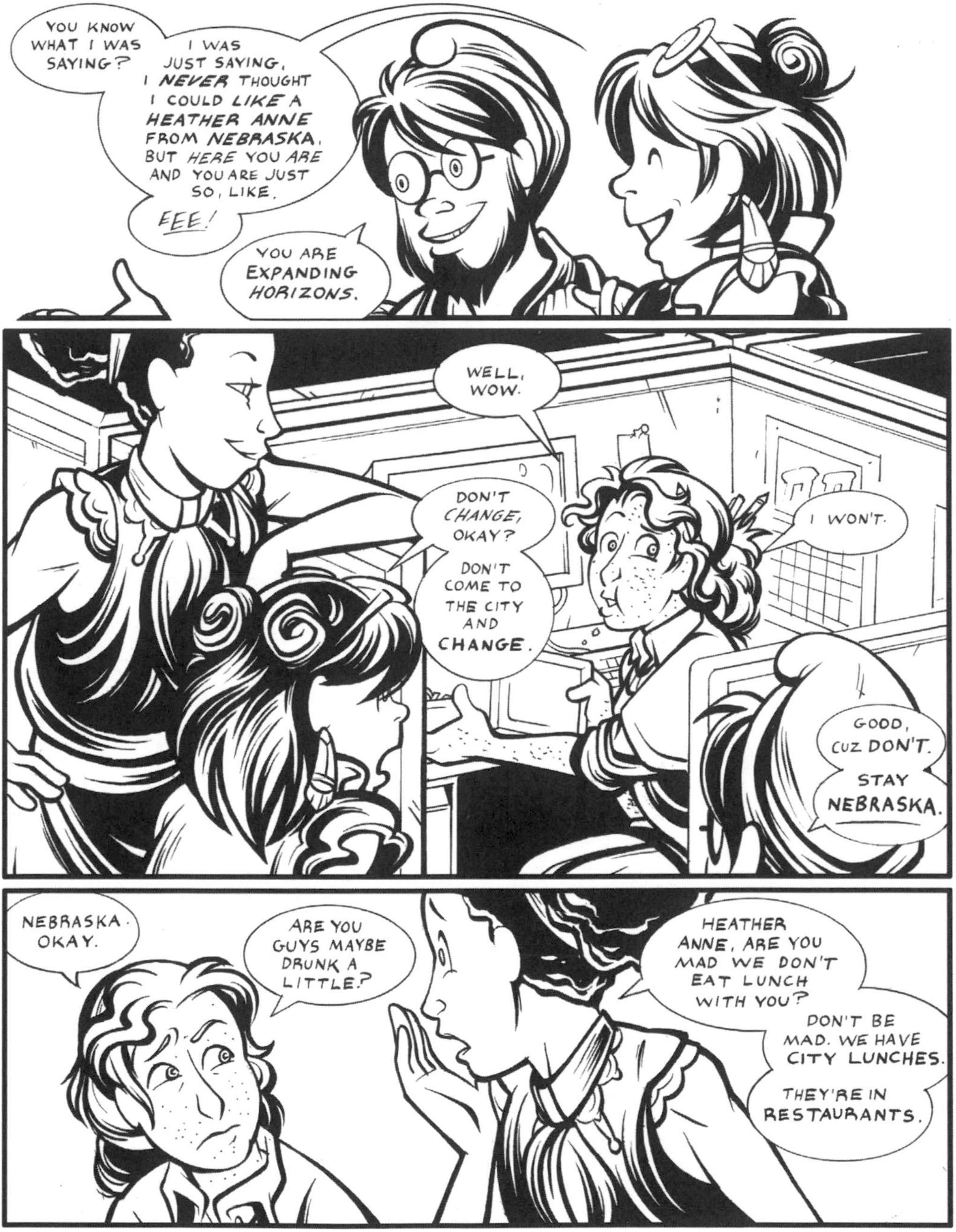
YOU KNOW WHAT I WAS SAYING?
I WAS JUST SAYING, I NEVER THOUGHT I COULD LIKE A HEATHER ANNE FROM NEBRASKA. BUT HERE YOU ARE AND YOU ARE JUST SO, LIKE.
EEE!
YOU ARE EXPANDING HORIZONS.
WELL, WOW.
DON'T CHANGE, OKAY?
DON'T COME TO THE CITY AND CHANGE.
I WON'T.
GOOD, CUZ DON'T.
STAY NEBRASKA.
NEBRASKA. OKAY.
ARE YOU GUYS MAYBE DRUNK A LITTLE?
HEATHER ANNE, ARE YOU MAD WE DON'T EAT LUNCH WITH YOU?
DON'T BE MAD. WE HAVE CITY LUNCHES.
THEY'RE IN RESTAURANTS.

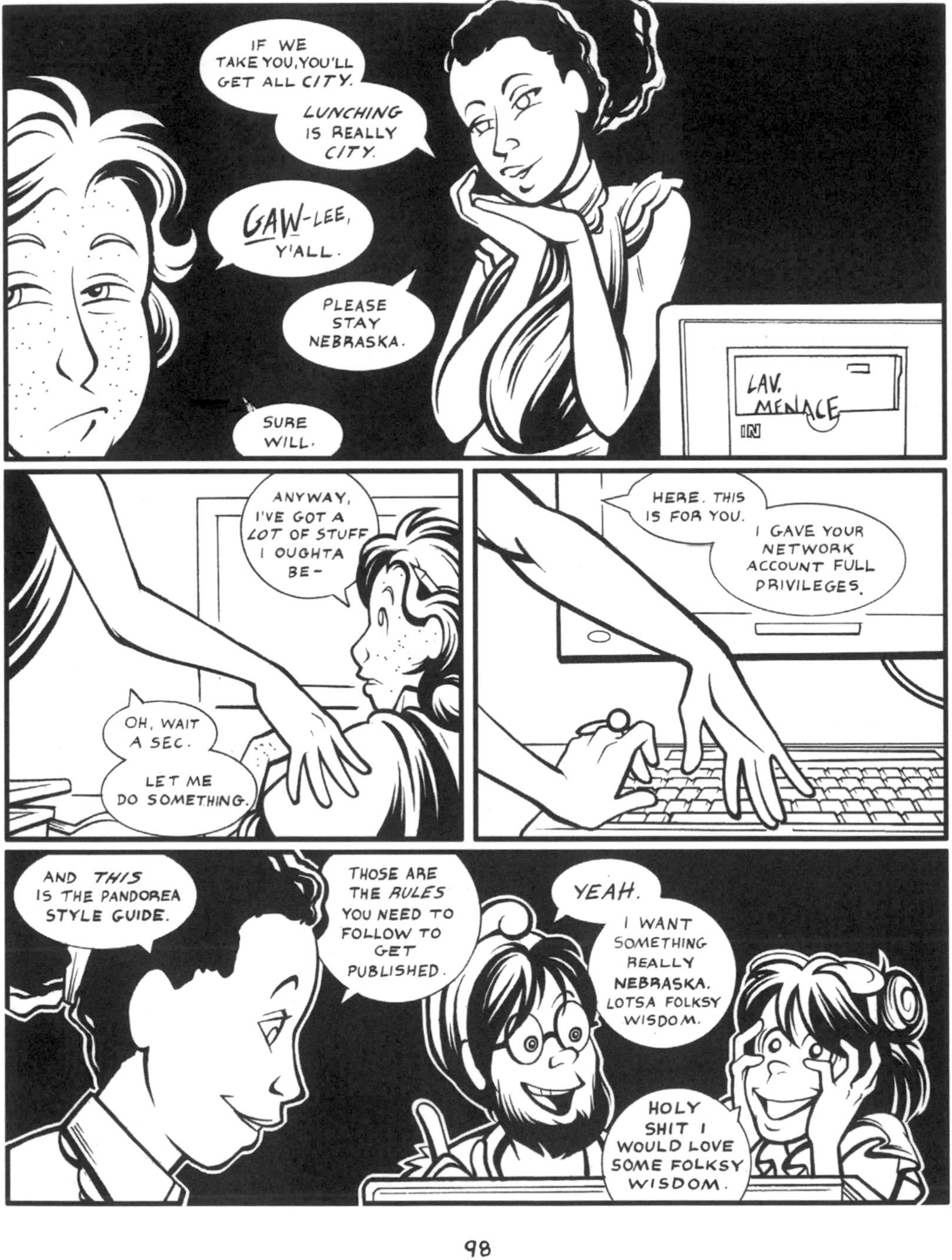
IF WE TAKE YOU, YOU'LL GET ALL CITY.
LUNCHING IS REALLY CITY.
GAW-LEE, Y'ALL.
PLEASE STAY NEBRASKA.
SURE WILL.
LAV. MENACE
IN
ANYWAY, I'VE GOT A LOT OF STUFF I OUGHTA BE-
OH, WAIT A SEC.
LET ME DO SOMETHING.
HERE. THIS IS FOR YOU.
I GAVE YOUR NETWORK ACCOUNT FULL PRIVILEGES.
AND THIS IS THE PANDOREA STYLE GUIDE.
THOSE ARE THE RULES YOU NEED TO FOLLOW TO GET PUBLISHED.
YEAH.
I WANT SOMETHING REALLY NEBRASKA. LOTSA FOLKSY WISDOM.
HOLY SHIT I WOULD LOVE SOME FOLKSY WISDOM.

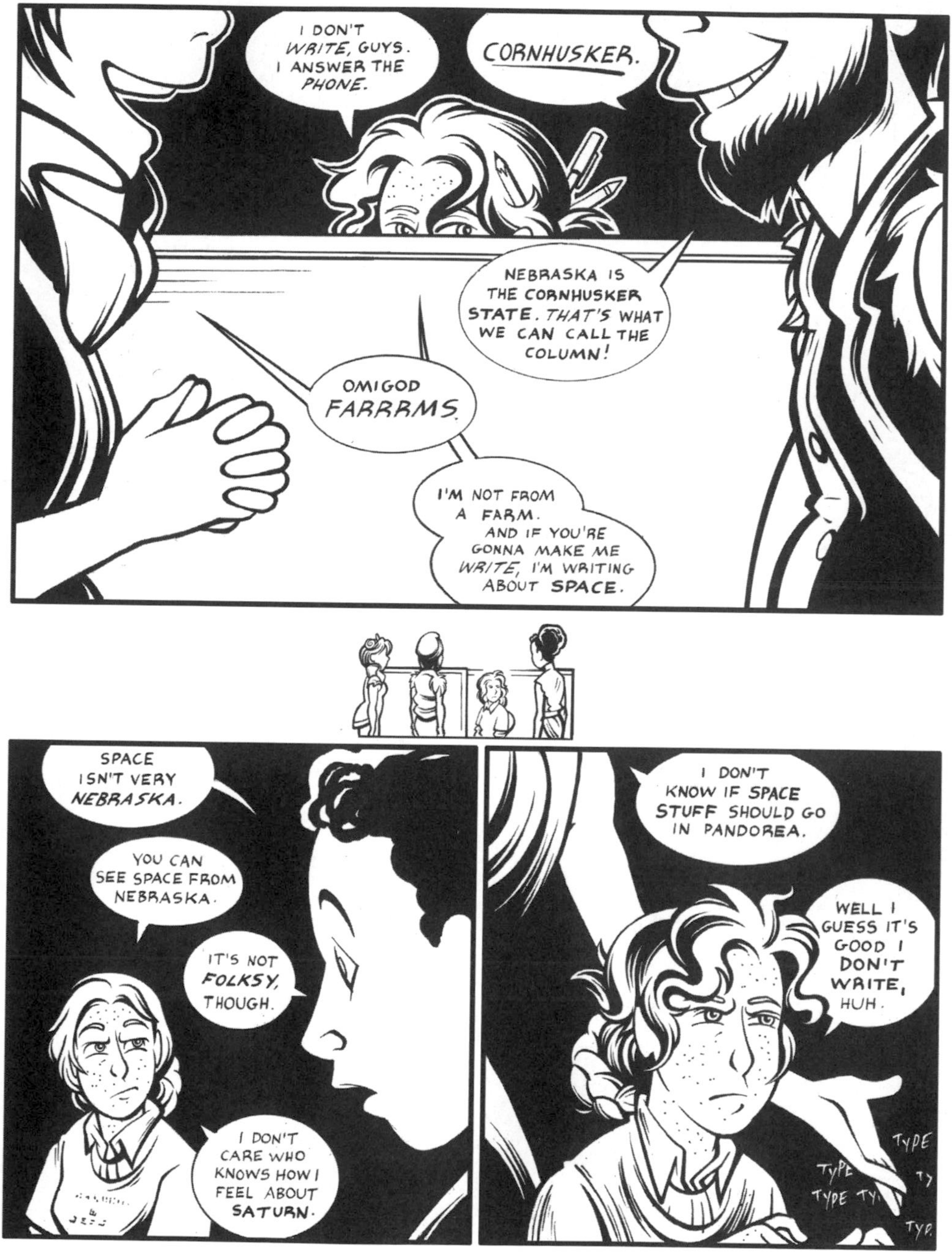
I DON'T *WRITE*, GUYS. I ANSWER THE *PHONE*.
CORNHUSKER.
NEBRASKA IS THE CORNHUSKER STATE. *THAT'S* WHAT WE CAN CALL THE COLUMN!
OMIGOD *FARRRMS*.
I'M NOT FROM A FARM. AND IF YOU'RE GONNA MAKE ME *WRITE*, I'M WRITING ABOUT SPACE.
SPACE ISN'T VERY *NEBRASKA*.
YOU CAN SEE SPACE FROM NEBRASKA.
IT'S NOT *FOLKSY*, THOUGH.
I DON'T CARE WHO KNOWS HOW I FEEL ABOUT SATURN.
I DON'T KNOW IF SPACE STUFF SHOULD GO IN PANDOREA.
WELL I GUESS IT'S GOOD I DON'T WRITE, HUH.
TYPE
TYPE
TY
TYPE TY
TYP

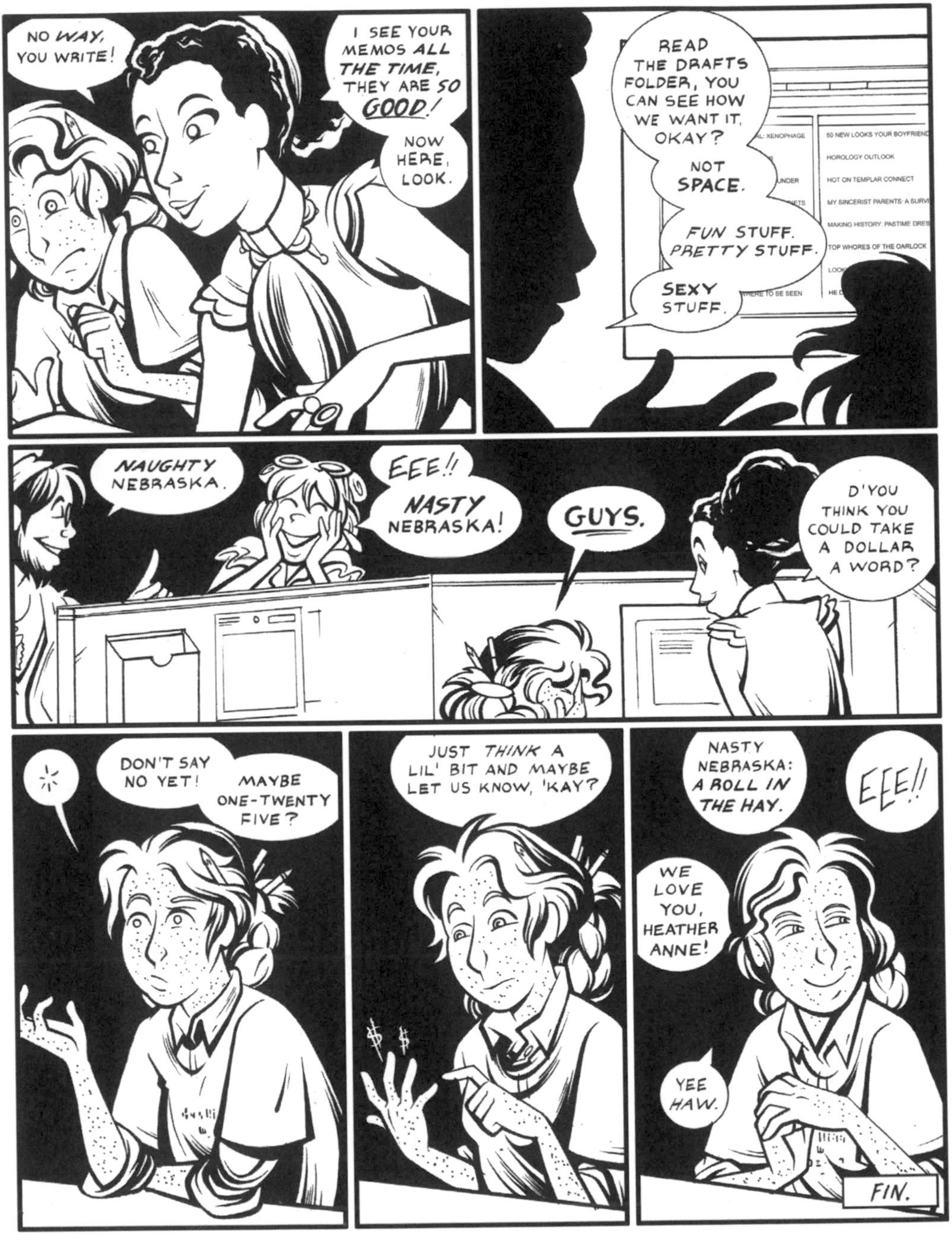

NO *WAY*, YOU WRITE!
I SEE YOUR MEMOS *ALL THE TIME*, THEY ARE *SO GOOD*!
NOW HERE, LOOK.
READ THE DRAFTS FOLDER, YOU CAN SEE HOW WE WANT IT, OKAY?
NOT SPACE.
FUN STUFF. PRETTY STUFF.
SEXY STUFF.
50 NEW LOOKS YOUR BOYFRIEND
HOROLOGY OUTLOOK
HOT ON TEMPLAR CONNECT
TOP WHORES OF THE OARLOCK
NAUGHTY NEBRASKA.
EEE!!
NASTY NEBRASKA!
GUYS.
D'YOU THINK YOU COULD TAKE A DOLLAR A WORD?
DON'T SAY NO YET!
MAYBE ONE-TWENTY FIVE?
JUST *THINK* A LIL' BIT AND MAYBE LET US KNOW, 'KAY?
NASTY NEBRASKA: *A ROLL IN THE HAY.*
EEE!!
WE LOVE YOU, HEATHER ANNE!
YEE *HAW*.
FIN.

Footnotes.

Page 1

The Veritas, and one of its drudges, Kasper. We last saw this cafe, and this cafe employee, in the first book's intermission.

Page 3

The Israelite wet house. I considered adding the refuge's motto ("So that every mouth can be fed") to the sign, but I hit you guys over the head with too many music references as it is. In the center: an Ethiopian-style, crowned Lion of Judah.

Wet houses are shelters designed to house homeless, chronic alcoholics. (Regular homeless shelters don't allow alcohol.) The focus is on harm reduction: improving the health, hygiene, and nutrition of residents, while providing them with a fixed address. This keeps them out of the street and, consequently, out of parks, alleys, doorways, bad weather, and emergency rooms. Some wet houses even provide their residents with alcohol on-site. Getting sober is not the point.

In Templar, wet houses are also "safe injection sites," where junkies on needle drugs can shoot up undisturbed. I imagine Biggs has to go out and find his own smack, though.

Page 4

Lots of cartoonist buddy cameos on this page. Hi, cartoonist buddies.

By some strange quirk of chance, one of the cartoonists I originally drew in the third panel looks a lot like a Caucasian version of Ben. He also acts a lot like Ben. He is also actually *named* Ben. That took some getting used to.

Real Ben was being confused for Templar Ben, so I went back and turned Real Ben middle-aged and brownish for print. Sorry, Real Ben.

Page 5

The last cartoonist cameo, and the end of Tuesday's disembodied assault on Nan, the madam-glorifying author.

Nan was partially inspired by the compulsion some people have to consider any gender-atypical behavior by historical women to be a proto-feminist blow struck against the patriarchy, no matter how wildly deviant.

Sheesh.

Robbing a bank is not feminist. Running a street gang is not feminist. Burying your numerous husbands in the cow pasture and disappearing to Canada with their money is *not feminist*.

Page 6

Normalcy is subjective. For most people, it's what they were born to and raised in. And EJ just told us a whole hell of a lot about what he considers normal.

Whatever you think he's been though, you're probably right. People already on the street at his age are running away from something. He has no happy stories.

Page 8

Biggs is very good at hiding his addiction. Part of that is how fastidious he is about shooting up. Sterilizing wipes, cotton filters, clean water, disposable needles. Cutting his chances of contracting some disgusting blood or skin infection has helped him fly under the radar.

Page 9

It also helps that he shoots up in his groin. Visible track marks tend to give a guy away.

Some readers thought Biggs was shooting up in his penis, but he's going for his femoral vein. This is pretty horrible, since the femoral vein in notoriously difficult and dangerous to hit in. If he misses, that needle's going into the femoral artery or the femoral nerve. Bad news.

Biggs has been at this for a while. He's probably shooting in the only discrete vein he hasn't managed to burn out and collapse.

Page 11

Looks like Kasper the Sincerist spilled his guts real good.

Page 14

Panel three: kind of like suicide.

The Jakes sent Jackie in alone because they never dreamed this is would happen. Anyone who knew anything about Jakeskin would have permitted Jackie to drag them out to an uncertain fate in the street. EJ was, unfortunately, clueless.

Page 19

Part army ants, part hyena pack, part tsunami. Jake field tactics are executed with two principles in mind:
- If violence must be practiced, it must be overwhelming.
- City people are not actually people at all. Killing one has all the moral significance of squashing a tick.

Page 24

With the exception of Jackie, Marcus, and Apollo, you're not supposed to be able to tell all these Jakes apart. Their uniform appearance is pretty standard stuff for cults, which discourage individuality by definition. It'll also help if any of the surviving rummies try to describe their attackers.

"Yep. That's the guy who ruptured my

kidney, officer. The bald one with the knife."

Page 31

Deep-fried guinea pig on a bun. Yum.

Page 32

Despite the recurrent, head-to-toe flapper wear, Flannery would vehemently deny being a Pastime.

Flappers don't get enough credit for redefining the role of women in American society, in my opinion. They drove cars, bobbed their hair, dated, snubbed corsetry, and wore sleeveless dresses that bared their knees. That was all terribly shocking and contrary to the mainstream values of the 1920s.

Page 35

Reagan's outfit was inspired by something Freddie Mercury once wore. In case you were raised by wolves, Freddie was the lead singer of Queen. And the man could dress.

You can see the original get-up on the cover of Queen's *Live at Wembley '86*.

Page 37

Reagan's managerial style could best be described as "Older Sister Who Is Annoyed With You."

Page 45

I re-drew Mesmer's entire outfit for print. The lacy, spaghetti-strap tank top he's wearing is a little twee for his tastes, but I needed to put him in an obviously feminine article of clothing, and there wasn't enough of him in the panel to show you he's wearing a skirt.

I don't think of Mez as a cross-dresser, though. That would suggest to me that he's trying to pass, or at least create a believably female overall look. He's not. He's a dude who likes to wear girl clothes. Sometimes with dude clothes. He mixes and matches. And he doesn't like girl clothes because they're for girls; he likes them because he likes them. The fact that they freak people out and get him stares doesn't hurt, either.

Page 46

I strongly suggest going back and re-reading the last scene of book two, now. And maybe Ben's scene with Eli in book three.

Page 48

There aren't enough post-sex clean-up scenes in comics.

Page 49

Tuesday doesn't expect exclusivity, and Moze doesn't want to give it to her. They would be the perfect couple, if they considered this a relationship.

I imagine Tuesday eschews monogamy for deliberate, socially avant-garde reasons that allude to the patriarchy. Moze just likes sleeping with as many girls as he can.

Page 50

The image of Tuesday and Moze walking down the street, hand in hand, amuses me a lot. A painstakingly put-together, hyper-sensitive, self-satisfied stick insect, and her huge, hairy, sloppy, relentlessly tranquil gentleman friend. I'll have to draw it some day.

And Curio's given name wasn't meant as a big reveal. "Prabhjot Kaur" is just a really Sikh name. A lot of people have it.

Page 51

If there's a Sikh Maharajah, that means the Sikh Empire is still intact, somewhere in the northwest of the Indian subcontinent. In our world, it fell in 1849, after the Second Anglo-Sikh War. In Templar's world, it's still going. Sikh isn't just Curio's religion; it's her ancestral nationality. She would probably describe herself as "Sikh-American."

I like Sikh philosophy. It's hard not to. It preaches universal human equality, good deeds, duty, and charity, and discourages ritual, superstition, castes, and consumerism. Sikhs have no priests, monks, or nuns. They don't veil their women. They consider truth

and "truthful living" holy. They worship a refreshingly non-anthropomorphic God: shapeless, timeless, sightless, and genderless. And their temples serve free vegetarian meals to all comers, twice daily. If you're going to be religious, you could do a lot worse.

Page 52

In case you weren't tipped off by the papyrus column door frame, the reed motif on the cabinets, the stars on the ceiling, and the sign in hieroglyphics outside the kitchen window, Moze and Tuesday are at Moze's place.

Moze's place is in Little Cairo. The sign is advertising a relative's store, which is on the ground floor. The building is probably owned by another relative.

Little Cairo is an ethnic enclave, like Chinatown or Little Italy. It's a landing strip for new Nile immigrants, a religious and cultural hub, a business center, and a tourist attraction. Moze and Sunny grew up here.

And this page demonstrates why I had to get Moze and Tuesday together. *Had to*. Tuesday comes from the land of Cares-Too-Much. Moze hails from the fantastic, far-away shores of Couldn't-Care-Less. They've got a fun dynamic, like Reagan and Scipio.

Page 53

My husband owns some punk compilation albums from a series called *Give 'Em the Boot*. They're meant to promote new bands signed to the series' label, Hellcat Records. *Heavy Metal Poisoning* works on the same principle, except it's less professional and features metal acts, most of which had the lifespans of mayflies.

Gracequake is the "wanna-be prog rock jerk circle" Sunny is badmouthing in book two.

Page 54

The deportation of foreign-born criminal offenders is pretty standard stuff. It happens in our America all the time. The crime doesn't have to be violent, or even serious. People have been deported over minor drug possession charges, or driving without a license.

Sunny's official status, like that of a lot of legal immigrants, is murky. He's culturally American, but he's not a citizen, and he has a criminal record. There's a justifiable fear that he wouldn't be allowed to walk back out of an immigration office if he ever walked in trying to clarify matters.

Page 58

In Moze's bedroom: A ton of Bes figures.

I bet Tuesday designs her own clothes.

Page 63

Scipio is unusually oblivious to how people perceive him. It would never occur to him that his mere presence is intimidating.

Page 68

Guess Eddie isn't coming.

Page 73

Did Pippi lie? Did the cops get the story right? Is Pippi hiding in the bathroom because this is completely fucking traumatic, or because she's been found out and the gig is up?

Dunno. Good questions, though.

Page 78

This is a common hustle. Guy's caught trying to sleep with someone, is made to pay hush money by an offended party threatening to blab his indiscretion. Unbeknownst to the guy, the "offended party" and the gal who got him in bed are in cahoots. It's called the badger game. No one knows why.

Just catching someone having extramarital relations used to be enough to squeeze 'em for a few bucks, but not these days. Phony affairs are more likely to result in cash if the girl is underage – like Pippi – or the affair is homosexual and the guy (or gal) is a closet case.

Page 81

On the mug: the Australian Aboriginal flag.

Page 82

"Gamarada" means "comrades" in Cadigal (or Gadigal). The Cadigal were among the native inhabitants of what eventually became Sydney, Australia. Things didn't go well for them.

"Tully," in this context, is the equivalent of "whitey" or "cracker."

Lots of weapons lying around. This was inspired by an online forum post where a man was bragging that he was never more than five feet from a gun when he was at home. He was very proud of this fact.

Page 84

Someone is very concerned about their security.

By the way, if you ever have a significant other that acts like EJ, you should probably leave them before they start hitting you.

Note EJ's chewed-up knuckles. Things do not bode well for Marcus.

Page 85

Templar's Australia isn't our Australia. I always get kind of cowardly when it comes to cementing the nuts and bolts of this alternate timeline, but hey, I kinda owe you guys an explanation, here.

In Templar's version of World War II, the Japanese advance in the southwestern Pacific was more successful, particularly aggressions against Australia. A few less duds, a few more bullseyes, some luckier bombardiers. The Battle of Midway came a little too late to save the country. The government fractured into numerous squabbling factions, and never fully reunited.

Australia still exists, but not as the stable nation we know. The New South Wales Aboriginal Resistance is only one of several competing groups currently making the place unbearable. Japan doesn't run the country – they still lost the war – but neither does anybody else. Not effectively.

Page 86

Remember Gordon? He was giving Flannery a hard time at Kingdom Come in book two. Had to be shooed away by Reagan.

He probably had a gun on him at the time.

Page 88

And now they know how to *use* that thing. Good job, Gordon.

Page 89

In panel three: Did you see it? Hope you saw it.

And as related in panel four, Gordon and Biggs met in rehab. It shouldn't be surprising a guy like Gordon would try self-medicating at some point.

Page 92

Like I said, no happy stories. Whoever raised EJ should be horse-whipped.

EJ's co-dependence with Biggs is probably the result of Biggs being halfway-decent to him, just once, several months ago. It was such a profoundly unusual event in EJ's life that it's gone on to elicit some truly spooky, incompetent, and threatening loyalty.

Page 94

In case you were wondering when these two threads of plot were going to meet: they just did.

Page 96

I once read an article about Sarah Jessica Parker, the star of *Sex and the City*. It was about why women considered her pretty, why men *didn't* consider her pretty, and why it bothered women that men didn't like her. The crux of the argument was that Sarah followed all the rules – dressed fashionably, put on flattering make-up, had her hair done – and women appreciated that. But following the rules didn't actually make her pretty. Sarah's female-only appeal revealed men ultimately didn't consider fashionable clothing and well-applied make-up factors in who they found attractive, which is the exact opposite of what marketing tells us, and the exact opposite of what self-conscious women want to hear.

Interesting theory. I had it in mind when I was drawing the woman on the far right.

She's trying. She is *really trying*. But Morgan has come to work disguised as a pile of laundry, and she still looks better. And she always will.

Life is unfair.

Page 97

Pandorea's most obnoxious male employee is wearing a Phrygian cap. It's a soft, red, conical hat, symbolically associated with liberty and the defeat of oppression. It played an iconic role in the American Revolution, but is most frequently associated with the French Revolution.

Smurfs are wearing these in white. Maybe that's why some people consider them allegorical propaganda for communism.

Page 100

There are writers who would walk through fire to get paid a dollar a word. And I can tell you one thing: there's no way Ben's getting that much over at the *Crusade*.

And that's chapter four. Thanks again, guys. As usual, there's lots more to read online at http://www.templaraz.com.

Bye!

Sketches.

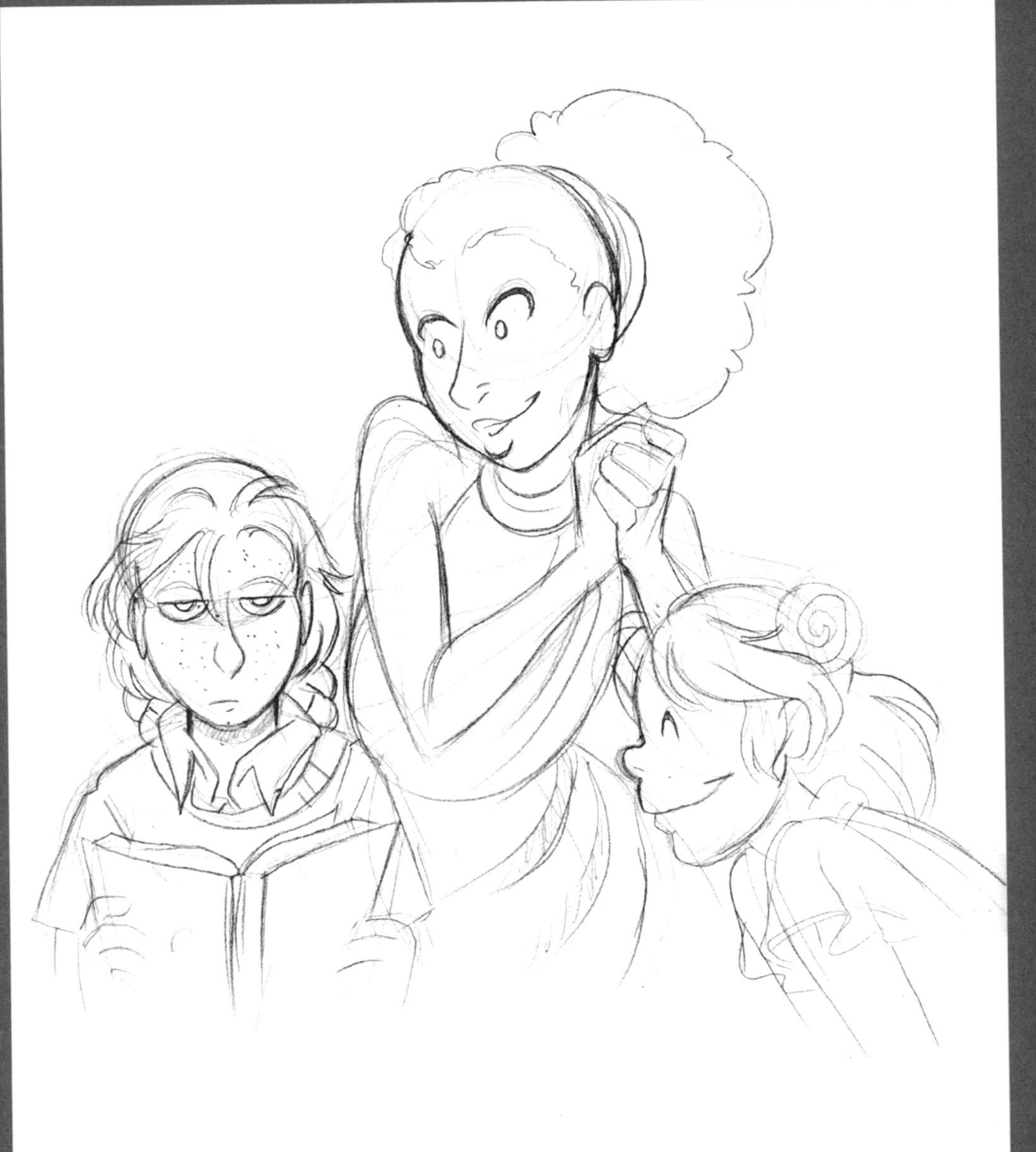

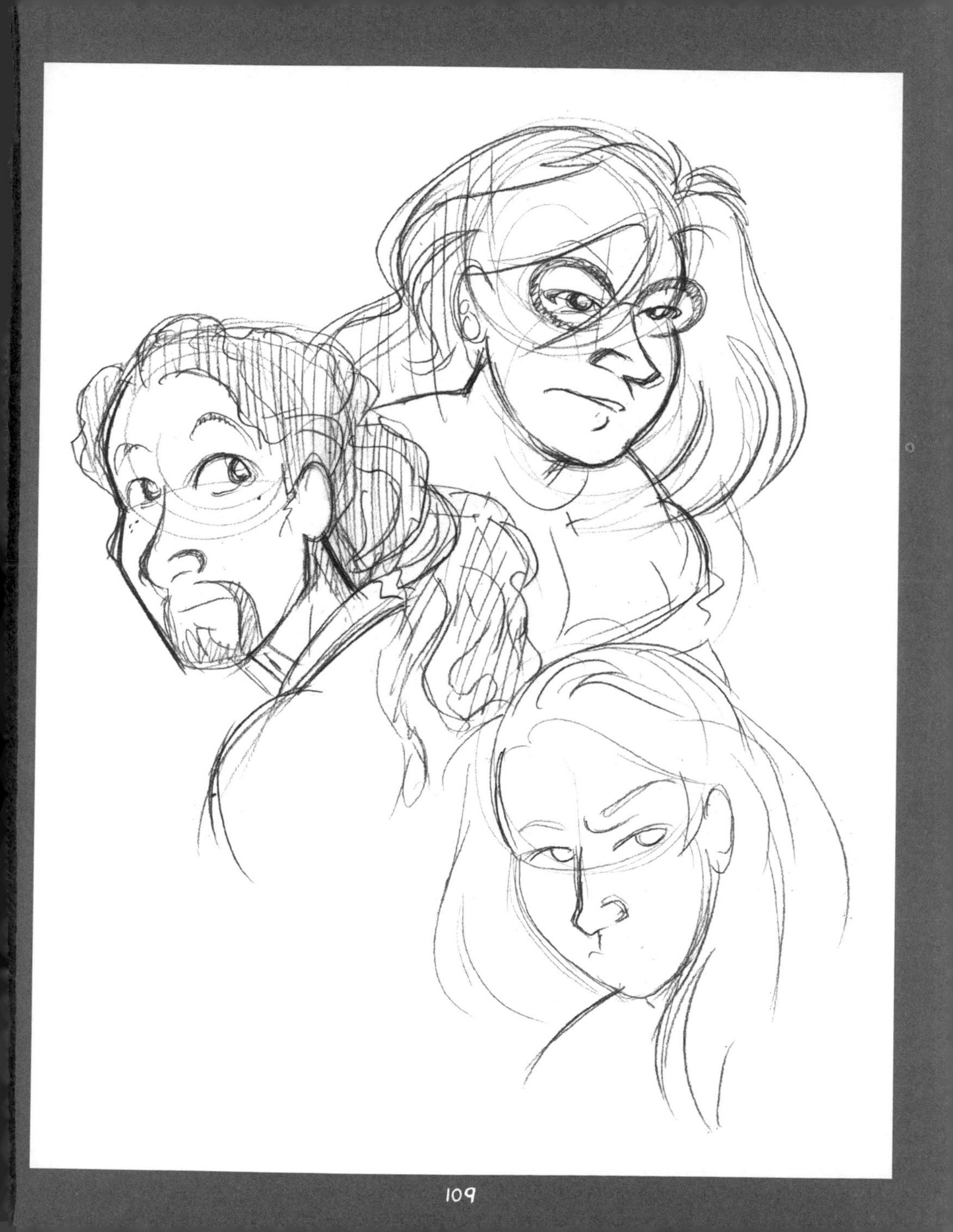

About the artist.

Spike still lives in Chicago.

Nothing has changed.

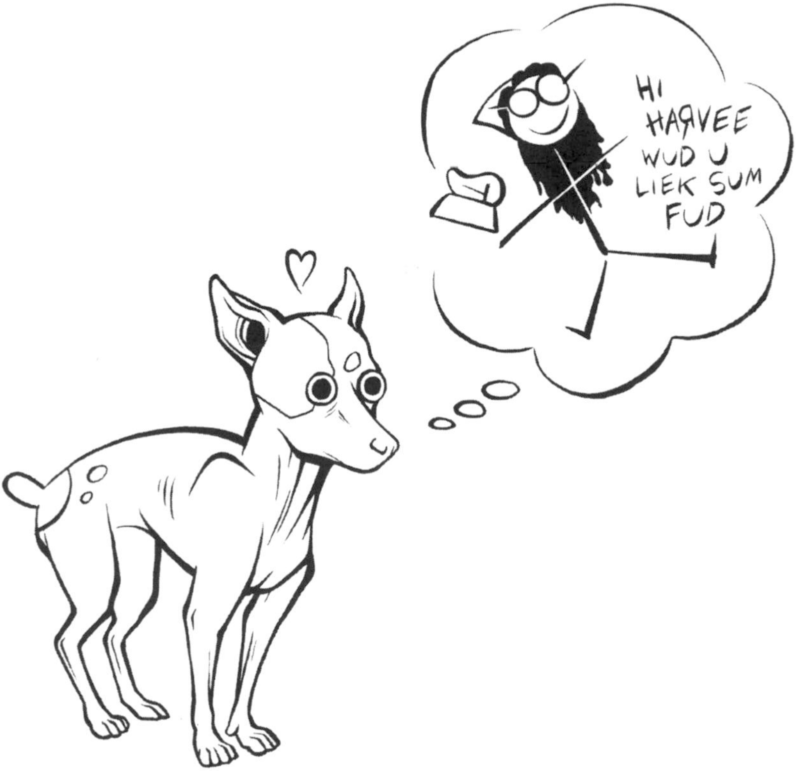
HI
HARVEE
WUD U
LIEK SUM
FUD